Christian Faith and the Bible of Judaism

The Judaic Encounter with Scripture

JACOB NEUSNER

WILLIAM B. EERDMANS PUBLISHING COMPANY
Grand Rapids, Michigan

Copyright © 1987 by Wm. B. Eerdmans Publishing Co.
255 Jefferson Ave. S.E., Grand Rapids, Mich. 49503
Printed in the United States of America

Library of Congress Cataloging-in-Publication Data

Neusner, Jacob, 1932-

  Includes index.
    1. Midrash rabbah.   Genesis — Criticism, interpretation, etc.
  2. Midrash rabbah.   Leviticus — Criticism, interpretation, etc.
  3. Sifrei.   Numbers — Criticism, interpretation, etc.
  4. Bible.   O.T. Genesis — Criticism, interpretation, etc., Jewish.
  5. Bible.   O.T. Leviticus — Criticism, interpretation, etc., Jewish.
  6. Bible. O.T.   Numbers — Criticism, interpretation, etc., Jewish.
  7. Judaism — Relations — Christianity.
  8. Christianity and other religions — Judaism.
  I. Title.
BM517.M65N478   1987   296.1′4   87-20177

ISBN 0-8028-0278-8

For
JAMES H. CHARLESWORTH
Princeton Theological Seminary

who has devoted his life to restoring to the world the treasures of ancient Israel in the apocryphal and pseudepigraphic scriptures and who generously and wisely offers counsel to colleagues who turn to him for guidance. He is a model of faith seeking understanding and of understanding seeking faith.

Contents

Preface

The Bible of Judaism—that is, Scripture as read and interpreted by the rabbis who flourished in the early centuries of the Common Era (Christian Era in common speech)—makes one contribution to Christian faith. It is the profound conviction of these ancient rabbis, whom Jews revere and call "our sages, of blessed memory," that Scripture forms a commentary on everyday life—as much as everyday life brings with it fresh understanding of Scripture. That theological conviction forms the basis for how our sages read Scripture. When we follow their efforts to give concrete meaning to that belief, we find for the faithful Jew and Christian today a model of the way to read Scripture. In this book I want to provide a significant example, for Christian faithful, of ways in which the Bible of Judaism may help us all to worship, serve, and love God through the study of the Torah, God's word to Israel and the world. This simple, but profound conviction epitomizes what I think is to be learned from our sages.

There is a constant interplay, an on-going interchange, between everyday affairs and the word of God in the Torah (Scripture). What we see reminds us of what Scripture says—and what Scripture says informs our understanding of the things we see and do in everyday life. That is, in my view, the meaning of the critical verse of Scripture: "In all thy ways, know Him." And the deep structure of human existence, framed by Scripture and formed out of God's will as spelled out in the Torah, forms the foundation of our everyday life. Here and now, in the life of the hour, we can and do know God. So everyday life forms a commentary on revealed Scripture (on the Torah), and Scripture (the Torah) provides a commentary on everyday life. Life flows in both directions.

The founders of Judaism as we know it, who flourished in the first seven centuries of the Common Era, brought Scripture into their world, and their world into Scripture. They therefore show us how people shaped their understanding of the world out of the resources of God's revelation concerning the beginnings of humanity, and especially of God's people, Israel. That example serves Jews and Christians today, struggling as they do to hold together (for Jews) the Torah and the demands of modern life, and (for Christians) the Word and the world. The great sages—honored with the title of rabbi—transformed the To-

rah into a plan and design for the world, the everyday as an instance of
the eternal. When we see how they did it and reflect upon the profound
results, for faith, they achieved, we learn an important lesson.

The lesson is how we may turn what we are into what we may become,
following the example of Israel's ancient sages, who found in Scripture
the message for their age and the model of what they might attain. They
read Scripture as God's picture of creation and humanity. They read the
life of the streets and marketplaces, the home and the hearth, the nations and the world, as an on-going commentary on Scripture and the
potentialities (not all of them good) of creation. So, as I have said, life—
truth—flows in both directions. Reading Genesis as the sages did,
against the background of their world, we encounter the story of the
beginnings of humanity in a new way. It is now an account not of a
distant past, but of a living and abiding present. Reading Leviticus as
acutely relevant to their world, understanding Numbers as an urgent
message for their particular human setting, the sages come to Scripture as
God's living word for their day. For our sages of blessed memory teach us
to turn Scripture into a paradigm of truth even for our own time.

In this book I introduce Judaic approaches to the life of Scripture with
special reference to Genesis, Leviticus, and Numbers. Genesis of course
takes precedence, because it is the story of beginnings. To make sense of
today, we look back at the way things got started: the plan and program
for all time. In the account of God's creation of the world, formation of
humanity and disappointment with the result, search for man and woman on whom to build the world, discovery of Abraham and Sarah, and in
the history of the family of Abraham and Sarah and formation of Israel,
God's first love, we regain our own roots. Leviticus and Numbers also
direct our attention to the origins, this time of the mode of service to
God in sacrifice and worship, in the cult described in Leviticus, and the
origins of God's people, wandering in the wilderness and seeking the
promised land, in Numbers. The importance of Leviticus and of Numbers will not prove self-evident until we see how our sages have found in
those somewhat forbidding accounts of the tabernacle in the wilderness
and the wandering to the promised land important messages as well.

Searching for those beginnings with the model of our sages in mind
will not fulfil that quest—no one brings us to the end. But it will uncover
paths we might otherwise not find, because I believe the ancient rabbis of
Judaism teach important lessons to believing people today. These lessons
are of two kinds, the how and the what: how to read Scripture, and what

to find there. Specifically, the ancient rabbis show us how to read Scripture in a way that we can follow. They show us ways of responding to Scripture that we may not have imagined. They also teach us dimensions of scriptural meaning that we may not otherwise grasp. We Jews and Christians, revering Scripture as the Written Part of God's one whole Torah (for the Jewish part) or as the Old Testament (for the Christian part), do well to seek in our encounter with the teachings of the living God the wisdom, imagination, and insight of the ages. Ours is a task no prior generation, back to the beginnings, have had to take up.

In an age of militant secularism and hostility to the biblical origins of the civilization of the West—and of the world—we come together to sustain one another's faith. In this book I want to contribute some modest measure of my own faith, Judaism, as that faith may add to the faith of our Christian neighbors, for all of us now dwell together in the new catacomb, the darkness of disdain for our common faith in one God, creator of heaven and earth, judge of all humankind. This is a book of religious faith. I draw as a rabbi on treasures I mean to share with Christians. I come with humility to the faith of others. I hope to give, as others have in our day given of their faith, their grace, to us Jews.

This book is not a scholarly examination of how ancient rabbis read Scripture, but rather focuses on how from their example we may derive a more profound understanding of ourselves through Scripture, the Torah in particular. At stake here is not what was going on in the fourth century of the Common (Christian) era, when Genesis Rabbah and Leviticus Rabbah were written, but what will happen in the twenty-first century. For to us Jews the Hebrew Scriptures, the Written Torah, forms the record of God's picture of humanity. We encounter the Written Torah not (in anthropological terms) as humanity's projection of itself onto eternity, but (in theological ones) as God's picture of humanity in time. So in this book we shall take up choices explored by the founders of Judaism, learning from them through their example the freedom to bring our world to Scripture and to reshape our world in the encounter with Scripture. That kind of freedom I think Christians will find liberating and honest.

In the pages that follow, I show what the doctrine of inerrant Scripture meant to our sages, for they believed that Scripture was, and is, God's word. But we have now to go beyond the issue of inerrancy. If we believe that the Torah reveals God's will to humanity (as we Jews do) or that the Bible records God's word (as Christians do), then we affirm Scripture and undertake the task of finding meaning in that affirmation: how does Scripture teach us to understand our lives and the times in which we live. Inerrancy as test of faith misses the point. Once by our choice of Scripture we believe, what truths does belief entail? It is time to move beyond the limiting issues of academic learning, which divide the world into believers (sometimes called "fundamentalists") and scholars. Believers learn, and scholars believe. There are other approaches to Scripture, besides the narrowly academic, the philological and historical.

Seeing Scripture as a commentary on life and the everyday as a systematic exegesis of Scripture presents us with a new and, I think, fruitful way of reading Scripture—and the everyday as well. The approach of our sages, exemplified in this book, will prove intellectually rigorous, but humanly relevant as well. What matters in Scripture is not the history of Scripture or even the historicity of the events portrayed in Scripture. What matters is the authority of Scripture, and that rests upon the community of the faithful today, not the events that (we may "prove") took place so long ago. At issue is not history in the sense that the world really was made in six days, but eternity: that God sanctifies and rests on the seventh, the Sabbath of creation. Under debate, after all, is not whether or not archaeology proves that things happened in the way in which Scripture says they did (or in some other way), but Scripture's method and message for history. What counts is not what happened then—did Sodom really perish in fire and brimstone, or was it an earthquake?—but what Scripture teaches us to make of what is happening now. All of us for nearly two hundred years have suffered the abuse to think that Scripture answers a set of historical questions: did it really happen? But the questions that draw us to Scripture are not questions about what happened long ago, but what is happening now—and what, in Scripture, God wants of me. And to people who ask Scripture to explain what is happening now, the lessons and example of the sages of Judaism have much to say.

In remarking that I find in our sages' understanding of Genesis a model for ourselves, I meant something very simple. I aim to show Christian readers how the faithful of Israel, exemplified by the sages who wrote the documents we shall meet as Genesis Rabbah, Leviticus Rabbah, and Sifré to Numbers, for fifteen hundred years have brought their world to Scripture and read their world in the light of Scripture. In this way I hope to legitimate for another generation the human right of asking Scripture our questions, and not only the questions of philology or of history. The particular reading of Genesis, Leviticus, and Numbers presented here derives from Judaic sages who lived in the Land of Israel in the third and fourth centuries. The work reached a conclusion sometime after the Roman Empire had become Christian, and took up profound questions that troubled Israel's sages on account of that unexpected event. But, as noted earlier, what we wish to learn does not lead us to historical questions, concerning either if Abraham really lived or how the fourth century rabbis responded to the challenge represented by Christianity's political triumph. These are not important issues here. Rather, the Jews in the fourth century asked the books of Genesis, Leviticus, and Numbers to explain what was happening with the advent of Christianity—an enormous shock. They asked Scripture to supply them with insight into the meaning of history. The sages devoted their attention to all of the books of the Hebrew Scriptures, but we concentrate on only three, since they serve to show us types of approaches to Scripture.

The interest and importance of their reading of Genesis, Leviticus, and Numbers transcend the age in which the sages did their work. For how the great Judaic sages of that time taught the interpretation of the stories of Genesis, Leviticus, and Numbers, as well as other works of Scripture, would guide later Judaic exegetes of the same biblical books. So when we follow the work before us, we gain entry into the way in which Judaism in its normative and classical form, from that day to this, would understand more than these stories (the creation of the world, Adam's sin, Noah, and especially the founding family of Israel, in its first three generations, Abraham, Isaac, and Jacob, as well as Joseph). We learn how they mediated those accounts to their own day, turned them into acutely relevant messages of truth for their times, facts for all times. In an age in which the book of Genesis, in particular, attracts remarkable interest and in which a literal mode of reading enjoys the authority of true religion, the supple and creative approach of the ancient rabbis, founders of Judaism, provides a valuable choice. The sages show the profound depths of the stories of the creation of the world and Israel's founding family. They systematically relate the history of the people Israel to the lives and deeds of the founders, the fathers and the mothers of this book of the Torah. But their work on Leviticus and Numbers is equally suggestive for us. It shows how even the most particular and dry biblical books can yield a rich and universally nourishing harvest of scriptural truth.

Once we have read Genesis, Leviticus, and Numbers (as well as other books of the Hebrew Scriptures) as "our sages of blessed memory" teach us, we gain the freedom to follow our imagination as they arouse it. We no longer need to deal with those who claim to dictate how, in what they deem a literal and fundamental sense, we must receive the story of the creation of the world and of Israel. What to some proves fundamental, to us, having heard the story as the third and fourth century sages of Israel retell it, appears shallow. What these sages find in the text opens our minds to possibilities beyond imagining. The sages' way of reading the first book of the Bible shows that faithful exegetes may uncover deep layers of meaning and discover truth entirely consonant with the concerns of a given age. That is so, whether it is the fourth century or the twenty-first century, to the heritage of which, with God's help, I hope to hand on these books of mine. The interest of the Church in all this is obvious. The Church long ago identified itself as Israel and, through the shared Scriptures, with Israel. Consequently, the experience of Israel spoke to the heart of the Church. In our own day, all the more so, the Church joins suffering Israel. We live in a moment of reconciliation, which, with God's help, will encompass Islam as well, the third religion of the family of Abraham. *This is the day that the Lord has made. Let us rejoice and be happy in it.*

This work draws on my translations and studies of the rabbinic compilations of scriptural exegesis ("*midrashim*") as follows.

Genesis Rabbah: The Judaic Commentary on Genesis, A New American Translation. Brown Judaic Studies. Atlanta: Scholars Press, 1985.

    Vol. 1, *Parashiyyot One through Thirty-three. Genesis 1:1– 8:14.*

    Vol. 2, *Parashiyyot Thirty-four through Sixty-seven. Genesis 8:15– 28:9.*

    Vol. 3, *Parashiyyot Sixty-eight through One Hundred. Genesis 28:10– 50:26.*

Judaism and Scripture: The Evidence of Leviticus Rabbah. Chicago: University of Chicago Press, 1986. This study of how Scripture makes its way into Judaism as framed by our sages includes a complete translation of Leviticus Rabbah, the first of the great critical text of Mordecai Margulis.

Sifra: The Judaic Commentary on Leviticus, A New Translation. The Leper, Leviticus 13:1–14:57. Brown Judaic Studies. Chico: Scholars Press, 1985. Based on the translation of *Sifra Parashiyyot Negaim* and *Meso-*

ra in my *History of the Mishnaic Law of Purities*. Vol. 6, *Negaim: Sifra*.
[With a section by Roger Brooks]
Sifré to Numbers: An American Translation. Brown Judaic Studies. Atlanta: Scholars Press, 1986.

Vol. 1, *1-58*.
Vol. 2, *59-115*.

Note the forthcoming completion of this translation.

William Scott Green, *Sifré to Numbers: An American Translation*. Vol. 3, *59-115. Brown Judaic Studies*. Atlanta: Scholars Press, 1988.

This book furthermore takes its place among several anthologies I have published on Judaism and Scripture, as follows.

Comparative Midrash: Genesis Rabbah and Leviticus Rabbah. Brown Judaic Studies. Atlanta: Scholars Press, 1986.
Reading Scriptures: An Introduction to Rabbinic Midrash, with Special Reference to Genesis Rabbah. Chappaqua: Rossel, 1986. This anthology with an introduction on how the sages read the book of Genesis serves synagogue worship and study, and runs parallel in spirit to the present book, which I offer to the Christian Church.
Genesis and Judaism: The Perspective of Genesis Rabbah. Brown Judaic Studies. Atlanta: Scholars Press, 1986. An analytical anthology. The structure of values rabbis brought to the biblical text, as portrayed in Genesis Rabbah, together with analysis of the categories at hand. The anthology comprises materials different from those included in this book and addresses its own agenda of issues.

Finally, I turn to the larger historical question that initially brought me to the writings that reached closure in the fourth and early fifth centuries. In the following works I have laid out a theory of the history of Judaism.

The Foundations of Judaism: Method, Teleology, Doctrine. Philadelphia: Fortress Press, 1983-1985.

Vol. 1, *Midrash in Context: Exegesis in Formative Judaism*
Vol. 2, *Messiah in Context: Israel's History and Destiny in Formative Judaism*.
Vol. 3. *Torah: From Scroll to Symbol in Formative Judaism*

These books have been summarized in a one-volume abridged edition.

The Foundations of Judaism. Philadelphia: Fortress Press, 1987.

I have drawn the historical implications and spelled out my theory of the beginnings of Judaism as we know that religion in the following.

Judaism in the Matrix of Christianity. Philadelphia: Fortress Press, 1986. This book treats the formation of Judaism in the fourth century in response to the challenge of the political triumph of Christianity in the age of Constantine.

The following work carries forward in a specific way the analysis of the terms of the theological confrontation.

Judaism and Christianity in the Age of Constantine: History, Messiah, Israel, and the Initial Confrontation. Chicago: University of Chicago Press, 1987. This book argues that the formation of Judaism in the fourth century responded to the challenge of the triumph of Christianity in that same period.

My basic thesis on the history of Judaism then emerges in the next work. The thesis is that Judaism in its classical form—the Judaism of the dual Torah, oral and written—flourished in Christendom and in Islam because it answered the urgent questions posed to Jews by the dominion of Christendom and Islam. That same Judaism for some Jews lost its hold as self-evident truth when Christianity for some Christians ceased to provide a self-evidently valid construction of the world.

The Death and Birth of Judaism: The Impact of Christianity, Secularism, and the Holocaust on Modern Judaism. New York: Basic Books, 1987. This book maintains that Judaism in its classic formulation endured so long as the issues presented by Christianity defined the world in which Jews lived. For that long period of time the questions answered by Judaism proved urgent, and the answers, to Jews self-evidently correct. When Christianity lost its hold on the West, Judaism among Jews no longer enjoyed the status of self-evident truth. That accounts for the birth, in the nineteenth and twentieth centuries, of new forms of Judaism.

Given the multiplicity of Judaisms in modern times—for as readers know, not all Jews are religious, and many religious Jews are religious in ways different from the received, traditional way—we want to know how we may define Judaism beyond all of its manifestations. For that purpose I return to Scripture, and argue that the Torah of Moses defined the enduring paradigm, even for those forms of Judaism that did not draw on its texts to substantiate their self-evidently valid answers to the urgent program of questions they had chosen. This argument is in the following book.

Judaism: Past, Present, Future. Boston: Beacon Press, 1987. This book offers a general theory of the entire history of Judaism, explaining how diverse Judaisms (traced in *Judaism in the Matrix of Christianity* and *Death and Birth of Judaism,* cited above), each in its own distinctive way, actually recapitulate a single generative paradigm, that of the Torah of Moses.

In conclusion, I offer both a personal and a theological reason for bringing the present anthology into being.

The personal one is simple. I have spent my life in the free and open society of America, a country that has accorded to Jews, among all other citizens, the dignity of equality. Christians (not merely Gentiles) in that free society have honored and respected Judaism, as well as Jews, in ways hitherto uncommon. Only in America—so I deeply believe—have Judaism and Christianity found it possible to transcend the issues of confrontation and conflict and to meet in mutual regard and esteem. In my life that has meant, in concrete terms, an on-going encounter with men and women of deep Christian faith, both Protestant and Catholic and Orthodox, and also profound regard and esteem for Judaism and for me as a serious Jew. My closest and dearest colleagues in Judaic Studies, Ernest S. Frerichs, Methodist, and Wendell S. Dietrich, Presbyterian, spend their scholarly and academic lives on the serious study of Judaism. And, if in my view the best and the brightest, they stand for many others whom I have known and appreciated through my life. I want in this book to pay my tribute to their faith, as they have spent their lives paying their tribute to mine. For they took up the study of Judaism out of respect and regard. They came as faithful Christians to honor the faith of Judaism. Let me then honor their faith too.

That motive also explains the dedication of this book. James H. Charlesworth, a Bible-believing Christian, has spent his life restoring to the Jewish people the treasures of the ancient Jewish writers of books now classified as Apocrypha and Pseudepigrapha of the Old Testament. Not only has he given his entire scholarly career to that demanding task, he also has shown to colleagues an uncommon generosity of spirit. I first met his work, and then him, when I was working on my earliest scholarly projects. It was a joy to wander into a field tended by so splendid a master. He knew his subject and all of its literature, and he also shared what he knew generously and unstintingly. Later on I was able to know the man and his faith, to honor the one and to appreciate the other. In this dedication I wish to pay him back in some small way for what he has contributed to my life and to my faith as a believing Jew.

The second reason for presenting this anthology is public and not personal. Judaism and Christianity in the age of holocaust and in the aftermath of the murder in factories built for that purpose of six million Jews in Christian Europe come together as they have not since the beginning, and as they have not been able to since the fourth century. The relationship of subordinated, patient Judaism and world-possessing Christianity—a relationship that began in the age of Constantine—has ended. The confrontation has ceased. In their contemporary encounter Judaism and Christianity have entered a new epoch of relationship—not yet dialogue, but no longer confrontation. For that, at least, we have— all of us—to give thanks. Why at just this time, in just this dreadful way, God has brought us to the threshold of mature reconciliation, no one knows. Perhaps it is for a blessing, held back until, mourning unspeakable tragedy, we rejoined ranks—not before "Auschwitz" or Golgotha but before Sinai. There in a cleft in the rock we shall shelter before the Presence. There we shall hear, after the mighty noise, a voice of silence. And that is all: *In the beginning, God created the heaven and the earth.*

JACOB NEUSNER

Program in Judaic Studies
Brown University
Providence, Rhode Island

June 12, 1986
For Erev Shavuot, 5746/Pentecost, 1986

PART ONE

GENESIS

Introduction to Genesis as Read in Genesis Rabbah

I offer this sample of Genesis Rabbah (and the other compilations of scriptural exegeses to follow) not because I believe Christians should know something about the history of Judaism, let alone to tell you about the fourth century, when Genesis Rabbah and Leviticus Rabbah took shape (the date for Sifré to Numbers is indeterminate but possibly third century). I do claim that Genesis Rabbah, Leviticus Rabbah, and Sifré to Numbers, among the many great commentaries to Scripture by our sages, teach us how we too can and should—in their model—approach Scripture. I offer not so much their message—though it is relevant to our day—but, rather, their model. Still, to begin with, we understand what they accomplished as a model for us only when we grasp what they said as a message to their own day.

Genesis, the story of beginnings, lays forth the meaning and end of humanity. In the book of Genesis, as the sages of the fourth century see things, God set forth to Moses the entire scope and meaning of Israel's history among the nations and of Israel's salvation at the end of days. They read Genesis not as a set of individual verses, one by one, but as a single and coherent statement, whole and complete. So in a few words I will restate the conviction of the framers of Genesis Rabbah about the message and meaning of the book of Genesis.

We now know what will be in the future. How do we know it? Just as Jacob had told his sons what would happen in time to come, just as Moses told the tribes their future, so we may understand the laws of history if we study the Torah. And in the Torah, we turn to beginnings: the rules as they were laid out at the very start of human history. These we find in the book of Genesis, the story of the origins of the world and of Israel.

The Torah tells us not only what happened but why. The Torah permits us to discover the laws of history. Once we know those laws, we may also peer into the future and come to an assessment of what is going to happen to us—and especially of how we shall be saved from our present existence. Because everything exists under the aspect of a timeless will, God's will, and all things express one thing, God's program and plan, in the Torah we uncover the workings of God's will. Our task as Israel is to accept, endure, submit, and celebrate.

2

That message must strike you as surprising, for in general people read the book of Genesis as the story of how Israel saw the past, not the future. People find in Genesis an account of the beginning of the world and of Israel—humanity from Adam to Noah, then from Noah to Abraham, and the story of the three patriarchs and four matriarchs of Israel (Abraham, Isaac, Jacob, Sarah, Rebekah, Leah, and Rachel), and finally Joseph and his brothers—from creation to the descent into Egypt. But to the rabbis who created Genesis Rabbah, the book of Genesis tells the story of Israel, the Jewish people, in the here and now. The principle behind their approach to the book is important for Christians and Jews alike. It is this: what happened to the patriarchs and matriarchs signals what will happen to their descendants; the model of the ancestors sends a message for the children. So the importance of Genesis, as the sages of Genesis Rabbah read the book, derives not from its lessons about the past but its message for Israel's and humanity's present—and, especially, future. Their conviction is that what Abraham, Isaac, and Jacob did shaped the future history of Israel. If, therefore, we want to know the meaning of events now and tomorrow, we look back at yesterday to find out.

This appears to be a kind of "historical" reading of Scripture. But it is history with a substantial difference. The interest is not merely in history as a source of lessons. It is in history as the treasury of truths about the here and now, and especially about tomorrow: the same rules apply. What the patriarchs did supplies the model, the message, the meaning for what we should do. That is why I offer for Christian readers a sizable example of what it means to read Genesis in light of today and tomorrow.

Why did the sages of the Jewish people come to Genesis with the questions of their own day? Because, they maintained, the world reveals not chaos but order, and God's will works itself out not once but again and again. If we can find out how things got going, we also can find meaning in today and method in where we are heading. So did our sages believe. And that is why they looked to a reliable account of the past and searched out the meaning of their own days. Bringing to the stories of Genesis that conviction that the book of Genesis told not only the story of yesterday but also the tale of tomorrow, the sages whose words are here before us transformed a picture of the past into a prophecy for a near tomorrow.

In terms of its literary character, Genesis Rabbah is a composite of paragraphs rather than a sustained essay. Each paragraph takes up a verse of the book of Genesis in sequence. So the whole book is organized around the order of another book; that is, Genesis Rabbah (as its name— "the great Midrash, or exposition, on Genesis"—tells us), follows the sequence of verses of the book of Genesis. Then who speaks through the book before us? I hear two different voices: (1) the voice of the author of the paragraph, and (2) the voice of the one who selected the paragraph and put it in the document, so speaking *through* choosing and including the paragraph but not through writing it. What sort of voice is this? It is the voice of the compiler, editor, arranger. As the editor of a newspaper speaks through the selection and arrangement of stories, so the framers of Genesis Rabbah talk to us through what they have chosen and how they have laid things out. It is the picture created by a great arrangement of flowers, the tableau deep with meaning created in choreography. It is as if you determined to write a book by selecting paragraphs from letters you have received; your book would have two voices, the voice of your correspondents and, as the one who selected and arranged their messages, your voice too. It is like the place of the artist in creating a collage; the artist does not create the materials, but the artist does see and convey the message. So Genesis Rabbah speaks through selection and arrangement, and also through what is chosen. That is why, for our part, when we want to know from whom we hear in this book we turn first of all to the people who made the choices and assembled the book's materials as we now have them. We do not know who wrote the paragraphs before us, or where, when, or why someone composed them as we have them. But we do have the document itself, and the document as a matter of fact accurately represents the selection and arrangement of the writings— and therefore the mind and imagination of the people responsible for them.

We shall read our sages' comments as they address the common human condition. Knowledge of when and where they made those comments is not essential to an appreciation of what they have to say about the existential facts that we share with them. Still, readers may wish to know what precipitated the sages' interest in the book of Genesis. And once we know where and when the document reached its conclusion, we also can see more clearly to whom its message to begin with made a difference. Taking as fact the conclusions of people who have worked hard on the problem, we can place the document in one location (time, country) and not some other—namely, in the Land of Israel!, toward the end of the fourth century of the Common Era. What made that particular time crucial in the life of Israel, the Jewish people, in the Land of Israel, is an event that also shaped the entire history of Western civilization. We may, in fact, locate the sages' rereading of the Torah's account of the beginnings of the world and of Israel—the book of Genesis—at exactly that moment at which Western civilization also came to its genesis. In other words, the fourth century marked the beginning of the West as it reached its continuing and enduring definition.

What made all the difference, and what happened in that turning point in time? It was, first, the conversion of the Roman emperor Constantine to Christianity and the legalization of Christianity, then its designation as the state's favored religion, and finally, by the end of the century, the establishment of Christianity as the religion of Rome. To the Christians, it was an age of vindication and validation. Some of the Church's leading figures had met persecution and imprisonment in the decades just prior to Constantine's conversion, and then ended their lives as high officials of the Roman Empire at his court. If the great German rabbi Leo Baeck had been taken out of the concentration camp where he was located in 1945 and, by the end of 1947, had become prime minister of Germany under the successor of Adolph Hitler, we could begin to imagine the power of events as Christians experienced them. The triumph of Christianity changed the history of the West, because from that point onward the principal institutions of politics, culture, and social organization in Western civilization found definition and meaning in the Christian religion—pure and simple. Since Rome encompassed the greater part of then-known civilization in the West, the fourth century therefore encompassed the redefinition of the West. What happened may be summarized very simply: Rome became Christian, and a formerly despised and illicit religious group took power.

But that event, by itself, need not greatly have confounded Israel and its sages. A second event, at the same critical time, did matter. To understand it, we must recall that the Jewish people had hoped, from the destruction of the Temple in 70 c.e., to witness its rebuilding, together with the restoration of Israel's government in its land and the advent of Israel's righteous and correct ruler, the Messiah. Reason for that hope derived from the destruction of the first Temple, built by Solomon, when after the passage of a few generations Israel returned to its land, the Levites to their platform, and the priests to the altar of God. So hope persisted that the same pattern would find renewal, and the prophets' promises of redemption—which the Christians claimed had already been kept in the restoration after 586 B.C.E.—would once more be kept. Then Israel's faith as the ancient prophets had formed it would find that vindication which Christianity (from Israel's viewpoint, momentarily) now enjoyed. As the years passed, from Constantine's conversion in 312 C.E. onward, Israel's thinkers may well have pondered the meaning of events. We know that the counterparts in the Christian world found they had to revise and rewrite the entire history of the world, from creation onward, to provide an explanation of the new age in the continuity of time. It would be speculative to claim that Israel as a whole expected the Messiah just now, as the claim so long rejected that Jesus had been Christ and that Christ now triumphed made its way. For Christians claimed, quite plausibly for many, that the conversion of the hated Rome to Christianity both validated and vindicated their original conviction about Jesus as the Christ.

Whether or not Israel in its land worried over that matter we do not know. But we do know one stunning fact. In 360, a generation beyond Constantine's conversion, an emperor came to the throne who threw off Christianity and reaffirmed paganism. Julian, whom Christians called from then to now "the apostate," reestablished the overthrown idols, reopened the philosophical schools of pagan tradition, and presented paganism in its elegant and cultured form to a startled empire. At the same time Julian undertook to embarrass and humiliate the Christians. Since the Christians had by no means gained a majority of the population when Julian revealed this stunning turn in world history, the Christian dream seemed to turn into a nightmare. For the worst thing that can happen, beyond remission, is a new growth of cancer, and for those who recalled the miracle of Constantine's conversion and the consequent upward move of Christianity the moment foreboded a miserable end.

Why all this affected Israel is simple. As part of his program to embarrass Christianity and disprove its claims, Julian announced that the Jews might go back to Jerusalem and rebuild their Temple. The Gospels represent Jesus as predicting that no stone on stone would remain, for the Temple would be destroyed and never rebuilt. Indeed, no stone did remain on another. But now, it appeared, Jesus' prediction would be shown a lie. Then what would come of the rest of his other claims, as these circulated in the New Testament and in the Church? And how would the Christians now disprove the Jews' insistence that the prophets' promises of old would yet be kept? Since the Christians had long pointed to the destruction of the Temple and the loss of Jerusalem as marks of

Israel's punishment for rejecting Jesus' claim to be the Messiah (that is, the Christ), Julian's action certainly pointed toward a malicious intent. Here, in Julian's mind, people could find yet another cause to reject Christianity and all its claims. For the Jews, of course, Julian's move stood for something quite the opposite: the vindication of Israel's patience, endurance, and hope. Now it all seemed to come true—and that on the eve of the three hundredth anniversary of the destruction. By the Jews' reckoning the Temple had been destroyed in the year 68, so if it took a few years, from 360 onward, by the year 368 Israel would regain its holy altar and sacred city, as would God the sacrifices so long suspended, and—by Israel's hopeful reckoning—the world would conclude the sorry history and celebrate the coming of the Messiah.

But it was not to be. Within the year Julian died on a battlefield in far-off Iran, near the waters of Babylon where so large a portion of Israel then lived. Christians reported that on his lips, as he breathed his last, were the words, "Galilean, thou hast triumphed." Whatever he actually said—if anything—hardly matters, for that was precisely what the Christian world concluded: Jesus now was finally vindicated as the Christ. Julian's death in his campaign against the Iranian Empire under its most brilliant ruler, Shapur II, of the dynasty known as the Sassanian (hence, in the history books, Sassanian Iran), for all time wiped out the last hope of pagan renaissance in Rome. For Israel in its land the disappointment proved only the least problem.

Ahead, over the next generation, lay a trial the Jewish people in the Roman Empire had never before known. Judaism in Rome, from the beginnings of Roman rule in the Middle East before the time of the Maccabees, had enjoyed the status of a protected, completely licit religion. Jews enjoyed freedom to practice their religion. They could not, for example, be forced to violate the Sabbath. Buildings built for Judaic worship enjoyed the protection of the state. Constantine had done little to limit the Jews' rights, either as citizens or as believers in their faith. But now that freedom for the first time faced abridgement—and worse. What was happening was simple. After Julian, the initial policy of toleration of both paganism and Judaism shifted. The once-more-Christian Roman government determined to make certain that the Christian grasp on power never again would weaken. So laws against paganism in all its forms went forth from Constantinople to the entire Empire, placing severe restraints on all forms of pagan worship and imposing heavy penalties on those who fostered paganism.

When Christian zealots attacked pagan temples, just as in times past pagan zealots had harassed and murdered Christians, they went after synagogues and Jews as well. For in the counterattack on paganism, the net that was cast caught Israel too. Before Constantine, of course, Christianity had no politics, and therefore no policy for the Jewish people either. Afterward in a matter of a few generations Christianity had to develop a politics, a view of history, and a policy of a political character regarding the Jewish people. As a matter of theology, there had been a Christian policy of toleration for Israel, meant to await the second coming and the last judgment as witness to the truth of Christianity. That, in general, yielded a political policy that Jews were not to be exterminated, as pagans in time to come would be exterminated, and Judaism was not to be extirpated, as in the future paganism would be destroyed. This was to be the general policy for the long haul.

What in particular happened now, toward the end of the fourth century, from Julian's death after 260 to the turn of the fifth century? A policy, drawn from the program against paganism, limited Israel's right to the security and freedom that the nation had enjoyed in its land with only a few (if bitter) periods of persecution, from the coming of Roman governance and rule in the first century B.C.E. Specifically, synagogues were destroyed, Jews lost the right to convert slaves whom they purchased, Jews who became Christians enjoyed the protection of the state, and in various other ways Jews' former privileges and rights were abridged or revoked. By the turn of the fifth century, around 410, the Jews' institution of self-government in the land of Israel, the rule by their patriarch, came to an end. In all, it was a very difficult time—not because of trouble alone, not even because of the unprecedented character of the new laws and outrages, but because of the disappointment and despair that followed the high hopes kindled by Julian's abortive scheme. But we must take note of a simple fact: paganism was extirpated, Judaism was not. So in the long run, the Christian policy of limited toleration of Judaism did take effect. If it had not, Judaism too would have disappeared.

To revert to our sad analogy, if in 1937 Hitler had given way to a democratic government that restored Jewish rights, and in 1939 a new Nazi government had come back to power and annulled those rights again, we might have a relevant analogy to the awful dread that affected despairing Israel. What now? And what of the brief hope of yesterday? In consequence of the restoration of Christian rule and the disappointment attached to the failure of Julian's scheme to rebuild the Temple, Israel's hope for the restoration of the holy Temple and the drawing near of the Messiah turned into disaster. Not only would the Temple not be rebuilt, but the Christian claim that Israel's hope was lost, its land beyond its grasp, and its future in doubt enjoyed renewed self-evidence for those who believed it—and they were now many. Historians tell us that by the end of the fourth century the Land of Israel, the Holy Land, possessed a Christian and not a Jewish majority. Whether or not that is so I cannot say, but it does suggest what happened.

Why have I had to tell this tale? The fourth century in fact presented the West, including Israel, with its first "Christian" century. While the Jewish people had managed on the whole to ignore the Christians' slow but steady rise to power, they no longer could pretend Christianity constituted a temporary setback in the journey to the end of time. It was not temporary, it was far more than a setback, and it had to be dealt with. The fact that Genesis Rabbah came to closure toward the end of the fourth century matters for one reason: the Land of Israel now found itself in the domain of Christianity, an enormous and historical shift in the status of the land and of the Jewish people—therefore also of the Torah. In Genesis Rabbah every word is to be read against the background of the world-historical change that had taken place in the time of the formation of the document. The people who compiled the materials we shall now see made a statement through what they selected and arranged. This then is their collage, their creation. Genesis Rabbah in its final form emerges from that momentous first century in the history of the West as Christian, the century in which the Roman Empire passed from pagan to Christian rule, and in which, in the aftermath of the Emperor Julian's abortive reversion to paganism in 360, Christianity adopted that policy of repression of paganism which rapidly engulfed Judaism as well.

At the beginning I claimed that the sages who created Genesis Rabbah, Leviticus Rabbah, Sifré to Numbers, and the other great readings of Scripture in the third and fourth centuries offer us a model as much as a message. And it is the model that I alleged is relevant to all of us who revere Scripture as God's word, as do I and as do you, the reader. If we listen to the messages of Genesis Rabbah, we hear how Israel's sages reopened the book of Genesis and reconsidered its story of beginnings. And that is the model that they offer to us. Let me be specific.

In that story they hoped to find—and they did find—the counterpart, namely the story of the day at hand, which they anticipated would indeed form the counterpart and conclusion to the story of beginnings. From creation to conclusion, from the beginnings of salvation in the patriarchs and matriarchs to the ending of salvation and its fulfilment in their own day: this is what our sages sought to discover. And in the book of Genesis, in the doings of the founders, they found models for deeds of the descendants. And we can do the same. That is my message: *we can do the same*. Genesis Rabbah presents us with a model we can emulate. It teaches us to exercise freedom in responding to the written Torah, Scripture. It shows us how the sages of ancient times read Scripture in light of their own concerns. We too can follow their model and emulate their example. So Genesis Rabbah shows us a method and teaches us a message, and in both aspects it speaks directly to us. For the deepest conviction of our sages is that Scripture speaks to us, to Israel, in all ages and all the time. Accordingly, they recognize no single and original meaning that dictates for all time to come what Scripture is permitted to say. To the contrary, they exercised a freedom of interpretation, by insisting that God speaks through the Torah to Israel everywhere and continually. So they both exemplify for us how to read Scripture, and they also teach us some lessons that Scripture has to offer them and us. The power of Genesis Rabbah is not only its message, therefore, but also its method. What is the method? To take up Scriptures, and bring to the written Torah the deepest anguish of the age. Allow the Torah to speak to us here and now.

What is the message? It is to address the circumstance of historical crisis. In its own day, this message generated remarkable renewal, a rebirth of intellect in the encounter with Scripture, not in quest of the rules of sanctification—these had already been found by the framers of earlier rabbinic writings—but of salvation. So the book of Genesis, which portrays how all things had begun, would testify to the message and the method of the end: the coming salvation of patient, hopeful, enduring Israel. The deepest conviction of Judaism and Christianity today imparts relevance to that same message. It is to bring our burden and our crisis to Scripture, and to Genesis in particular, where it all began. There we shall seek the lessons of the coming salvation of eternal Israel—both parts of the one people of God.

How, exactly, does Genesis Rabbah work? Various verses of Scripture come to illuminate one another. A favorite exercise of our sages is to draw upon one verse to tell the meaning of an entirely distinct and separate passage. For example, in many passages we shall begin with a verse from one of the prophetic books or the writings, and only then work our way back to the verse of the book of Genesis that concerns us. This effort to see one verse in light of another provides a model of the mind of the sages. They see one verse in light of another because they are used to seeing one thing in light of another—today in the aspect of yesterday and tomorrow, one of the patriarchs in the aspect of the Jewish people, embodied in that man's life and times. The principal mode of thinking demonstrated here requires us to look deeply at something, for in the depths we find something else, as each thing stands for another and all things possess a potentiality of meaning never close to the surface, always in the depths.

This translation of Genesis Rabbah (in Hebrew, Bereshit Rabbah) takes as its text and systematic commentary J. Theodor and Ch. Albeck, *Midrash Bereshit Rabba: Critical Edition with Notes and Commentary* (Berlin and Jerusalem: 1893-1936), vols. 1-3. That text is critical, so far as contemporary Judaic scholarship can produce a critical text, and I have treated it as authoritative in every detail. I have furthermore had the advantage of an excellent translation, already available, and have made ample use of it. I systematically consulted H. Freedman, *Genesis*, in *Midrash Rabbah: Translated into English with Notes, Glossary, and Indices*, ed. Freedman and Maurice Simon (London: Soncino Press, 1939), vols. 1-2. Where I have adopted Freedman's translation verbatim or nearly so, I have indicated by adding his name in square brackets. But I have taken full account of his rendering of nearly every line. I learned from him on each occasion on which I consulted him. It is a splendid piece of work. As to the translation of verses of Scripture, I took an eclectic approach, sometimes copying Freedman's, sometimes relying on the fine English of the RSV, and sometimes making my own translation.

I have made up most of the system of identifying each sentence and paragraph. Specifically, I have labeled each sentence, paragraph, and larger composite, so as to facilitate ready reference to the entire document. The first Roman numeral refers to the *parashah*, or chapter; the second, to the paragraph of the *parashah*. These two matters are already signified in the printed text and in Freedman's translation. Many of the so-called paragraphs in fact are made up of two or more complete and autonomous thoughts. In my use of an Arabic numeral after the Roman, I indicate the divisions within paragraphs as I propose to differentiate them. I then indicate, by a letter, each individual stich, that is, the smallest whole unit of thought. Thus I:I.1.A stands for the first *parashah*,

the first paragraph of the first *parashah,* the first complete composition of
the first paragraph of the first parashah, and the first sentence of the first
complete composition of the first paragraph of the first *parashah*—and so
on. The same system is used in Leviticus Rabbah and Sifré to Numbers,
which follow.

To conclude, Genesis told about beginnings so as to point to happy
endings, and in reading the book of Genesis Israel could find reason to
hope for its future in the certain facts of a long-ago past. And so will our
generation now find hope in a trying age. That, in a single sentence,
states the astonishing achievement of the sages. Brought into being in
the age of crisis, Genesis Rabbah told Israel the meaning of its day and of
many days to come. For Genesis Rabbah, the first statement of Judaism
on the meaning of Genesis to be written down, formed the source for
centuries to follow. When for the coming, difficult centuries Israel would
turn to Genesis, the Jewish people would encounter that book through
the eyes of the sages who originally assembled the passages before us.
And when Israel faced disappointment in its messianic hope, when Israel
wondered where events were heading, when Jews asked why they should
go on and what their duties were, they found answers to their questions
in the book of Genesis. That was because the sages of Genesis Rabbah
had made that book a message for Israel's living history. No longer about
long-dead ancestors, the genealogy and family history of Genesis, imposed on the house and destiny of Israel, explained not a distant past but
an immediate moment: today, tomorrow, the drawing near of redemption. As I was working my way through Genesis Rabbah, with this
understanding of whom I heard and what I witnessed, I found myself
deeply moved by the human triumph of our sages. I do not mind saying
that there are passages in Genesis Rabbah that have moved me to tears. I
should be glad if the reader found here passages that move to faith, prayer
to the one God of Israel and all humanity, but—in the context of our
difficult century, which now comes to a close—above all to hope.

I conclude with a passage of Genesis Rabbah that, in my view, states
the center and heart of Judaism, and therefore the heritage of Judaism for
Christianity. The fundamental theological conviction that gives life to
the sages' search of Scripture is that the task of Israel is to hope, and the
message of Genesis—there for the sages to uncover and make explicit—
is always to hope. For a Jew it is a sin to despair. This I think defines the
iron law of meaning, telling the sages what matters and what does not,
guiding their hands to take up those verses that permit expression of
hope—that above all.

Genesis Rabbah XCVIII:XIV

4. A. "I hope for your salvation, O Lord" (Gen. 49:18):

B. Said R[abbi]. Isaac, "All things depend on hope, suffering depends on hope, the sanctification of God's name depends on hope, the merit attained by the fathers depends on hope, the lust for the age to come depends on hope.

C. "That is in line with this verse: 'Yes, in the way of your judgments, O Lord, we have hoped for you; to your name, and to your memorial, is the desire of our soul' (Isa. 26:8). 'The way of your judgments' refers to suffering.

D. "'. . . to your name': this refers to the sanctification of the divine name.

E. "'. . . and to your memorial': this refers to the merit of the fathers.

F. "'. . . is the desire of our soul': this refers to the lust for the age to come.

G. "Grace depends on hope: 'O Lord, be gracious to us; we have hoped for you' (Isa. 33:2).

H. "Forgiveness depends on hope: 'For with you is forgiveness' (Ps. 130:4), then: 'I hope for the Lord' (Ps. 130:5)."

Creation and Creationism: There Are Things We Cannot Know from Scripture

Let us start with a burning issue of our own time, the matter of creation-ism. Some people maintain that Scripture provides an inerrant account of how the world actually came into being. The sages affirm that Scrip-ture reveals some things, not others. In their day, as much as in ours, people speculated about the beginnings of things. The sages took the view that beyond one fact, that God made the world, no propositions about creation carried weight. In the passage at hand, the sages charac-terize as arrogant people who seek to penetrate beyond the limits that the human mind can reach. Opening with a verse that affirms that some things lie beyond our powers of understanding, the sages point out the limitations of our minds, our dependence—for knowledge and under-standing—upon the Torah. The lesson of creation is simple: creation testifies to the glory of God, Creator of heaven and earth. Science, including geology, only enhances our awe and wonder at God's work.

The passage that follows underlines the view that some questions cannot be answered. That point is made through a study of the meaning of the word "dumb." The pertinent theme of the verse cited at the outset is the notion that there are things about which one must not speak, hence in the repertoire of meanings attributed to the key word—"be dumb"—the important one is "silenced." The continuation of the verse carries forward the same idea, namely that one should not speak ar-rogantly against the righteous, meaning God. The combination of the two ideas is then clear. That is, it is arrogant to expound the works of creation, and these are matters about which one must remain silent. About what must we speak? About the glories of the Creator of heaven and earth. God alone made heaven and earth.

At the end we move toward a passage of special interest. People today open Scripture in search of the secrets of nature. Our sages did the same, and we see an example of how they did it. They found in the characteristics of the letters of the Hebrew alphabet special messages. Since the account of creation begins with the Hebrew letter *b* (beth, the second letter of the Hebrew alphabet) and not the Hebrew letter corresponding to the *a* (aleph, the first letter of the Hebrew alphabet), our sages seek the message conveyed by the *b*. What they find is a series of important lessons—all of them having to do with theological and moral matters, none of them dictating facts of creation.

I:V

1. A. R. Huna in the name of [that is, "on the authority of"] Bar Qappara commenced [discourse by citing the following verse]: "'Let the lying lips be made dumb [which arrogantly speak matters kept secret against the righteous]' (Ps. 31:18 [Hebrew v. 19]).

    B. "[Translating the Hebrew word for 'dumb' into Aramaic one may use words meaning] 'bound,' 'made dumb,' or 'silenced.'

    C. "'Let [the lying lips] be bound,' as in the following verse: 'For behold, we were binding sheaves' (Gen. 37:7).

    D. "'Let the lying lips be made dumb,' as in the usage in this verse: 'Or who made a man dumb' (Exod. 4:11).

    E. "'Let them be silenced' bears the obvious meaning of the word."

    F. "Which arrogantly speak matters kept secret against the righteous" (Ps. 31:18):

    G. ". . . which speak against the Righteous," the Life of the Ages, matters that he kept secret from his creatures [Freedman: the mysteries of creation].

    H. "With pride" (Ps. 31:18):

    I. That is so as to take pride, saying, "I shall expound the work of creation."

    J. "And contempt" (Ps. 31:18): Such a one treats with contempt the honor owing to me.

    K. For R. Yose b. R. Hanina said, "Whoever gains honor through the humiliation of his fellow gains no share in the world to come.

    L. "For one does so through the honor owing to the Holy One, blessed be he, how much the more so!"

    M. And what is written after the cited verse [Ps. 31:18]?

N. "How abundant is your goodness, which you have stored away
for those who revere you" (Ps. 31:19 [Hebrew v. 20]).

O. Rab said, "Let one [who reveals the mysteries of creation] not
have any share in your abundant goodness.

P. "Under ordinary circumstances, if a mortal king builds a palace
in a place where there had been sewers, garbage, and junk, will
not whoever may come and say, 'This palace is built on a place
where there were sewers, garbage and junk,' give offense? So
too, will not whoever comes and says, 'This world was created
out of chaos, emptiness, and darkness,' give offense?"

Q. R. Huna in the name of Bar Qappara: "Were the matter not
explicitly written in Scripture, it would not be possible to state
it at all: 'God created heaven and earth' (Gen. 1:1)—from
what? From the following: 'And the earth was chaos' (Gen.
1:2). [Freedman: God first created chaos and emptiness, and out
of these he created the world, but this is not to be taught
publicly.]"

I.III

1. A. R. Tanhum commenced discourse: "For you are great and do
wonderful things, you alone are God" (Ps. 86:10).

B. Said R. Tanhum b. R. Hiyya, "As to a skin, if it has a hole as
small as the eye of a needle, all of the air will escape from it.

C. "But as to a human being, a person is made with many apertures
and holes, but the spirit does not go forth through them.

D. "Who has done it in such a way? 'You alone are God' (Ps.
86:10)."

2. A. When were the angels created?

B. R. Yohanan said, "On the second day of creation [Monday]
were they created.

C. "That is in line with this verse of Scripture: 'Who lays the beams
of your upper chambers in the waters' (Ps. 104:3), after which it
is written, 'Who makes the spirits of your angels' (Ps. 104:4).
[The waters were divided into upper and lower parts, and on
that same day the angels were created.]"

D. R. Hanina said, "They were created on the fifth day of creation
[Thursday]. For it is written, 'Let fowl fly above the earth' (Gen.
1:20), and it is written, 'And with two did the angel fly' (Isa.

6:2). [Freedman, p. 5, n. 3: Thus angels too fall within the category of beings that fly and were created on the same day as all flying creatures.]"

E. R. Luliani b. R. Tabari in the name of R. Isaac: "Both from the viewpoint of R. Hanina and from that of R. Yohanan, there is agreement that nothing at all was created on the first day.

F. "That is so that you will not reach the false conclusion that Michael was there, stretching out the heaven at the south, with Gabriel at the north, and the Holy One, blessed be he, measuring from the middle.

G. "Rather: 'I the Lord do everything by myself, stretching out the heaven on my own and spreading forth the earth by myself' (Isa. 44:24).

H. "'By myself' is written [in Scripture, as if to mean 'who is with me?']. [That is, God asks, 'Who was my partner in creating the world?']

I. "In ordinary affairs when a mortal king is honored by a province the nobles of the province are honored with him. Why? Because they bear the burden with him.

J. "But that is not how it is with the Holy One, blessed be he.

K. "But he on his own created his world, so he on his own is glorified in his world."

3. A. Said R. Tanhuma, "'For you are great and do wonderful things' (Ps. 86:10).

B. "Why so? Because: 'You alone are God' (Ps. 86:10).

C. "You by yourself created the world.

D. "'In the beginning God created' (Gen. 1:1)."

I:IX

1. A. A philosopher asked Rabban Gamaliel, saying to him, "Your God was indeed a great artist, but he had good materials to help him."

B. He [Gamaliel] said to him, "What are they?"

C. He [the philosopher] said to him, "Unformed [space], void, darkness, water, wind, and the deep."

D. He [Gamaliel] said to him, "May the spirit of that man [you] burst! All of them are explicitly described as having been created by him [and not as pre-existent].

    E. "Unformed space and void: 'I make peace and create evil' (Isa.
        45:7).

    F. "Darkness: 'I form light and create darkness' (Isa. 45:7).

    G. "Water: 'Praise him, you heavens of heavens, and you waters
        that are above the heavens' (Ps. 148:4). Why? 'For he com-
        manded and they were created' (Ps. 148:5).

    H. "Wind: 'For lo, he who forms the mountains creates the wind'
        (Amos 4:13).

    I. "The deep: 'When there were no depths, I was brought forth'
        (Prov. 8:24)."

I:X

1. A. ["In the beginning God created" (Gen. 1:1):] R. Jonah in the
      name of R. Levi: "Why was the world created with [a word
      beginning with the letter] *b*?

    B. "Just as [in Hebrew] the letter *b* is closed [at the back and sides]
      but open in front, so you have no right to expound concerning
      what is above or below, before or afterward."

    C. Bar Qappara said, "'For ask now of the days past which were
      before you, since the day that God created man upon the earth'
      (Deut. 4:32).

    D. "Concerning the day *after* which days were created, you may
      expound, but you may not make an exposition concerning what
      lies before then.'

    E. "'And from one end of the heaven to the other' (Deut. 4:32).

    F. "[Concerning that space] you may conduct an investigation,
      but you may not conduct an investigation concerning what lies
      beyond those points."

    G. R. Judah b. Pazzi gave his exposition concerning the story of
      creation in accord with this rule of Bar Qappara.

2. A. Why with a *b*?

    B. To tell you that there are two ages [this age and the age to come,
      for the letter *b* bears the numerical value of two].

3. A. Another matter: Why was the world created [with a word be-
      ginning with the letter] *b*?

    B. Because that is the letter that begins the word for "blessing."

    C. And why not with an *a*?

    D. Because that is the first letter of the Hebrew word for "curse."

4. A. Another matter: Why not with an *a*?

   B. So as not to give an opening to the *minim* [heretics] to claim, "How can the world endure, when it has been created with a word meaning 'curse'!"

   C. Rather, said the Holy One, blessed be he, "Lo, I shall write it with a letter standing for the word 'blessing,' and may the world endure!"

5. A. Another matter: Why with a *b*?

   B. Because the letter *b* has two points, one pointing upward, the other backward, so that [if] people say to it, "Who created you?" it will point upward.

   C. It is as if to say, "This one who is above has created me."

   D. "And what is his name?" And it points for them with its point backward: "The Lord is his name" [pointing to the first letter in the alphabet, backward from the second, which is the *a*, standing for the One].

6. A. R. Eleazar b. Abinah in the name of R. Aha: "For twenty-six generations the letter *a* made complaint before the Holy One, blessed be he, saying to him, 'Lord of the world! I am the first among all the letters of the alphabet, yet you did not create your world by starting with me!'

   B. "Said the Holy One, blessed be he, to the *a*, 'The world and everything in it has been created only through the merit of the Torah. Tomorrow I am going to come and give my Torah at Sinai, and I shall begin only with you: "I [beginning with the *a*] am the Lord your God" (Exod. 20:2).'"

7. A. Bar Hutah said, "Why is it called "*alef*"? Because that is the word for a thousand: 'The word which he commanded for a thousand (*'elef*) generations' (Ps. 105:8)."

Chaos and Order, Nature and History

What God did in creating heaven and earth was to bring order to chaos. That is the principal point at hand. But it concerns the chaos not only of unformed nature, but also of incomprehensible history. Events yield patterns and conform to rules, God's rules, even though we do not always understand the order of reality. That is one principal message of our sages. For them, it follows, nature and history conform to the will of one God, and each forms the counterpart and complement of the other. When faced with events that break all the rules, the prophet Jeremiah invoked the enduring covenant between God and Israel and compared it to the sands on the seashore. God's covenant lasts so long as God's creation endures. Sages in the time at hand reaffirmed what the events of the day called into question: God's rule, in accord with principles of order and sense. The world beginning to end bears meaning, makes sense, and the rules of nature testify to the character of the rules of history: both conform to God's eternal rule and will. That is the message our sages uncovered in the story of creation.

The earth was unformed and void—until it obeyed God's will. So II:I. The earth furthermore stands for Adam, created without form, as well as Cain, the generation of the flood, and on and on. What our sages are telling us is that the condition of nature and the condition of humanity and its history form a corresponding and complementary whole. The work of salvation begins with the creation of light, which stands for the saints, Abraham, Isaac, Jacob, and so on. In a further, stunning exercise our sages move on from the correspondence of nature and history to the specific salvation-history of Israel. The creation of the world stands for the history of Israel, so that each moment of creation invokes what would happen in the story of God's people. Thus "the earth was unformed" refers to Babylonia. Our sages review the four kingdoms (Babylonia, Media, Greece, and Rome) that lead ultimately to the dominion of Israel, God's rule worked out through that of supernatural and holy Israel, God's people.

Identifying itself as Israel, the Church too would find in the history of Israel the meaning of the world from creation to ultimate redemption. This leads, at the end, to the coming of the Messiah. At the moment of creation God foresaw all that would happen, the deeds of the righteous and the wicked. In this way too, our sages maintain, the story of creation is also the story of the world, beginning, middle, and end.

II:I

1. A. "And the earth was unformed [and void, and darkness was upon the face of the deep]" (Gen. 1:2).
   B. R. Berekhiah opened [discourse by citing the following verse]: "Even a child is known by what he does, whether his work be pure and whether it be right" (Prov. 20:11).
   C. Said R. Berekhiah, "While [the earth] was as yet unripe, it yielded thorns.
   D. "[This accords with] what in the future will be prophesied in regard to it, 'I saw the earth, and lo, it was unformed' (Jer. 4:23)."

II:III

1. A. ["And the earth was unformed . . ." (Gen. 1:2):]
   B. R. Judah b. R. Simon interpreted the verse as referring to coming generations [as follows]:
   C. "'The earth was unformed' refers to Adam, who was [Freedman:] reduced to complete nothingness [on account of his sin].
   D. "'And void' refers to Cain, who sought to return the world to unformedness and void.
   E. "'And darkness was upon the face of the deep' (Gen. 1:2) refers to the generation of Enosh: 'And their works are in the dark' (Isa. 29:15).
   F. "'Upon the face of the deep' (Gen. 1:2) refers to the generation of the flood: 'On the same day were all the fountains of the great deep broken up' (Gen. 7:11).
   G. "'And the spirit of God hovered over the face of the water' (Gen. 1:2): 'And God made a wind pass over the earth' (Gen. 8:1).

H. "Said the Holy One, blessed be he, 'For how long will the world make its way in darkness. Let light come.'

I. "'And God said, "Let there be light"' (Gen. 1:3). This refers to Abraham. That is in line with the following verse of Scripture: 'Who has raised up one from the earth, whom he calls in righteousness to his foot' (Isa. 41:2-3).

J. "'And God called the light day' (Gen. 1:5) refers to Jacob.

K. "'And the darkness he called night' (Gen. 1:5) refers to Esau.

L. "'And there was evening' refers to Esau.

M. "'And there was morning' refers to Jacob.

N. "'One day'—for the Holy One, blessed be he, gave him one day, and what is that day? It is the Day of Atonement. [Freedman, p. 17, n. 1: It is the one day over which Satan, symbolizing the wickedness of Esau, has no power.]"

II:IV

1. A. R. Simeon b. Laqish interpreted the verses at hand to speak of the empires [of the historical age to come].

   B. "'The earth was unformed' refers to Babylonia: 'I beheld the earth, and lo, it was unformed' (Jer. 4:23).

   C. "'And void' refers to Media: 'They hastened [using the letters of the same root as the word for 'void'] to bring Haman' (Esth. 6:14).

   D. "'Darkness' refers to Greece, which clouded the vision of the Israelites through its decrees, for it said to Israel, 'Write on the horn of an ox [as a public proclamation for all to see] that you have no portion in the God of Israel.'

   E. "'. . . upon the face of the deep' refers to the wicked kingdom [of Rome].

   F. "Just as the deep surpasses investigation, so the wicked kingdom surpasses investigation.

   G. "'And the spirit of God hovers' refers to the spirit of the Messiah, in line with the following verse of Scripture: 'And the spirit of the Lord shall rest upon him' (Isa. 11:2)."

2. A. On account of what merit will the Messiah come? [It will be on account of the merit represented by the verse:] ". . . over the face of the water" (Gen. 1:2).

   B. It is, specifically, on account of the merit of repentance, which is compared to water: "Pour out your heart like water" (Lam. 2:19).

II:V

1. A. R. Abbahu and R. Hiyya the Elder:
   B. R. Abbahu said, "At the beginning of the act of creating the world, the Holy One, blessed be he, foresaw the deeds of the righteous and of the wicked.
   C. "'And the earth was unformed' refers to the deeds of the wicked.
   D. "'And God said, "Let there be light"' refers to the deeds of the righteous.
   E. "But I do not know which of the two God prefers, the deeds of this sort or the deeds of that.
   F. "On the basis of what is written, namely, 'And God looked upon the light, seeing that it was good,' one has to conclude that God prefers the deeds of the righteous to the deeds of the wicked."
2. A. Said R. Hiyya the Elder, "At the beginning of the creation of the world the Holy One, blessed be he, foresaw that the Temple would be built, destroyed, and rebuilt.
   B. "'In the beginning God created' [refers to the Temple] when it was built, in line with the following verse: 'That I may plant the heavens and lay the foundations of the earth and say to Zion, You are my people' (Isa. 51:16).
   C. "'And the earth was unformed'—lo, this refers to the destruction, in line with this verse: 'I saw the earth, and lo, it was unformed' (Jer. 4:23).
   D. "'And God said, "Let there be light"'—lo, it was built and well constructed in the age to come.
   E. "That is in line with this verse: 'Arise, shine, for your light has come, and the glory of the Lord is risen upon you' (Isa. 60:1)."

Nature Obeys, Humanity Rebels

What strikes our sages in the story of the creation of the world is how faithful nature carried out God's word, while rebellious humanity did not. The story of creation then presents a contrast, from which humanity draws its lesson, and nature today teaches us that same lesson. Its order, its regularity, its obedience to rules tell humanity how things should be. Then humanity, with its disorder, its disobedience, its incapacity to carry out God's word and will, is shamed. The fundamental lesson of creation, as our sages read the narrative, therefore concerns humanity rather than details of the natural world. When the Psalmist says, "The heavens declare the glory of God," the message is somewhat different from what we hear. It is not the celebration of nature, but the celebration of God by nature, and that is what we now contemplate.

Once more our sages link the story of creation to the history of humanity and of Israel. In the present case the creation of water points toward the punishment, by water, of sinful humanity. The opening passage provides a striking parable to draw the link between water and the generation of the flood. Although the water did not want to do what God commanded (V:IV), it did what it was told. This then draws the contrast to sinful Adam. But Israel, obedient to the covenant, would be saved by water (V:V) at the splitting of the sea. The message of creation, then, is that nature obeyed the will of the Creator, and humanity has that same task. The principal virtue is humility, acceptance of God's will, conciliation with one's fellow. That attitude of humility toward God will then yield as well good will toward others. How we feel and act toward God governs also our behavior toward our fellow human beings.

Here also in the systematic effort to interrelate the story of creation with the history of Israel there is a close correspondence between the natural world and the historical world of Israel. The repertoire of historical events of course is hardly random, since it lays emphasis upon moments at which Israel was saved. So the main point is that Israel will be saved by God's intervention into its history, just as the world was brought into existence through God's act of creation. I take the emphasis therefore to stress the power of God to do his will in the natural and in the historical world, but in context that power also takes form through the obedience of the water to God's word. Time and again Israel will be compared to dirt and to water, to indicate its virtue: submission and obedience. The message is clear.

The composition contains an important proposition, that the natural world links itself up to Israel's history. Just as, when a miracle is done for Israel, Israel sings a song of praise, so too will the day or the night, depending on circumstance. That proposition far transcends a single setting, since it forms a main-beam of the argument of the compositors of Genesis Rabbah. The obvious implication is that Israel, now accepting lesser status than Rome, will gain stature and merit on that account. So the subjugated condition of Israel now enhances its greatness in time to come.

V:I

1. A. "And God said, 'Let the waters under the heaven be gathered together into one place and let the dry land appear'" (Gen. 1:9).

   B. It is written, "At your rebuke they fled" (Ps. 104:7).

   C. "And God said, 'Let the waters under the heaven be gathered together into one place . . .'" (Gen. 1:9).

2. A. ["Let the waters be gathered together into one place" (Gen. 1:9):] R. Berekhiah in the name of R. Abba b. Yama: "'Let there be a line set for the water,' in accord with this verse of Scripture: 'And a line shall be stretched forth over Jerusalem' (Zech. 1:16). [Freedman, p. 34, n. 2: The radicals of the Hebrew word for 'let . . . be gathered' thus derive from the word for a measuring line and are to be translated: 'let the waters be confined to a definite measure of quantity.']"

   B. [Explaining the language for "be gathered together" differently,] R. Abba b. Kahana in the name of R. Levi: "'Let the water be gathered together to me [that is, in the sense of the dative, 'for my purpose,' 'so that'] I may do with them what I plan in the future [specifically, the flood I shall make of the waters].'

   C. "The matter may be compared to the case of a king who built a palace and gave residences in it to people who lacked the power of speech. They would get up in the morning and greet the king by making appropriate gestures with their fingers and with flag-signals. The king thought to himself, 'Now if these, who lack the power of speech, get up in the morning and greet me by means of gestures, using their fingers and flag-signals, if they had full powers of speech, how much the more so!'

D. "So the king gave residences in the palace to people possessed of full powers of speech. They got up and took possession of the palace [and siezed it]. They said, 'This palace no longer belongs to the king. The palace now belongs to us!'

E. "Said the king, 'Let the palace revert to its original condition.'

F. "So too, from the very beginning of the creation of the world, praise for the Holy One, blessed be he, went upward only from water. That is in line with the verse of Scripture which states, 'From the roar of many waters' (Ps. 93:4). And what praise did they proclaim? 'The Lord on high is mighty' (Ps. 93:4).

G. "Said the Holy One, blessed be he, 'Now if these [waters], which have neither mouth nor power of speech, so praise me, when mortals are created, how much the more so!'

H. "The generation of Enosh went and rebelled against him, the generation of the flood went and rebelled against him, the generation of the dispersion went and rebelled against him.

I. "The Holy One, blessed be he, said, 'Let these be taken away and let those [that were here before, that is, the primeval waters] come back.'

J. "That is in line with the following verse of Scripture: 'And the rain was upon the earth forty days and forty nights' (Gen. 7:12)."

V:III

1. A. Said R. Levi, "The waters were saying to one another, 'Let us go and obey the command of the Holy One, blessed be he.'

B. "That is in line with the following verse of Scripture: 'The floods have lifted up their voice' (Ps. 93:3).

C. "They said, 'Where shall we go?'

D. "Scripture says, 'Let the floods take up their roaring' (Ps. 93:3)."

E. R. Levi said, "The reference [to the place set aside] is 'the way of the sea' [a play on the word 'their roaring']."

F. R. Abba b. Kahana said, "The word [for 'roaring'] means 'to such and such a place,' 'to such and such a corner.'"

G. R. Huna said, "It means 'to this sea.'"

H. R. Joshua b. Hananiah said, "'to the receptacle of the sea' [Freedman]."

I. R. Eliezer says, "The sea drew them in, in line with this verse of Scripture: 'Have you entered into the springs of the sea' (Job 38:16). The sense is, to the place of waters absorbed by the sea."

J. Our rabbis [explain the same usage] in this way, "[The waters say,] 'We are crushed, so receive us, we are crushed, so receive us.'"

V:IV

2. A. Said R. Berekhiah, "The upper water separated from the lower water only with great anguish, in line with this verse: 'He holds the streams back from weeping' (Job 28:11)."

B. R. Tanhuma provides proof of the same proposition from the following: "'He has made the earth by his power . . . at the voice of his giving a multitude of waters in the heavens' (Jer. 10:12-13). The word 'voice' refers only to weeping, in line with this verse: 'A voice is heard in Ramah, moaning, bitter weepings' (Jer. 31:15)."

V:V

1. A. Said R. Jonathan, "The Holy One, blessed be he, made a stipulation with the sea to split open before the Israelites.

B. "That is in line with this verse of Scripture: 'And the sea returned to its former strength', which word may be read, 'in accord with the stipulation that it had given' (Exod. 14:27)."

C. Said R. Jeremiah b. Eleazar, "It was not with the sea alone that the Holy One, blessed be he, made such a stipulation, but he made the same stipulation with everything that was created in the six days of creation.

D. "That is in line with this verse of Scripture: 'I, even my hands, have stretched out the heavens, and all their host have I commanded' (Isa. 45:12).

E. "'I commanded' the sea to divide.

F. "'I commanded' the heaven to be silent before Moses: "Give ear, heaven" (Deut. 32:1).

G. "'I commanded' the sun and the moon to stand still before Joshua.

H. "'I commanded' the ravens to bring food to Elijah.

I. "'I commanded' the fire not to harm Hananiah, Mishael, and Azariah.

J. "'I commanded' the lions not to harm Daniel, the heaven to open before Ezekiel, the fish to vomit up Jonah."

V:IX

1. A. "And God said, 'Let the earth put forth grass'" (Gen. 1:11):

B. It has been taught on Tannaite authority [that is, of the compilers of the Mishnah] in the name of R. Nathan, "Three came in for judgment but four went out guilty: Adam, Eve, and the snake went in for judgment, but [in addition] the earth was condemned along with them: 'Cursed is the ground' (Gen. 3:17).

C. "[That is to say,] the ground would produce for man accursed things, such as gnats, insects, and fleas."

D. Then let the ground produce a camel for him?

E. Said R. Isaac of Magdala, "Even in such a beast there is benefit to be derived."

F. Why was the ground accursed?

G. R. Judah b. R. Shalom said, "It was because the earth violated the commandment [that had been assigned to her]. For this is what the Holy One, blessed be he, had actually said: 'Let the earth put forth grass, herbs yielding seed, and fruit-trees bearing fruit' (Gen. 1:11). [The sense of the commandment is as follows:] just as the fruit of the tree is eaten, so the wood of the tree should be edible. [But that is not the case, and hence the ground did not carry out its orders.]

H. "But the ground did not do it that way, rather: 'And the earth brought forth grass, herbs yielding seed after its kind, and trees *bearing* fruit' (Gen. 1:12). The fruit of the tree could be eaten, but the wood of the tree could not be eaten."

I. R. Phineas says, "What the earth did wrong was to add to the commandment that had been given it, supposing that in doing so, [the earth] would do the will of her creator: 'A tree bearing fruit' (Gen. 1:11) meant [to the earth] that even barren trees should produce fruit."

J. In accord with the view of R. Judah, there is no problem [in understanding the curse], but in accord with that of R. Phineas, why should the earth have been cursed? [It improved on its assignment.]

K. It is in line with what people say: "Cursed be the breast who suckled such a one as this."

3. A. When iron was created, the trees began to fret.

B. [God] said to them, "Why should you fret? Let wood that comes from you not enter it [as the heft of an ax], and none of you will have to worry about injury. [You are responsible for your own problems.]"

VI:II

1. A. "And God made the two great lights" (Gen. 1:16):

B. "Yours is the day, yours also is the night" (Ps. 74:16).

C. [Israel speaks:] "To you [God], the day gives praise, to you the night gives praise.

D. "Just as the day falls into your dominion, so the night falls into your dominion. When you do miracles for us by day, then 'Yours is the day.' And when you do miracles for us by night, then 'Also yours is the night.'

E. "When you do miracles for us by day, we say a song of praise before you by day. When you do miracles for us by night, we say before you a song of praise by night.

F. "You did miracles for us by day, so we sang a psalm before you by day: 'Then sang Deborah and Barak the son of Abinoam on that day' (Judg. 5:1).

G. "You did miracles for us by night, so we sang a psalm before you by night: 'You shall have a song as in the night when a feast is hallowed' (Isa. 30:29).

H. "For you it is fully right to recite a song by day and by night.

I. "Why so? For: 'You have established light and sun' (Ps. 74:16)," and "you made the two great lights" (Gen. 1:16).

VI:III

1. A. ["And God made the two great lights" (Gen. 1:16):]
R. Tanhum, R. Phineas in the name of R. Simon: "Since [God]

calls them 'great,' how is it possible that he then goes and diminishes [one of] them by saying, 'the great light and the lesser light' (Gen. 1:16)?

B. "It is because [the latter] entered the territory of its fellow. [The moon sometimes appears by day, not only by night.]"

2. A. Said R. Phineas, "In reference to all offerings, it is written: 'And a he-goat for a sin-offering' (Num. 28:22; 29:5). But with reference to the offering for the new month, it is written: 'A he-goat for a sin-offering for the Lord' (Num. 28:15).

B. "[What sin has the Lord committed, that a he-goat has to be brought as a sin-offering in behalf of the Lord?] Said the Holy One, blessed be he, 'I am the one who made him enter the territory of his fellow.'

C. "Now if this one entered the territory of his fellow with permission nonetheless is disparaged by Scripture, one who enters the territory of his fellow without permission—how much the more so!"

3. A. R. Levi in the name of R. Yose b. R. Ilai: "It is merely natural that someone who presently is great should count by what is great, and someone who presently is small should count by what is small.

B. "Esau [Rome] counts by the sun, because it is great, while Jacob [Israel] counts by the moon, for it is small."

C. Said R. Nahman, "That really is a good omen. Esau counts by the sun, because it is great. But just as the sun rules by day but does not rule by night, so Esau will have something in this world but nothing in the world to come.

D. "Jacob counts by the moon, which is small, and just as the moon rules by night and also by day [making its appearance both by night and by day], so too will Jacob have a portion in this world and in the world to come."

E. R. Nahman made a further statement on the same matter. R. Nahman said, "So long as the light of the great luminary lasts, the light of the lesser luminary is not going to be noted. Once the light of the great light sets, then, and only then, the light of the lesser one shines forth.

F. "So too, as long as the light of Esau lasts, the light of Jacob will not be seen. Once the light of Esau sets, then the light of Jacob will shine forth.

G. "That is in line with this verse: 'Arise, shine [for behold, darkness shall cover the earth, and gross darkness the peoples, but upon you the Lord will arise, and his glory shall be seen upon you]' (Isa. 60:1)."

VI:IV

1. A. "And the stars" (Gen. 1:16):

   B. Said R. Aha, "The matter may be compared to the case of a king who had two governors, one of whom governed a city, the other an entire province. Said the king, 'Since this one has accepted a lesser position, ruling over a city, I decree in his regard that, when he goes forth, the council and people shall go forth with him, and when he comes back in, the entire council and people will come back with him.'

   C. "So said the Holy One, blessed be he, 'Since the moon has accepted a diminished position, ruling only by night, I decree concerning the moon that, when the moon comes out, the stars should come out with it, and when [the moon] comes in, the stars should come in with it.'"

   D. And along these same lines: "And his brother's name was Yoktan" (Gen. 10:25) [that is, "he shall be small"].

   E. Said R. Aha, "Why was he called 'He shall be small'? For he diminished himself [by his modest actions]. And what on that account did he merit? [On account of the merit attained by his modesty,] he had the merit of raising up thirteen families.

   F. "Now if that is the case with a small person, if a great person diminishes his stature, how much the more so [will he gain merit on that account]!"

   G. Along these same lines: "And Israel put forth his right hand and placed it on the head of Ephraim, while he was the younger" (Gen. 48:14).

   H. Said R. Huna, "Now do we not know on our own the order of the generations [of Joseph's household], that Scripture should have to tell us that he was the younger?!

   I. "But rather, he is called 'the lesser' because he diminished himself. And what did he merit on that account? He gained the merit of being awarded the blessing of the first-born. If a great person diminishes his stature, how much the more so [will he gain merit on that account]!"

"Let Us Make Man"

The sages understood that the Hebrew word Adam, translated as "man," really refers to the human being, male and female, as Scripture itself makes clear. That androgynous character of the first human being marked only one of the ways in which we are twin-beings. We are dual not only in our male and female sexuality, but, in a deeper sense, in our capacity to do good and our power to do evil. And we are dual, also, in our fate: in this world and in the world to come. That is God's view of humanity, as Genesis lays matters out. The story of the creation of the human being opens the tragic account of Genesis. From this point onward, the story unfolds as the tale of God's disappointment. The high hopes—"Let us make man in our image, after our likeness"—gradually give way to despair: "For the inclination of the heart of man is only evil. . . ."

And yet, our sages underline the hopeful side: the human being was made of heaven and earth—capacity for evil, power to do good. Both dimensions take the measure of humanity, and the choice is ours: with grace to do the good.

Our sages lay stress on the utter uniqueness of Adam (man/woman, born androgynous). God took counsel with heaven and earth in creating Adam. God recognized that humanity would sin, but also that there would be saints among Adam's and Eve's descendants. This mixed character of humanity was part of Adam's nature. The debates among the angels, the argument between Truth and Righteousness that we shall witness all testify to the combination, in Adam, of good and evil, both of them part of human nature. The vision of humanity formed by our sages came to them not out of the everyday facts of the streets and marketplaces as the sages observed them. We are not guided by people who knew nothing of the real world.

This vision, so grand and so transcendant, comes from sages who believed despite the evidence of the day that humanity is in God's image, after God's likeness. Their vision rested on God's image in humanity, and that is why they could imagine humanity as they did. The message is that in creating man God expressed his special love for him. I call special attention to VIII:X: since man is in God's image, the angels did not know man from God. Only that man sleeps distinguishes man from God. I cannot imagine a more daring affirmation of humanity. The theme derives from the verse that states, ". . . in our image, after our likeness" (Gen. 1:26), but this passage is not cited in the present construction. Clearly VIII:X simply carries forward the concluding entry of VIII:IX, in which the relevant verse is cited. We have, then, no mere anthology on the cited verse. We have a profoundly polemical statement about the true character and condition of man.

Accordingly, "In our image" yields the view that the complete image of man is attained in a divine union between man and woman, and, further, the syllogism that what makes man different from God is that man sleeps, and God does not sleep. Given the premise of the base verse and the issues inherent in the allegation that man is in God's image, the treatment here proves extraordinary. Man has traits of angels and traits of beasts. When he is righteous, his angelic and heavenly traits mark him as in God's image, and when he sins he is not in the likeness and the image of God.

VIII:II

1. A. R. Hama b. Hanina opened [discourse by citing this verse]: "You know this of old time, since man was placed upon the earth" (Job 20:4).

   B. Said R. Hama b. Hanina, "The matter may be compared to a province which drew its sustenance from ass-drivers [who brought food from the countryside], and the drivers would say to one another, 'What market price shall we set today for the province?' Those who came on the sixth day [Friday] would ask those who came on the fifth, those who came on the fifth would ask those who came on the fourth, those who came on the fourth would ask those who came on the third, those who came on the third would ask those who came on the second, those who came on the second would ask those who came on the first. But as to those who came on the first [Sunday, after the Sabbath, on which the markets were closed,] whom did they have to ask? Would it not be the residents of the province, who were engaged in the conduct of public business for the province?

C. "So as to the works of creation of each day, the one would ask the other, 'What sort of creatures did the Holy One, blessed be he, create on you today?' Accordingly, those of the sixth day would ask those of the fifth, those of the fifth, those of the fourth, those of the fourth day would ask those of the third, those of the third would ask those of the second, those of the second day would ask those of the first. But as to the first day, whom could it ask? Is it not the Torah, which came before the creation of the world by two thousand years, in line with this verse: 'Then I was by him as a nursling and I was his delight day after day' (Prov. 8:30).

D. "Since a day, so far as the Holy One, blessed be he, is concerned, is a thousand years, as it is said: 'For a thousand years in your sight is like a day when it is passed' (Ps. 90:4), [we know that, because the passage in Proverbs refers to day after day, two thousand years were involved].

E. "That is in line with this verse: 'Do you know this of old time?' (Job 20:4).

F. "[The sense then is:] 'The Torah knows what came before the creation of the world, but you have no business in investigating such questions, attending rather to 'what has happened since man was placed upon earth' (Job 20:4)."

G. R. Eleazar in the name of Bar Sirah said, "Concerning what is greater than yourself do not seek,

H. "concerning what is stronger than yourself do not pursue knowledge,

I. "concerning what is more wonderful than yourself do not seek to know,

J. "concerning what is hidden from you do not ask,

K. "but concerning what has been permitted to you, look deeply, for you have no business in dealing with hidden things."

VIII:III

1. A. "And God said, 'Let us make man'" (Lev. 1:26):

   B. With whom did he take counsel?

   C. R. Joshua b. Levi said, "With the works of heaven and earth he took counsel.

   D. "The matter may be compared to the case of a king who had two advisers, and he would do nothing without their express approval."

E. R. Samuel b. Nahman said, "It was with the things that he had created each prior day that he took counsel.

F. "The matter may be compared to the case of a king who had a privy counsellor, and he would do nothing without his express approval."

G. R. Ammi said, "He took counsel with his own heart.

H. "The matter may be compared to the case of a king, who had a palace built by an architect. When he saw it, it did not please him. To whom could he then address his complaint? Would it not be to the architect? So too: 'And it grieved him in his heart' (Gen. 6:6)."

I. Said R. Yose, "The matter may be compared to the case of a king who conducted his affairs through a trust officer and incurred a loss. To whom should he address his complaint? Is it not to the trust officer? Accordingly: 'And it grieved him in his heart' (Gen. 6:6)."

VIII:IV

1. A. Said R. Berekhiah, "When God came to create the first man, he saw that both righteous and wicked descendants would come forth from him. He said, 'If I create him, wicked descendants will come forth from him. If I do not create him, how will the righteous descendants come forth from him?'

B. "What did the Holy One, blessed be he, do? He disregarded the way of the wicked and joined to himself his quality of mercy and so created him.

C. "That is in line with this verse of Scripture: 'For the Lord knows the way of the righteous, but the way of the wicked shall perish' (Ps. 1:6).

D. "What is the sense of 'shall perish'? He destroyed it from before his presence and joined to himself the quality of mercy, and so created man."

2. A. R. Hanina did not explain the cited verse in this way. Rather, [he said,] "When the Holy One, blessed be he, proposed to create the first man, he took counsel with the ministering angels. He said to them, 'Shall we make man' (Gen. 1:26)?

B. "They said to him, 'What will be his character?'

C. "He said to them, 'Righteous descendants will come forth from him,' in line with this verse: 'For the Lord knows the way of the righteous' (Ps. 1:6), meaning, the Lord reported concerning the ways of the righteous to the ministering angels..

D. "'But the way of the wicked shall perish' (Ps. 1:6), for he destroyed it [to keep it away] from them.

E. "He reported to them that righteous descendants would come forth from him, but he did not report to them that wicked descendants would come forth from him. For if he had told them that wicked descendants would come forth from him, the attribute of justice would never have given permission for man to be created."

VIII:V

1. A. Said R. Simon, "When the Holy One, blessed be he, came to create the first man, the ministering angels formed parties and sects.

   B. "Some of them said, 'Let him be created,' and some of them said, 'Let him not be created.'

   C. "That is in line with the following verse of Scripture: 'Mercy and truth fought together, righteousness and peace warred with each other' (Ps. 85:11).

   D. "Mercy said, 'Let him be created, for he will perform acts of mercy.'

   E. "Truth said, 'Let him not be created, for he is a complete fake.'

   F. "Righteousness said, 'Let him be created, for he will perform acts of righteousness.'

   G. "Peace said, 'Let him not be created, for he is one mass of contention.'

   H. "What then did the Holy One, blessed be he, do? He took truth and threw it to the ground. The ministering angels then said before the Holy One, blessed be he, 'Master of the ages, how can you disgrace your seal [which is truth]? Let truth be raised up from the ground!'

   I. "That is in line with the following verse of Scripture: 'Let truth spring up from the earth' (Ps. 85:2)."

   J. All the rabbis say the following in the name of R. Haninah, R. Phineas, R. Hilqiah in the name of R. Simon: "'Very' [at Gen. 1:31], 'And God saw everything that he had made, and behold it was very good,' refers to man.

K. "The sense is, 'And behold, man is good.'"

L. R. Huna the elder of Sepphoris said, "While the ministering angels were engaged in contentious arguments with one another, keeping one another preoccupied, the Holy One, blessed be he, created him.

M. "He then said to them, 'What good are you doing [with your contentions]? Man has already been made!'"

VIII:VI

1. A. R. Huna in the name of R. Aibu: "It was with considerable thought that he created him. [How so?] Only after he had created what was needed for his food, he created him.

B. "So the ministering angels said before the Holy One, blessed be he, 'Lord of the ages, "What is man that you should give so much thought to him, and the son of man that you should think about him?" (Ps. 8:4 [Hebrew v. 5]). How come you went to all this trouble in creating him?'

C. "He said to them, 'If so, "Sheep and oxen, all of them" (Ps. 8:7 [Hebrew v. 8])—why were they created? "The birds of the heaven and the fish of the sea" (Ps. 8:8 [Hebrew v. 9])—why were they created too?

D. "If there is a tower filled with all sorts of good things but no guests [for the owner to entertain], what good is it all to the owner who filled it up?'

E. "They said to him, '"Lord, our Lord, how glorious is your name in all the earth" (Ps. 8:9 [Hebrew v. 10])! Do what pleases you!'"

VIII:VII

1. A. R. Joshua of Sikhnin in the name of R. Levi: "He took counsel with the souls of the righteous, in line with the following verse: 'These were the makers, and those that dwelled among plantations and hedges; there they dwelt with the king in his work' (1 Chr. 4:23).

B. "'These were the makers' corresponds to the verse: 'And the Lord God made man' (Gen. 2:7).

C. "'And those that dwelled among plantations' to the verse: 'And the Lord God planted a garden eastward' (Gen. 2:8).

D. "'And hedges,' in line with: 'I have placed the sand for the bound of the sea' (Jer. 5:22).

E. "'There they dwelt with the king in his work': They dwelt there with the King of kings of kings, the holy one, blessed be He.

F. "With the souls of the righteous among them he took counsel and created the world."

VIII:VIII

1.

A. R. Samuel b. Nahman in the name of R. Jonathan: "When Moses was writing out the Torah, he wrote up the work of each day [in sequence]. When he came to the verse, 'And God said, "Let us make man . . . ,"' (Gen. 1:26), he said, 'Lord of the age, in saying this you give an opening to heretics [to claim that there are two dominions in heaven, so the Creator-God had to consult with others in making the world, because he was not alone and all-powerful].'

B. "He said to him, 'Write it anyhow, and if someone wants to err, let him err.'

C. "The Holy One, blessed be he, said to him, 'Moses, as to this man whom I am going to create, will I not bring forth both great and unimportant descendants from him?

D. "It is so that, if a great man has to get permission from a lesser person and says, 'Why in the world should I have to get permission from an unimportant person,' people will say to him, 'Learn a lesson from your creator, who created the creatures of the upper world and the creatures of the lower world, but when he came to create man, went and took counsel with the ministering angels.'"

2. A. Said R. Layyah [Hila], "There is no taking counsel here. Rather the matter may be compared to the case of a king who was walking about at the door of his palace and saw a clod tossed [on the ground]. He said, 'What should we do with it?'

B. "Some say, 'Use it for public baths,' and others, 'For private baths.'

C. "The king said, 'I shall make a statue [of myself] with it, and who is going to stand in my way?'"

VIII:X

1. A. Said R. Hoshiah, "When the Holy One, blessed be he, came to create the first man, the ministering angels mistook him [for God, since man was in God's image,] and wanted to say before him, 'Holy, [holy, holy is the Lord of hosts].'

   B. "To what may the matter be compared? To the case of a king and a governor who were set in a chariot, and the provincials wanted to greet the king, 'Sovereign!' But they did not know which one of them was which. What did the king do? He turned the governor out and put him away from the chariot, so that people would know who was king.

   C. "So too when the Holy One, blessed be he, created the first man, the angels mistook him [for God]. What did the Holy One, blessed be he, do? He put him to sleep, so everyone knew that he was a mere man.

   D. "That is in line with the following verse of Scripture: 'Cease you from man, in whose nostrils is a breath, for how little is he to be accounted' (Is. 2:22)."

VIII:XI

2. A. R. Joshua b. R. Nehemiah in the name of R. Hinena b. Isaac and rabbis in the name of R. Eleazar: "He created in him four traits applicable to beings of the upper world and four of the lower world.

   B. "As to traits applicable to creatures of the upper world, he stands up straight like ministering angels, he speaks as do ministering angels, he has the power of understanding as do ministering angels, and he sees as do ministering angels."

   C. But does a beast not see?

   D. [That indeed is the case,] but a man sees from the side.

   E. "As to traits applicable to creatures of the lower world, he eats and drinks like a beast, he has sexual relations like a beast, he defecates like a beast, and he dies like a beast."

3. A. R. Tipdai in the name of R. Aha: "The creatures of the upper world were created in the image and likeness [of God] and do not engage in sexual relations, while the creatures of the lower world engage in sexual relations and were not created in the image and likeness [of God].

B. "Said the Holy One, blessed be he, 'Lo, I shall create him in the image and likeness [of God], like the creatures of the upper world, but he will engage in sexual relations, like creatures of the lower world."

C. R. Tipdai in the name of R. Aha: "The Holy One, blessed be he, said, 'If I create him solely with traits of creatures of the upper world, he will live and never die, and if I do so solely with traits of creatures of the lower world, he will die and not live. Instead, I shall create him with traits of creatures of the upper world and with traits of creatures of the lower world.

D. "'If he sins, he will die, and if not, he will live.'"

VIII:XIII

1. A. Said R. Abbahu, "The Holy One, blessed be he, took the cup of blessing [for the benediction of the marriage of Adam and Eve] and said the blessing for them."

B. Said R. Judah b. R. Simon, "Michael and Gabriel were the best men of the first man."

C. Said R. Simlai, "We have found that the Holy One, blessed be he, says a blessing for bridegrooms, adorns brides, visits the sick, buries the dead, and says a blessing for mourners.

D. "What is the evidence for the fact that he says a blessing for bridegrooms? As it is said: 'And God blessed them' (Gen. 1:28).

E. "That he adorns bride? As it is written: 'And the Lord God built the rib . . . into a woman' (Gen. 2:22).

F. "Visits the sick? As it is written: 'And the Lord appeared to him' (Gen. 18:1).

G. "Buries the dead? As it is written: 'And he buried him in the valley' (Deut. 34:6)."

H. R. Samuel b. Nahman said, "Also he concerns himself for the mourner. It is written, 'And God appeared to Jacob again, when he came from Paddan-aram, and blessed him (Gen. 35:9).

I. "What was the blessing that he said for him? It was the blessing for mourners."

"And Behold, It Was Very Good"

The sages' paramount stress affirms creation: it is very good. Creation testifies to the greatness, the wisdom, the perfection of the Creator. That lesson, we recall, comes from leaders of a defeated people, who even now have seen their rivals come to power. Yet we hear no bitter message, no rejection of creation or of the Creator. Quite to the contrary, Scripture affirms—and the sages will not then deny—God's essential goodness. The study of creation, moreover, demands from humanity the best efforts, because "from this point forward, the glory of kings is to search out a matter." That means that those who through science uncover the glory, the perfection of creation serve the Creator of the world best of all. Not only is creation perfect, it also conformed to the rules of right timing: not too soon, not too late. Every aspect of creation reveals its miracle.

And yet, there is a subterranean theme before us, since our sages contrast the joy that God felt with creation and the sorrow that lay before. For God made humanity, which would sin and disappoint and lead God to despair. The contrast, then, sets the perfection and goodness of creation once more against the imperfection and evil done by humanity. We see a profound theodicy, blaming on humanity the imperfections of creation—surely the message that to begin with Scripture wishes to convey to us.

What our sages want to know is what, in particular, about creation was "very good." The answer they find is that everything was done at the right time, in the right way. God experimented in world-creation before settling on the world that is ours. Our sages further stand back and draw pleasure from God's evident pleasure in creation. They find in the powerful affirmation a profound moment, a deep judgment. But this calls to mind what some find as flaws in creation—death, for example. For if creation is "very good," then why is death in the world? Why sleep? Why the impulse to do evil? The list goes on: the balance between the traits in creation we appreciate and those that trouble us. All are explained, each in its way, as part of the perfection of creation. Keep in mind that this judgment comes not from people in command of their fate, but from the leaders of a defeated, disappointed nation, subjugated now to the rule of those they regard as heretics and sinners. And yet, they could conclude that "And behold, it was very good" means "and behold, man is good." In this age beyond the Holocaust, the power of Israel, the Jewish people, to live on and to build attests to that same attitude of mind which we see before us.

If we look ahead to the sequence of propositions from IX:I onward, what do we find? First, the mystery of creation is sealed and not to be revealed. Second, it is true that God made worlds before this one. But the reason is that only with the creation of this world did God know that the world he created was very good. God fully inspected this world and found it very good. God knew full well what he was doing from the beginning. If people maintained that the Creator-God was an evil bungler, the present sequence would present a systematic reply. God not only did not bungle creation but knew precisely what he was doing from beginning to end.

The reference to God's inspecting creation and finding it very good, then, contains no implication that God did not know what he was doing, since he knew full well from before creation precisely what he was doing. Obviously, were we to reconstruct the argument against which the sages direct their counterargument, we should once more find ourselves in the midst of a gaggle of gnostics. But that observation seems altogether too general, for "gnostic" stands for many positions sharing few indicative traits. All we can identify are the most general, hence commonplace, propositions. Without a theory on the particular sort of gnostic position against which argument flows, we cannot materially advance the large-scale interpretation of our document. Shortly we shall have reason to identify the holders of the position contrary to the one advanced by the sages.

The impulse to do evil draws in its wake the suffering that people undergo. Is this too very good? Indeed so, for the reason that is given: it is what brings people to the world to come. That is why Gehenna is very good, in line with the foregoing. Just as the suffering of people prepares them for the life of the age to come, so the promise of Gehenna makes them wish to avoid failures in performing religious deeds. From suffering and Gehenna we move on to the angel of death, also encompassed in the perfection of creation. The world is "very good" because there is an exact justice in what happens in the world. "Measure for measure" marks creation and its rules. While some maintain that the world presents marks of imperfection and of the Creator's incompetence of malicious spirit, the contrary is the case.

For at issue throughout is the simple question, "How can creation be 'very good' if there is evil in the world?" So we systematically review the challenges to the view that creation is "very good." These encompass death (IX:V.1), sleep (IX:VI), the impulse to do evil (IX:VII), suffering (IX:VIII), Gehenna (IX:IX), the angel of death (IX:X), and the measure of punishment (IX:XI). All of these negative aspects of creation mar the goodness of the work of the Creator-God and point to the conclusion that the Creator was evil, not good. By repeating the matter in a protracted catalogue and in a single form, the compositor makes his point. Everything people think mars creation in fact marks its perfection. Death is good because it prevents the wicked from getting what they have not earned, hence death insures justice in creation. Sleep is good because it permits the sage to study Torah all the more effectively when he awakes. The evil impulse produces good results. Suffering is the route to eternal life. Gehenna likewise insures justice for those who have earned a reward, by preventing those who have not earned a reward from getting one. The angel of death takes up the same task. And as to punishment? It is inflicted only with justice.

So in the end, there is a mete punishment for those who deserve it and a proper reward for those who earn it (so IX:XI.2). The crown of creation is man, and when God praises creation the intent focuses in the end upon humanity. We cannot treat as distinct from the foregoing the present, stunning conclusion. Rather, the passage that breaks the established form also presents the point of the antecedent catalogue. The purpose of the whole then leads us to conclude that the human being is "very good."

IX:II

1. A. R. Tanhuma opened [discourse by citing the following verse of Scripture]: "He has made everything beautiful in its time" (Eccl. 3:11).
   B. Said R. Tanhuma, "The world was created at the proper time. The world was not ready to be created prior to this time." [God admired the works of creation because the world was brought into being when it was ripe. Hence what has attracted the

exegete's attention, once again, is the question, What is it about the world that God found to be very good? The answer here is that the world was "beautiful in its time," the right one for God to create.]

2. A. Said R. Abbahu, "On the basis of the cited verse, we learn that the Holy One, blessed be he, had created worlds and destroyed them [as unsuccessful], until he created this world. He said, 'This one pleases me, the others did not please me.'"

B. Said R. Phineas, "The scriptural verse that supports R. Abbahu's view is this: 'And God saw all that he had made . . .' (Gen. 1:31)."

IX:III

1. A. ["And God saw all that he had made, and behold, it was very good" (Gen. 1:31):] R. Yohanan and R. Simeon b. Laqish:

B. R. Yohanan said, "A mortal king builds a palace, then examines the upper floors in one inspection and the lower ones in another; but the Holy One, blessed be he, could take in both the upper floors and the lower floors in a single look. [Freedman, p. 65, n. 1: Interpreting "And God saw *everything* that he had made"—in a single glance.]"

C. Said R. Simeon b. Laqish, "'Lo, it was very good' refers to this world. 'And lo, it was very good' [with the addition of *and*] encompasses the world to come. The Holy One, blessed be he, encompassed both of them with a single look."

2. A. R. Simeon b. Laqish in the name of R. Eleazar b. Azariah: "'Ah, Lord God, behold, you have made the heaven and the earth' (Jer. 32:17). From that moment: 'There is nothing too hard for you.' (Jer. 32:17)."

B. R. Haggai in the name of R. Isaac, "'And you, Solomon my son, know the God of your father, and serve him with a whole heart and with a willing mind; for the Lord searches all hearts, and understands all the imaginations of the thoughts' (1 Chr. 28:9). [Taking the root of the word for 'imaginations,' Hebrew *ysr*, which serves also as the root for the word 'form' or 'create,' we interpret as follows:] Before thought is formed in the heart of man, it already is revealed before you."

C. R. Yudan in the name of R. Isaac: "Before a creature is actually created, his thought is already revealed before you."

D. Said R. Yudan in his own name, "'For there is not a word on my tongue but lo, O Lord, you know it altogether' (Ps. 139:4). Before my tongue forms speech, already 'lo, O Lord, you know it altogether.'"

IX:IV

1. A. R. Hama b. Hanina and R. Jonathan:

B. R. Hama b. Hanina said, "The matter may be compared to the case of a king who built a palace. He saw it and it pleased him. He said, 'O palace, palace! May you always charm me as you charm me at this hour!' So said the Holy One, blessed be he, to his world, 'O my world, my world! May you always charm me as you charm me at this hour!'"

C. R. Jonathan said, "The matter may be compared to the case of a king who married off his daughter and arrayed for her a marriage canopy, a house, which he plastered, paneled, and painted. He saw [what he had made] and it pleased him. He said, 'O my daughter, my daughter, may this marriage canopy always charm me as it charms me at this hour.' So said the Holy One, blessed be he, to his world, 'O my world, my world! May you always charm me as you charm me at this hour.'"

IX:V

1. A. In the Torah belonging to R. Meir people found written, "And behold, it was very good" (Gen. 1:31) [means] "And behold, death is good." [The play is on the word "very," Hebrew *m'd*, and "death," Hebrew *mwt*.]

B. Said R. Samuel b. Nahman, "I was riding on my grandfather's shoulder, going up from my town to Kefar Hana through Bet Shean, and I heard R. Simeon b. Eleazar in session and expounding in the name of R. Meir, "'And behold, it was very good'— 'And behold, death is good.'"

2. A. R. Hama b. Hanina and R. Jonathan:

B. R. Hama b. Hanina said, "The first man was worthy not to have to taste the taste of death. And why was the penalty of death applied to him? The Holy One, blessed be he, foresaw that Nebuchadnezzar and Hiram were destined to turn themselves into gods. Therefore the penalty of having to die was imposed upon man. That is in line with this verse of Scripture: 'You were in Eden, the garden of God' (Ezek. 28:13). And was Hiram actually in Eden? But he said to him, 'You are the one who caused that one in Eden to have to die.'"

C. R. Hiyya, son of the daughter of R. Berekhiah, in the name of R. Berekhiah: "'You were the far-covering cherub' (Ezek. 28:14). He said to him, 'You are the one who caused that young man [Adam, a play on the words for 'young man' and 'cherub'] to have to die.'"

D. [Reverting to B, we continue:] Said R. Jonathan to him, "If so, God should have decreed death only for the wicked, but not for the righteous. Rather, it was so that the wicked should not be able hypocritically to pretend to repent, so that they should not have occasion to say, 'Are not the righteous living on and on? It is only because they form a treasure of merit accruing on account of the practice of doing religious duties as well as good deeds. We too shall lay up a treasure of merit accruing from doing religious duties and good deeds.' What would come out is that the things they do would not be done sincerely [for their own sake, but only for the sake of gaining merit]. [That is what is good about death. It prevents the wicked from perverting the holy life by doing the right thing for the wrong reason. Everyone dies, so there is no point in doing religious duties only so as to avoid dying.]"

3. A. R. Yohanan and R. Simeon b. Laqish:

B. R. Yohanan said, "On what account was a decree of death issued against the wicked? It is because so long as the wicked live they anger the Holy One, blessed be he. That is in line with the following verse of Scripture: 'You have wearied the Lord with your deeds' (Mal. 2:17). When they die they stop angering the Holy One, blessed be he. That is in line with the following verse of Scripture: 'There the wicked cease from raging' (Job 3:17). There the wicked cease angering the Holy One, blessed be he.

C. "On what account, however, is the decree of death issued against the righteous? It is because so long as the righteous live they have to conduct warfare against their impulse to do evil. When they die they find rest. That is in line with this verse: 'And there the weary are at rest' (Job 3:17). 'It is enough, we have labored long enough.'"

D. R. Simeon b. Laqish said, "It is so as to give an ample reward for the one, and to exact ample punishment from the other. To give ample reward to the righteous, who really never were worthy of having to taste the taste of death but accepted the taste of death for themselves. Therefore: 'in their land they shall possess double' (Isa. 61:7).

E. "'And to exact ample punishment from the wicked,' for the righteous had not been worthy of having to taste the taste of death but they had accepted the taste of death for themselves on account [of the wicked]. Therefore: 'And destroy them with a double destruction' (Jer. 17:18)."

IX:VI

1. A. Said R. Simeon b. Eleazar, "'And behold, it was very good' (Gen. 1:31) means: 'And behold, sleep is good.'

B. "But is sleep very good [under all circumstances]? Have we not learned in the Mishnah: 'Wine and sleep are a pleasure for them [the wicked] and also a pleasure for the world' [Mishnah *Sanhedrin* viii.5] [but sleep is not a pleasure for the world when the righteous go to sleep, since the world is then deprived of their righteous deeds. Accordingly, sleep is not invariably *very* good.]

C. "[Sleep is very good because] a person sleeps a bit and then gets up and works hard in Torah-study [accomplishing more than he would if he had not slept for a little while]."

IX:VII

1. A. R. Nahman in the name of R. Samuel: "'Behold, it was very good' refers to the impulse to do good. '*And* behold, it was very good' encompasses also the impulse to do evil.

B. "And is the impulse to do evil '*very* good'?

C. "[Indeed so, for] if it were not for the impulse to do evil, a man would not build a house, marry a wife, and produce children. So does Solomon say, 'Again I considered all labor and all excelling in work, that is rivalry with his neighbor' (Eccl. 4:4)."

IX:VIII

1. A. Said R. Huna, "'Behold, it was very good' refers to the measure that metes out good [things to people', while '*And* behold, it

was very good' refers to the measure that metes out] suffering as
well.

B. "And can anyone say that the measure of suffering is 'very
good'?

C. "Rather, on account of that measure people reach the life of the
world to come, and so does Solomon say, 'And reproofs of
chastisement are the way to [eternal] life' (Prov. 6:23).

D. "You may say: Go forth and see what is the path that brings a
man to the life of the world to come. You have to conclude, it is
the measure of suffering."

IX:IX

1. A. Said R. Zeira, "'Behold, it was very good' refers to the Garden
of Eden. 'And behold, it was very good' encompasses Gehenna.

B. "And can anyone say that Gehenna is 'very good'?

C. "Rather, the matter may be compared to a king who had an
orchard and brought workers into it, building a paymaster's hut
at the gate. He said, 'Whoever shows himself worthy through
hard work in the orchard may go into the paymaster's hut [and
collect his wages], and whoever does not show himself worthy
in the labor of the orchard may not go into the paymaster's hut.

D. "So for whoever stores up a treasury of merit through performing
religious duties and supererogatory good deeds, lo, there is the
Garden of Eden; and for whoever does not store up for himself a
treasury of merit through the performance of religious duties
and good deeds, lo, there is Gehenna."

IX:X

1. A. Said R. Samuel b. R. Isaac, "'Lo, it was very good' refers to the
angel of life. 'And lo, it was very good' refers to the angel of
death.

B. "And can anyone say that the angel of death is 'very good'?

C. "Rather, the matter may be compared to the case of a king who
made a banquet and invited guests and set before them a spread
of every good thing. He said, 'Whoever eats and says a blessing
for the king may eat and enjoy himself, but whoever eats and
does not say a blessing for the king will have his head cut off
with a sword.'

D. "So here, for whoever stores up a treasury of merit attained through performance of religious duties and good deeds, lo there is the angel of life. And for whoever does not store up a treasury of merit attained through performance of religious duties and good deeds, lo, there is the angel of death."

IX:XI

1. A. Said R. Simeon b. Abba, "'Behold, it was very good' refers to the measure that metes out good things to people. 'And behold, it was very good' refers to the measure that metes out punishment to people.
   B. "And can anyone say that the measure that metes out punishment is 'very good'?
   C. "What it means is that God reflected long on how to impose [the measure of punishment]."
2. A. R. Simon in the name of R. Simeon b. Abba, "All of the measures [of reward and punishment] have ceased, but the principle of measure for measure has not ceased."
   B. R. Huna in the name of R. Yose, "From the very beginning of the creation of the world, the Holy One, blessed be he, foresaw: 'By the measure that a person metes out to others, so by that measure is [his fate] meted out' [Mishnah Sotah i.7].
   C. "Therefore Scripture has said, 'And behold, it was very good,' meaning 'and behold, the measure is good' [a play on the word for 'very,' Hebrew m'd and 'measure,' Hebrew mdh.]"

IX:XII

1. A. All rabbis say the following in the name of R. Haninah, R. Phineas, R. Hilqiah in the name of R. Simon: "The word 'very' and the word for man are written with the same consonants [m'd, 'dm, respectively]. The letters for both are the same.
   B. "The meaning then is as follows: 'And God saw everything that he had made, and behold, it was very good' (Gen. 1:31)—and behold, man is good."

IX:XIII

1. A. Said R. Simeon b. Laqish, "'Behold, it is very good' refers to the kingdom of heaven. 'And behold, it is very good' encompasses the kingdom here on earth.

B. "And can anyone say that the kingdom here on earth is 'very good'?

C. "Rather, it exacts justice of mortals: 'I, even I, have made the earth and created man upon it' (Isa. 45:12). [The word for 'man,' Adam, may be read, 'Edom,' which then refers to Rome. So the point is that God affirms the legitimacy of Rome, the earthly kingdom (Freedman, p. 70, n. 2).]"

"Then the Lord God Formed Man"

For our sages humanity is made up of water and dirt, the two materials available for creation of humanity. And out of these humble materials came the one holy creature in creation: the human being in God's likeness, after God's image. For God's part there are also two components, justice and mercy. The world cannot endure without the one; humanity, without the other. But for sages no event takes place all by itself. Each relates to all others, so when we speak of the creation of "the man" we think of a particular one. And in sages' minds that is Abraham, counterpart of the first man. Further, the creation of humanity bears in its wake Eden and the fall, and sages read the creation of humanity in that context, as Scripture requires.

The sages' strength as exegetes derives from their power to see Scripture whole, as a set of interconnecting parts. So "the man" of Gen. 2:7 at XIV:VI refers to Abraham, with the further implication that the fall of Adam finds its counterpart in the rise of Abraham, progenitor of God's people. We proceed to the next element of the base verse, the reference to "the man," which, as we can have predicted on the basis of preceding materials, is taken to refer to Abraham. This is first proved and then explained. The underlying motif, the correspondence of the history of humanity to the history of Israel and of both to the character of creation, proceeds apace. Why, our sages ask, did God make man? It was on account of Abraham. In this way, sages once more link the creation of humanity to the history of Israel, seeing the salvation-history of Israel as the counterpart to the natural history of humanity. A further theme important to sages is the resurrection of the dead, and this too they seek to derive from the creation of man. Their third point of emphasis is on the mixed character of humanity, a point already familiar to us: heaven and earth, soul, matter joined. A point of interest to Christian readers follows: what precisely was the "tree of knowledge"? Since many have held that the "forbidden fruit" had to do with sexual knowledge, it is interesting to see that our sages view matters quite differently. The linking of Eden to Israel's history will not surprise us by this point in our

survey of our sages' approach to Scripture. But the interest of sages
extends to humanity at large, which is why they want to know what
religious duties were assigned to Adam, who stands for all humanity. In
this way sages lay out what they believe God—who loves all humanity—
wants of everyone. The religious duties—e.g., not to murder, not to
steal, not to fornicate—then pertain to everyone.

The paradise that God planned for humanity came about through
much reflection. God's intent was honorable; God's plan, perfect. Humanity corrupted the perfection of nature; humanity turned eternal life
into the history of misery and sorrow. That is the basic motif our sages
find in the narrative of Eden and the fall. XV:III stresses that God had
prepared Eden in advance, and humanity's salvation is made ready in
advance: "He had already worked salvation." The important side is that
the Garden had already been made ready for Adam. Creation was a
sequence of thoughtful and much-considered actions, leading to perfection.

XIV:VI

1. A. "Then the Lord God formed the man" (Gen. 2:7):
    B. It was on account of the merit accrued by Abraham [Freedman,
        p. 114, n. 2: The exegete interprets the definite article to indi-
        cate the outstanding man, that is, Abraham].
2. A. Said R. Levi, "It is written, 'The greatest man among the Ana-
        kim [giants]' (Josh. 14:15).
    B. "'Man' refers to Abraham, and why is he called a great man?
        Because he was worthy of being created before the first man
        [Adam].
    C. "But the Holy One, blessed be he, thought, 'Perhaps something
        may go wrong, and there will be no one to repair matters. Lo, to
        begin with I shall create the first Adam, so that if something
        should go wrong with him, Abraham will be able to come and
        remedy matters in his stead.'"
    D. Said R. Abba b. Kahana, "Under ordinary circumstances when
        someone has a pair of beams, he joins them so that they meet at
        a slope [and not flat] [following Freedman, translation and
        note]. And where does he join them? Is it not at the middle of
        the room [as a vault], so that they will bear the weight of the
        beams fore and aft?
    E. "So why did the Holy One, blessed be he, create Abraham at

the midpoint in the unfolding of the generations? It was so that he should support the weight of the generations fore and aft."

F. Said R. Levi, "People bring a virtuous woman into the household of a woman in disarray [to teach her proper conduct], but they do not bring a woman in disarray into the household of a virtuous woman."

XIV:VII

3. A. There was the case of one of the important personages of Sepphoris, whose son died. There are those who say that [the son died because] the man himself was a sectarian, and there are those who say that it was because a heretic took lodging with him. R. Yose b. Halapta went up to pay a call on him.

B. He [the sectarian] saw the bereaved man sitting and laughing. He said to him, "Why are you laughing?"

C. [Yose] said to him, "We trust in the Master of heaven that you will see his face in the world to come." [This formulation implies that Yose was speaking to the bereaved householder, hence the important man was a sectarian, not merely serving as the host for one.]

D. [The bereaved man] said to him, "Does not that man [I] have enough sorrow that you have come to make more? Can potsherds be glued back together? Is it not written, 'You shall dash them in pieces like a potter's vessel' (Ps. 2:9)?"

E. He said to him, "A clay utensil is made out of water and the work of making it suitable for use is done through fire. A glass utensil is made out of fire and is prepared for everyday utilization through fire. If the one is broken, it may be repaired, and if the other is broken, may it not be repaired? [If glass can be repaired once broken, so surely can man!]"

F. He said to him, "It is because [glass] is made through blowing [that glass can be repaired, but a clay utensil, such as man, cannot be repaired. There is no resurrection of the dead.]."

G. He said to him, "Should not your ears listen to what your mouth is saying? Now if this is made through having mortal man blow air into it and then can be repaired, what is made through the breathing of air of the Holy One, blessed be he, all the more so [can be repaired]!"

H. Said R. Isaac, "'You will dash them in pieces like earthenware' is not what is written, but 'like a potter's utensils,' meaning 'like those that have not yet been heated.' And these can be restored."

XIV:VIII

1. A. "[. . . of dust] from the earth . . ." (Gen. 2:7):
    B. R. Berekhiah and R. Helbo in the name of R. Samuel the elder: "He was created from the source of atonement [that is, from dirt, of which the altar was made].
    C. "This is in line with the following verse of Scripture: 'You shall make me an altar of earth' (Exod. 20:24).
    D. "Said the Holy One, blessed be he, 'Lo, I shall create him from the place at which he attains atonement, and may he endure!'"
3. A. Then he tossed the soul into him.
    B. For the creation in this world is through the breathing in of air, but in the world to come it will be through actually handing it over [Freedman: as a gift].
    C. "And I shall hand over my spirit as a gift to you, and you shall live" (Ezek. 37:14).

XV:III

1. A. "In the east" (Gen. 2:8):
    B. Said R. Samuel b. Nahman, "The word 'east' bears the sense of 'prior,' [so you may suppose that the meaning is that God had created the garden prior to the creation of the world, hence using the pluperfect, 'The Lord God *had* planted. . . .' But that is not the case,] for the sense is only that it was prior to the creation of the first man.
    C. "[How so?] Man was created on the sixth day, but the garden of Eden had already been created on the third, in line with the following verse of Scripture: 'Yet God is my king, working salvation beforehand in the midst of the earth' (Ps. 74:12)."
    D. "[Adam speaks,] 'He had already worked salvation, in that the Holy One, blessed be he, prepared my salary in advance, even before I had gotten up to do the work!'"

XV:IV

2. A. "[There he put] the man . . ." (Gen. 2:8):
    B. It was on account of the merit owing to Abraham [who is, we recall, the model and the perfect man].

C. So it is written, "You know my sitting down and my standing up. You understand my thought from afar" (Ps. 139:2).

D. "My sitting down" refers to my settling in the Garden of Eden.

E. "My standing up" refers to my being driven forth from it.

F. "You understand my thought from afar" (Ps. 139:2): on account of the merit of whom did you determine to create me? It was on account of the merit of him who came from a far place: "Calling a bird of prey from the east, the man of my counsel from a far country" (Isa. 46:11). [This is taken to refer to Abraham, who answered God's call from a far place.]

XV:V

1. A. "And there he put [the man whom he had formed]" (Gen. 2:8):

B. [The use of the word "there"] is in line with the following verse: "And there they are unto this day" (2 Chr. 5:9). [Freedman, p. 121, n. 5: Thus "there" implies "for all time." Hence man was created to live permanently in the Garden of Eden.]

C. R. Levi b. Zechariah said, "That is on condition that he remains as he is in the condition imparted to him by the creation at hand [hence in a state of grace and without sin]."

2. A. Said R. Isaac b. Merion, "It is written, 'These are the generations of heaven and earth' (Gen. 2:4). If the one who created them praises them, who can disparage them? If their Creator praises them, who will find fault in them?

B. "Accordingly, they are lovely and praiseworthy: 'These are the generations of heaven and earth when they were created' (Gen. 2:4)."

XV:VII

1. A. ". . . the tree of knowledge . . ." (Gen. 2:9):

B. What was the tree from which Adam and Eve ate?

C. R. Meir says, "In fact it was wheat. When someone has no knowledge, people say, 'That man has never in his life eaten bread made out of wheat.'"

2. A. R. Samuel b. R. Isaac asked R. Zeira, saying to him, "Is it possible that it was wheat?"

B. He said to him, "Yes."

C. He said to him, "But lo, what is written is 'tree,' [so how can it be wheat]!"

D. He said to him, "It was wheat that grew as high as cedars of Lebanon [and so fell into the classification of trees]."

3. A. Said R. Jacob b. Aha, "There was a dispute between R. Nehemiah and rabbis."

B. R. Nehemiah said, "[Before one eats bread, one says the blessing,] '. . . who has brought forth bread from the earth,' for [God] has already brought the bread forth from the earth."

C. Rabbis say, "'. . . who brings [forth bread from the earth],' for he will bring it forth in time to come, in line with this verse: 'There shall be a handful of grain in the land' (Ps. 72:16)." [Freedman explains the relevance of this passage as follows: They differ on the bringing forth of bread itself, not mere wheat which must be made into bread. Nehemiah holds that the phrase refers to the past, as God brought forth bread itself before Adam's sin, while the rabbis say that the word is said to refer to the future, for it is then that God will cause bread to grow (Freedman, p. 122, n. 5).]

4. A. As to the blessing one is to say for vegetables, between two Amoras, R. Hinena b. Isaac and R. Samuel b. Imi, there was a dispute on the word at hand, Hebrew *lpt*. One of them said that the word *lpt* stands for "not bread" (*l' pt*).

B. The other said that the word stands for "it will not be bread in the future." [Freedman, p. 123, n. 2: "Not bread": it was not food for man before he sinned, as bread fully seasoned grew out of the ground then.]

6. A. R. Judah b. Ilai said, "It was grapes [that Adam and Eve ate], as it is said: 'Their grapes are grapes of gall, they have clusters of bitterness' (Deut. 32:32).

B. "They were the grapes that brought bitterness into the world."

C. R. Abba of Acre said, "It was the *etrog* [a citron], in line with this verse: 'And the woman saw that the [wood of] the tree was good for food' (Gen. 3:6). Now go and find out what sort of tree produces wood that can be eaten just as much as its fruit can be eaten, and you will find only the *etrog*."

7. A. R. Yose said, "It was figs."

B. [Yose] derives the meaning of what is not stated explicitly from the meaning of what is made explicit, and that very meaning he derives from its context. [How so?]

C. The matter may be compared to the case of a prince who misbehaved with one of his slave girls. When the king heard about it, he drove him out of the palace; and the prince went begging at the doors of slave girls, but they would not accept him. But the one with whom he had misbehaved opened her door to him and accepted him. So at the moment at which the first man ate from that tree, [God] drove him out of the Garden of Eden, and man went begging among all the trees, but none would accept him.

D. What did they say to him?

E. Said R. Berekhiah, "'Here comes the thief who deceived his Creator, here comes the thief who deceived his Master.' That is in line with the following verse of Scripture: 'Let not the foot of presumption come to me' (Ps. 36:1 [Hebrew v. 12]), meaning 'the foot that presumed against its Creator' [Freedman], 'and let not the hand of the wicked shake me' (Ps. 36:11 [Hebrew v. 12]), meaning 'do not let it take a leaf from me.'"

F. But it was the fig, of the fruit of which they had eaten, that opened its door and accepted him. That is in line with this verse: "And they sewed fig leaves together" (Gen. 3:7).

8. A. What kind of fig was it?

B. R. Abin said, "It was a *bart sheba* fig, for it brought seven [Hebrew *shebaʿ*] days of mourning into the world."

C. R. Joshua of Sikhnin in the name of R. Levi: "It was a *bart ali* fig, because it brought mourning and crying into the world. [Freedman: Hebrew *ʾali* is connected with *ʾeli*, 'lamentation.']"

9. A. R. Azariah, R. Judah b. Simon in the name of R. Joshua b. Levi, "God forbid [that it was any of the types of trees just now listed]. In point of fact, the Holy One, blessed be he, did not reveal the name of that particular tree to man, and it is not destined to be revealed."

B. Note what is written in the Mishnah: "'And if a woman approach any beast and lie down with it, you shall kill the woman and the beast' (Lev. 20:16). Now if man has sinned, what sin did the beast commit [that it should be put to death too]? But it is so that that beast should not walk about in the market place, while people say, 'It was because of that beast that so-and-so was stoned to death.' Now if it is on account of the honor owing to [Adam's] descendants that God took account, on account of his own honor, how much the more so" [Mishnah *Sanhedrin* vii. 4].

[Freedman, p. 124, n. 6: Similarly, God did not reveal the nature of the tree that it might not be said, "Through this tree Adam brought death into the world."]

XVI:IV

1. A. R. Tanhuma in the name of R. Joshua b. Levi said to him, "In the future the Holy One, blessed be he, is destined to give a cup of bitterness to the nations to drink from the place from which this [river] goes forth. And what is the verse that so indicates? 'A river flowed out of Eden to water the garden' (Gen. 2:10).

B. "This refers to the four kingdoms, forming the counterpart to the four heads [into which the river is divided].

C. " 'The name of the first is Pishon' (Gen. 2:11) refers to Babylonia, in line with this verse: 'And their horsemen spread (*Hebrew pashu*) themselves' (Hab. 1:8). And it also responds to [Freedman:] the midget dwarf, who was smaller than a handbreadth [that is, Nebuchadnezzar].

D. " 'It is the one which flows around the whole land of Havilah' [again, referring to Babylonia,] for [Nebuchadnezzar] came up and encompassed the entire Land of Israel, concerning which it is written: 'Hope you in God, for I shall yet praise him' (Ps. 42:5 [Hebrew v. 6]). [There is a play on the words for 'Havilah' and 'hope.']

E. " '. . . where there is gold' (Gen. 2:11) speaks of words of Torah, which are 'more to be desired than gold and than much fine gold' (Ps. 19:10 [Hebrew v. 11]). [Compare above, XVI:II.3.B. "Actual gold, not something that symbolizes something else of great value."]

F. " 'And the gold of that land is good' (Gen. 2:12) teaches that there is no Torah like the Torah of the Land of Israel, and there is no wisdom like the wisdom of the Land of Israel.

G. " 'Bdellium and onyx stone are there' (Gen. 2:12) refers to Scripture, Mishnah, Talmud, supplementary teachings, and lore.

H. " 'And the name of the second river is Gihon' (Gen. 2:13) refers to Media, for Haman [who was a Median] had [because of his deranged hatred of Israel] inflamed eyes like those of a serpent, on the count: 'On your belly (Hebrew *ghwnk*) you will go, and dust you will eat all the days of your life' (Gen. 3:14).

    I. "'It is the one which flows around the whole land of Cush' (Gen. 2:13). This allusion is to [Ahasueros, the Median, as in this verse]: 'Who reigned from India even to Cush' (Est. 1:1).

    J. "'And the name of the third river is Tigris' (Gen. 2:14) refers to Greece, which was sharp and speedy in making evil decrees, saying to Israel, 'Write on the horn of an ox [as a public proclamation] that you have no share in the God of Israel.'"

2. A. ". . . which flows east of Assyria" (Gen. 2:14):

    B. Said R. Huna, "In three matters did the kingdom of Greece take precedence [a play on the words for 'east' and 'precedence'] over the wicked kingdom [Rome]: in navigation, in setting up camp, and in language."

3. A. R. Huna in the name of R. Aha, "All kingdoms bear the name of Assyria because they get rich on account of exacting their taxes from Israel [a play on the words for 'rich' and 'Assyria']."

    B. Said R. Yose b. Judah, "All kingdoms are called Nineveh because they ornament themselves at the expense of Israel."

    C. Said R. Yose b. Halapta, "All kingdoms are called 'Egypt,' because they oppress Israel [a play on the words 'oppress' and 'Egypt']."

4. A. "And the fourth river is the Euphrates" (Gen. 2:14):

    B. This refers to Rome.

    C. It is called the Euphrates (Hebrew *prt*) because it unsettled and harassed his world.

    D. It is called the Euphrates because it became abundant on account of the blessing of the old man [Jacob, who blessed Esau, standing for Rome].

    E. It is called the Euphrates because: "In the future I am going to destroy it, at the end."

    F. It is called the Euphrates because of what will happen at the end of it: "I have trodden the winepress alone" (Isa. 63:3).

XVI:V

1. A. "And the Lord God took the man [and put him in the garden of Eden to till it and keep it]" (Gen. 2:15):

    B. R. Judah and R. Nehemiah:

    C. R. Judah said, "He raised him up, in line with this verse [in which the use of the word 'take' bears the meaning of 'raise up']: 'And the peoples shall take them and bring them to their place' (Isa. 14:2)."

D. R. Nehemiah said, "He enticed him [to enter the garden] in line
with this verse: 'Take with you words and return to the Lord'
(Hos. 14:2)."

3. A. "And he put him" (Gen. 2:15) means that he gave him the
religious duty of observing the Sabbath [linking 'put' to the
meaning of 'rest,' which the same root yields].

B. This is in line with the following verse of Scripture: "And he
rested on the Seventh day" (Gen. 20:10

C. "To till it" (Gen. 2:15): "Six days shall you till" (Exod. 20:9).

D. "And to keep it" (Gen. 2:15): "Keep the Sabbath day" (Deut.
5:12).

4. A. Another interpretation: "To till it and to keep it" (Gen. 2:15):

B. This refers to the offerings [in the Temple]: "You shall serve
God upon this mountain" (Exod. 3:12). "You shall keep [the
obligation of] offering to me" (Num. 28:2).

XVI:VI

1. A. "And the Lord God commanded the man, saying, 'You may
freely eat of every tree of the garden; [but of the tree of the
knowledge of good and evil you shall not eat, for in the day that
you eat of it you shall die]'" (Gen. 2:16-17).

B. R. Levi said, "He made him responsible to keep six commandments.

C. "He commanded him against idolatry, in line with this verse:
'Because he willingly walked after idols' (Hos. 5:11).

D. "'The Lord' indicates a commandment against blasphemy, in
line with this verse: 'And he who blasphemes the name of the
Lord' (Lev. 24:16).

E. "'God' indicates a commandment concerning setting up courts
[and a judiciary]: 'You shall not revile the judges' [in the verse at
hand, 'God'] (Exod. 22:28).

F. "'. . . the man' refers to the prohibition of murder: 'Whoever
sheds man's blood' (Gen. 9:6).

G. "'. . . saying' refers to the prohibition of fornication: 'Saying, "If
a man put away his wife"' (Jer. 3:1).

H. "'Of every tree you may eat' (Gen. 2:16) indicates that he
commanded him concerning theft. [There are things one may
take, and there are things one may not take.]"

2. A. Rabbis interpret the passage in this way: "'And the Lord God commanded' (Gen. 2:16).
   B. "He said to him, 'What am I? I am God. I wish to be treated like God, so he may not curse me. [That proves only that Adam was commanded not to blaspheme.]
   C. "How do we know that he was commanded not to fornicate? 'And cleave to his wife' (Gen. 2:24), and not to the wife of his neighbor, to a male, or to an animal." [So rabbis find in the verse only two prohibitions, against blasphemy and fornication.]

3. A. "Of every tree of the garden you may freely eat" (Gen. 2:16):
   B. Said R. Jacob of Kefar Hanan, "When does [a beast] turn into food and become fit for eating? When it has been properly slaughtered. Accordingly, he gave man an indication that it is forbidden to eat a limb cut from a living beast." [Jacob here finds the commandment not to treat animals cruelly.]

4. A. "But of the tree of the knowledge of good and evil you shall not eat, for in the day that you eat of it you shall die" (Gen. 2:17):
   B. [Since the verb "you shall surely die" uses the root "die" more than once, what is indicated is] the death penalty for Adam, for Eve, and for coming generations.

"She Shall Be Called Woman"

Our sages in no way exhibited the misogynism characteristic of Greco-Roman antiquity. They regarded marriage as the sole natural condition of man and woman. They viewed the creation of woman as not only a necessity but a blessing. They held that man cannot enjoy life without woman, man is completed by woman, and woman by man. True, conceptions of our own day about the full and complete equality of man and woman will have surprised the sages, who lived in their age, not in ours. But viewed in their context, not in ours, the sages emerge with honor. What is interesting in their interpretation of the creation of woman is how they work not on the detail but on the theme.

The treatment of the relevant verses provides a sizable anthology of sayings and stories about woman, marriage, home, and family. By this point, we shall not find surprising the effort of the sages to find the links, the connections between one detail and another. So the creation of woman calls to mind the perfection of nature in the holy Temple. The sleep, or repose, of Adam calls to mind diverse kinds of sleep. Each moment in the unfolding of the creation of humanity prefigures some other, and the range of time and experience—personal, natural, supernatural, historical—infuses the account. Consequently, every part of the biblical narrative forms in microcosm the entirety of scriptural reality: each detail covers the whole, and the sages uncover everything all at once in each moment.

Our sages' utterly positive and affirmative view of women and of marriage comes to expression in many ways in the discussion of the creation of woman, Eve. It was part of man's glory to know the right name of every creature, something the angels could not boast. And integral to man's knowledge of right and wrong in the classification of creation was the creation of Eve as the only right mate for Adam. This is proved by the story of the power of woman to impart virtue to an evil man, or to bring into vice a good man. Everything depends on the woman.

XVII:II

1. A. "It is not good" (Gen. 2:18):
   B. It has been taught on Tannaite authority: Whoever has no wife lives without good, without help, without joy, without blessing, without atonement.
   C. Without good: "It is not good for man to be alone" (Gen. 2:18).
   D. Without help: "I will make him a helper fit for him" (Gen. 2:18).
   E. Without joy: "And you shall rejoice, you and your household" (Deut. 14:26).
   F. Without blessing: "That a blessing may rest on your house" (Ezek. 44:30).
   G. Without atonement: "And he shall make atonement for himself and for his house" [meaning his wife, so if he cannot make atonement for his wife, he also cannot make atonement for himself] (Lev. 16:11).
   H. R. Simon in the name of R. Joshua b. Levi: "Also without peace, as it is said: 'And peace be to your house' (1 Sam. 25:6)."
   I. R. Joshua of Sikhnin in the name of R. Levi: "Also without life, as it is written: 'Enjoy life with the wife whom you love' (Eccl. 9:9)."
   J. R. Hiyya b. Gomedi said, "Also he is not a complete man: 'And he blessed them and called their name Adam' (Gen. 5:2)."
   K. And some say, "Such a person also diminishes the image of God: 'For in the image of God made he man' (Gen. 9:6), after which it is written: 'And you, be fruitful and multiply' (Gen. 9:7). [Freedman, p. 133, n. 2: God's majesty, as it were, is impaired when man refuses to fulfil these functions.]"

XVII:III

1. A. "I will make him a helper as his counterpart" (Gen. 2:18):
   B. If a man has merit, the wife is a help, and if not, she is his counterpart [in opposition to him].
   C. Said R. Joshua b. R. Nehemiah, "If one has merit, his wife will be like the wife of Hananiah son of Hakhinai; and if not, she will be like the wife of R. Yose the Galilean." [Hananiah's wife is never mentioned again.]
2. A. R. Yose the Galilean had a bad wife, who was the daughter of

his sister [so it was an act of merit that he married her] but who used to embarrass him. His disciples said to him, "Master, divorce her, for she does not treat you with respect."

B. He said to them, "Her dowry is too big for me, so I cannot divorce her."

C. One time he and R. Eleazar b. Azariah were in session. When they had finished their studies, he him, "Master, will you allow me to go with you to your house?"

D. He said to him, "Yes."

E. When they got there, she looked down and left the house [angrily]. [Yose] looked into the pot that was standing on the range and asked her, "Is there anything in the pot?"

F. She said to him, "In the pot there is hash." But when he went and peeked, he found chicken.

G. R Eleazar b. Azariah understood what he was hearing. They sat down together and ate. He said to him, "My lord, did she not say that in the pot was hash, while we found chicken in it?"

H. He said to him, "It was a miracle."

I. When they had finished eating, he said to him, "My lord, divorce that woman, for she does not treat you with respect."

J. He said to him, "Sir, her dowry is too much for me to pay, so I cannot divorce her."

K. He said to him, "We [your disciples] will divide up her dowry so that you can divorce her." They did so and divided among themselves the cost of her dowry, and he divorced her and married another woman, far better than she had been.

L. The sins of that first wife caused it to happen that she went and married the town watchman. After some time trouble came upon the man, and [since he had become blind] she would lead him all over town [to go begging]. But when they would come in the neighborhood in which R. Yose the Galilean lived, she led him away from it.

M. Since that man had been the town watchman and knew the entire town, he said to her, "Why do you not bring us to the neighborhood in which R. Yose the Galilean lives? I heard that he carries out his religious duties [and so will support us, since we are poor]."

N. She said to her, "I am his divorced wife, and I haven't got the strength to face him."

O. One time they came begging to the neighborhood of R. Yose the Galilean, and the husband began to beat her, and her cries brought embarrassment all over town. R. Yose the Galilean looked out and saw that the couple was being ridiculed in the marketplaces of the town. He took them and gave them housing in a room that he owned and provided them with food so long as they lived.

P. This was on the count of the verse: "And that you do not hide yourself from your own flesh" (Isa. 58:7).

XVII:IV

2. A. Said R. Aha, "When the Holy One, blessed be he, came to create the first man, he took counsel with the ministering angels. He said to them, 'Shall we make man?' (Gen. 1:26).

B. "They said to him, 'What is his character?'

C. "He said to them, 'His wisdom will be greater than yours.'

D. "What did the Holy One, blessed be he, do [in order to make his point]? He brought before them domesticated beasts, wild beasts, and fowl. He said to them, 'As to this creature, what is its name?' but they did not know.

E. "'What is its name?' But they did not know.

F. "Then he brought them before man. He said to him, 'As to this, what is its name?' 'Ox.' 'And as to this, what is its name?' 'Camel.' 'And as to this, what is its name?' 'An ass.' 'And as to this, what is its name?' 'Horse.'

G. "That is in line with this verse: 'And whatever man called every living creature, that was its name' (Gen. 2:19).

H. "He said to him, 'And what is your name?'

I. "He said to him, 'As for me, what is proper is to call me 'Adam,' for I have been created from the earth, [which in Hebrew is called 'adamah].'

J. "'And as for me, what is my name?' He said to him, 'As for you, it is fitting for you to be called, "The Lord," for you are the Lord of all that you have created.'"

3. A. Said R. Hiyya, "'I am the Lord, that is my name' (Isa. 42:8). That is my name, which the first man called me.'"

4. A. [Reverting to the story interrupted by Hiyya's statement:] "He then went and brought before the first man each beast with its

mate. He said, 'Every creature has a mate, but I have no mate.'
'But for the man will there not be found a helper fit for him?'
(Gen. 2:20).

B. "And why did not he create her for him to begin with? The Holy
One, blessed be he, foresaw that later on man would complain
to him about [his wife, Eve], so he did not create her until [man]
himself had asked for her on his own.

C. "When he asked for her on his own, forthwith: 'So the Lord
God caused a deep sleep to fall upon the man, and while he
slept, [took one of his ribs and closed up its place with flesh]'
(Gen. 2:21)."

XVII:V

2. A. Rab said, "There are three kinds of repose: there is the repose of
sleep, the repose of prophecy, and the repose of unconsciousness [as in a trance].

B. "The repose of sleep: 'So the Lord God caused a deep sleep to
fall upon the man' (Gen. 2:21).

C. "The repose of prophecy: 'And as the sun set, a deep repose fell
on Abram' (Gen. 15:12).

D. "The repose of unconsciousness: 'And no man saw it, or knew
it, nor did any awake; for they were all asleep, because a deep
sleep from the Lord had fallen upon them' (1 Sam. 26:12)."

E. Rabbis say, "Also there is the repose of [drunken] silliness, as it
is written: 'Stupify yourselves and be stupid . . . for the Lord has
poured out upon you the spirit of deep sleep' (Isa. 29:9-10)."

3. A. R. Hinena b. Isaac said, "There are three kinds of partial
realization [of a complete experience].

B. "The partial realization of the experience of death is in sleep.

C. "The partial realization of the experience of prophecy is in a
dream."

D. "The partial realization of the world to come is in the Sabbath."

E. R. Abin added two more: "The partial realization of light from
above is in the orb of the sun, and the partial realization of
wisdom from on high is in the Torah."

XVII:VII

1. A. A noble lady asked R. Yose, saying to him, "Why was it through
theft [of a rib]?"

B. He said to her, "Here is a parable. If someone left with you an ounce of silver, doing so in secret, would you return to him a *litra* [twelve ounces] of silver in public? Would you call that theft? [God took the rib but returned Eve. How was that a theft?]"

C. She said to him, "But why was it done in secret? [Why did God not let Adam watch the making of Eve?]"

D. He said to her, "To begin with he did create her for him, and when he saw her filled with discharge and blood [he was not attracted to her, so God] took her away from him and then went and created her a second time."

E. She said to him, "I can indeed add to what you have said. I was planning to get married to my mother's brother, but since I had grown up with him in the same house, I became ordinary in his eyes, so he went and married someone else, who in fact is not so pretty as I am."

2. A. There is this case, involving a certain pious man, who was married to a pious woman, but the couple did not produce children. They said, "What good do we do for the Holy One, blessed be he [if we do not produce children, so increasing God's image]?"

B. They went and divorced one another. The man went and married a wicked woman, and she made him wicked.

C. The woman went and married a wicked man, and she made him righteous.

D. This proves that everything depends on the woman. [Freedman: This story takes the root for the word "closed up" and imputes to that root the meaning "deliver," hence the sense now is that through woman God delivered man from evil.]

XVIII:I

1. A. "And the rib which the Lord God had taken from the man he built into a woman and brought her to the man" (Gen. 2:22):

B. R. Eleazar in the name of R. Yose b. Zimra: "[Referring to the verb for 'build,' which uses the consonants that bear the meaning of 'understand,' we conclude that] understanding was given to the woman more than to the man."

C. We have learned in the Mishnah: "If a girl who is eleven years and one day old takes a vow, her vow is subject to investigation [to see whether she understands what she has done]. If she grasps the meaning of vowing, she is deemed subject to the vow she has taken. If she is twelve years and one day old, her vows stand, but she is examined throughout the twelfth year. In the case of a boy twelve years and one day old, if he takes a vow, he is subject to investigation. When he is thirteen years and one day old, his vows stand. But he is subject to investigation throughout his thirteenth year. [Mishnah *Niddah* v. 2]. [So a girl attains understanding earlier than does a boy.]

D. R. Jeremiah in the name of R. Samuel b. R. Isaac: "There are those who reverse the matter. It is usual for a woman to stay at home [where she learns nothing], while it is usual for a man to go out to the market place. So he learns understanding from his encounters with mature adults."

2. A. R. Aibu, and some say in the name of R. Benaiah, and it has been taught on Tannaite authority in the name of R. Simeon b. Yohai: "[God] adorned her like a bride and brought her to him."

B. There are places in which people call doing the hair "building" [and hence, when Scripture says that God built her into a woman, the meaning is that he fixed her hair].

3. A. Said R. Hama b. Hanina, "What do you think? Is it that he brought her to him from under a single carob or a single sycamore tree? Rather, he adorned her with twenty-four different adornments [Freedman: the twenty four enumerated at Isa. 3:18-24], and then brought her to him.

B. "That is in line with this verse: 'You were in Eden, the garden of God; every precious stone was your covering, the carnelian, the topaz, and the emerald, the beryl, the onyx, and the jasper, the sapphire, the carbuncle, and the *smaradg,* and gold; the workmanship of your settings and of your sockets was in you, in the day that you were created they were prepared' (Ezek. 28:13)." [Choice of the intersecting verse is dictated by the reference to "the day that you were created." We shall now examine the cited verse.]

XVIII:IV

1. A. "Then the man said, 'This time she [is bone of my bones and flesh of my flesh; she shall be called woman, because she was taken out of man]'" (Gen. 2:23):

B. R. Judah b. Rabbi said, "When to begin with, he created her, when [Adam] saw her full of sinews and blood, he sent her away from himself. Then [God] went and created her a second time. In that case, he said, '*This time* she is bone of my bones' (Gen. 2:23)."

XVIII:VI

1. A. "And the man and his wife were both naked and were not ashamed" (Gen. 2:25):
   B. Said R. Eleazar, "There were three who did not remain in their good fortune for six hours, and they are the first man, Israel, and Sisera.
   C. "The first man: 'and were not ashamed' (Gen. 2:25). [Reading the consonants differently:] six hours had not passed.
   D. "Israel: 'And the people saw that Moses had tarried' (Exod. 32:1). Six hours had passed [again a play on the Hebrew consonants].
   E. "Sisera: 'Why does his chariot tarry to come?' (Judg. 5:28): 'Every day he would routinely come home in three hours or in four hours, and today six hours have passed and he has not yet come.'"

2. A. "And they were not ashamed" (Gen. 2:25). "But the snake was more subtle [than any other wild creature that the Lord God had made]" (Gen. 3:1).
   B. It would have been quite sufficient for Scripture to say: "And the Lord God made for the man and his wife garments of skin" (Gen. 3:21), [since this was done prior to the sin, and not afterward, so that statement should have appeared right after Gen. 2:25, rather than the verse that comes as Gen. 3:1].
   C. Said R. Joshua b. Qorha, "It serves to let you know the sin that that wicked [creature] had got them to do. When he saw that they were having sexual relations, and he lusted after [the woman, he tried to kill Adam by getting him to sin]."
   D. Said R. Jacob of Kefar Hanan, "[The presentation of that detail] was postponed to that latter passage so as not to conclude the story of the creation of man with the matter of the snake. [So that detail was introduced only at the end of the narrative.]"

"Where Are You?"

The fall from grace forms the climax of the narrative of creation, leading inexorably to Noah, then Abraham. Our sages find the power to turn the familiar into something fresh and powerful. We can feel in their reading of the passage the growing horror of what is to come, anticipation of tragedy—but also, therefore, intimation of a redemption beyond. The exegesis follows a single line, which is to pursue both the surface-theme, the advantages of the serpent, and the subterranean one, the sorrow of learning. The serpent's remarkable intelligence was the greatness from which he fell. The syllogism comes at the outset: the sorrows of learning, the self-pity of the intellectual. We now understand a principal concern of the sages' reading of Scripture, namely to find the threads that link story to story, narrative into tableau. The upshot once more is to treat the creation-narrative as a prefiguring of Israel's history.

For the sages the sin of eating of the fruit of the tree of knowledge stands for arrogance toward God. What God wants is humility and obedience to God's commandments. The message to Israel at that particular moment cannot be missed. If Israel wishes to find redemption from the rule of the nations and the power of sin, what Israel must do is accept the yoke of the kingdom of heaven—that is, adhere to the rule of God rather than the lordship of the nations. So at issue is not freedom from rules, but humanity's power to choose its ruler: God or the nations. The role of wisdom in that choice then cannot escape attention. Knowledge in the service of God leads to redemption; knowledge used arrogantly, to destruction.

The fall of humanity begins in arrogance, and that is the point at which we start. The serpent had great gifts of intellect, and the serpent is the cause of suffering. The point is that the fall from the heights is greater than the fall from a low place. It was arrogant, too, to add to God's commandment. God had said not to eat the fruit, but woman said that God had said not to touch it either. The exegesis at XIX:III of the encounter with the snake, Gen. 3:1-13, picks up the discrepancy between God's instruction not to eat the fruit of the tree and the woman's report that God had forbidden even touching the tree. This is another good way of laying out a syllogism (that is, the principle, then the example). The underlying motif is that it is arrogant for man to demand more than God had already laid down. The story is made to focus upon the dangers of human arrogance—here, even in a good cause. What follows is yet another such statement, now that man should not compete with God in ruling over creation. The snake's arrogance toward God exceeded that of Eve. But both parties to the sin shared that same trait, and in emphasizing that the fall of humanity came about because of arrogance, the sages made their main point. The competition between God and humanity now emerges as the principal motif of the tale. The argument in favor of eating the fruit rested on humanity's belief that humanity took the place of God and had therefore to call a halt to creation. Since man was made in God's image and likeness, no wonder there was competition between man and God.

With each sin in the unfolding of human history, God took a step further away from the world. With each saint, God returned to earth, stage by stage. So the counterpart of the fall from grace, in the sages' view, is Sinai, the full and complete return of God to earth through the Torah. Christians may find in the Torah Israel's counterpart to Christ, God incarnate. Judaism sees the Torah as the incarnation of God's will for humanity: God in the flesh of humanity will take the form of the life of Torah. What is striking is the claim that while the wicked (Gentiles) drove God out of the world, the righteous (Israelites) brought God back into the world. This theme links the story of the fall of man to the history of Israel, with Israel serving as the counterpart and redemption. The consequence of the fall of humanity affected not only Adam and Eve but also the world. God left the world, stage by stage, in consequence of the sins of humanity, as these sins unfolded. Then God came back to the world, stage by stage, in response to the virtues of humanity, as these came to the surface from Abraham to Sinai. The sages' world viewed the firmament as marked by seven levels, and in their account of the fall of humanity the sages saw God gradually ascending upward, leaving the world; but then, in their picture of God's grace and salvation, the sages saw God coming downward, meeting humanity at Sinai. These are dimensions to the fall of humanity not commonly appreciated: the counterpart of Eden and its tragedy is Sinai and its salvation. This point is made more than once, and most powerfully at XIX:IX, where the life of Adam and Eve in Eden is compared to—but contrasted with—the life of Israel in its land.

The climax of the sages' understanding is reached at XIX:IX. Here we see God as tragic hero of creation, disappointed in what has happened in the fall of humanity. And yet, once more, the counterpart to sinful man is Israel, redeemed by God. Israel's history forms the counterpart and opposite, just as in the life of the Church the New Testament serves as counterpart and completion of the old, just as each event in the one finds its complement in the other. XIX:IX must be regarded as the single most representative interpretation supplied by our sages. Here we see, in microcosm, their basic reading of Scripture.

Every detail is in place, the articulation is perfect, and the result completely convincing as an essay in interpretation. All of this rests on the simple fact that the word for "where are you" may be expressed as "How . . . ," which, as is clear, invokes the opening words of the book of Lamentations. So Israel's history serves as a paradigm for human history, and vice versa. Then Israel stands at the center of humanity.

The sages' principal task lay in the ordering of the inner life of Israel. So while they found in the scriptural facts the fundamental laws of history, they also discovered more important, because more relevant, rules for the everyday life of the people. At XX:I they uncovered one of their favorite themes, the power of gossip or of evil speech to disrupt and destroy the community. The serpent is the model of the gossip, the one who uses language to destroy, speech to murder. The upshot of the exercise links Israel's history to the history of humanity in the garden of Eden. The passage again focuses upon the sacred history of Israel, making the point that slanderers in Israel cause the nation's downfall, just as the snake caused the downfall of humanity.

If we had to specify the repertoire of exegetical initiatives available to the authors, we could not do better than to follow the program before us. We find here five entirely familiar themes or polemics. First comes the inquiry into the relationship between the tale at hand and the paradigm of Israel's history. Second, we are asked to find, even in God's curse, a blessing. Third, we attend to the plain facts of philosophy—here, natural philosophy, of interest to the exegetes as shown in their observations about the gestation period of beasts and the like. Fourth, we turn to the coming or future age. Finally, we validate divine justice, showing its exactness. The order of entries before us indicates no clear logic, but the repertoire of interests surely encompasses types of points repeatedly made in the unfolding exegesis of the story of the world. XX:IX returns us to more humble matters. The exegesis of the curse of Adam at both No. 1 and No. 2 emphasizes the same syllogism, that it is difficult to make a living, and that God intervenes to provide humanity with sustenance.

Once more the tale of the garden is explicitly joined to the existential reality of humanity, the link being the story of Israel in particular.

XIX:I

1. A. "Now the serpent was more subtle [than any other wild creature that the Lord God had made]" (Gen. 3:1):

    B. "For in much wisdom is much anger, and he who increases knowledge increases sorrow" (Eccl. 1:18).

    C. If a person increases knowledge for himself, he increases anger against himself, and because he adds to learning for himself, he adds to anguish for himself.

    D. Said Solomon, "Because I increased knowledge for myself, I increased anger against myself, and because I added learning for myself, I added anguish for myself.

    E. "Did you ever hear someone say, 'This ass went out and caught "the sun"' [Freedman: ague] or 'caught a fever'?

    F. "Where are sufferings located? They are located among men."

2. A. Rabbi said, "A disciple of a sage does not require admonition [that a given act is prohibited, and if he does such an act, he will be penalized. Such a warning is required only for ordinary folk. A disciple of a sage is assumed to know the law and therefore may be penalized without prior admonition. This illustrates the point that learning increases one's exposure to anguish.]"

    B. Said R. Yohanan, "He is in the status of fine linen garments that come from Beth Shean. If they are only slightly soiled, they go to waste. But the coarse linen garments that come from Arbela, how much are they worth, and how much money does it take to buy them? [What is more valuable also can produce great loss. What is not valuable also produces no loss.]"

    C. R. Ishmael taught, "In accord with the strength of the camel is its load.

    D. "In this worldly circumstances, when two men go into a restaurant, one says, 'Bring me roast meat, white bread, and a decent wine.' The other says, 'Bring me bread and beets.' This one eats and gets a bellyache, and that one eats and does not get a bellyache. What follows is that for the one the burden is heavy, and for the other it is not."

    E. It was taught in the name of R. Meir, "Because the greatness that the snake had enjoyed was so considerable, so was the depth of his degradation: 'More subtle than all' (Gen. 3:1), 'More cursed than all' (Gen. 3:14). [This makes explicit the point of the foregoing observations.]"

3. A. "And the serpent was more subtle than any other wild creature" (Gen. 3:1):

   B. R. Hoshiah the Elder said, "He stood erect like a reed and had feet. [That is what indicated his intelligence.]"

   C. R. Jeremiah b. Eleazar said, "He was a disbeliever."

   D. R. Simeon b. Eleazar said, "He was like a camel. This world lost out on a great benefit, for if things had not happened the way they did, a man could send commerce through [a snake], who would come and go [doing his employer's business]."

XIX:III

1. A. "And the woman said to the snake. 'We may eat of the fruit of the trees [of the garden, but God said, "You shall not eat of the fruit of the tree which is in the midst of the garden, neither shall you touch it, lest you die"]'" (Gen. 3:3):

   B. Where was man when this conversation was going on?

   C. Abba Halpun b. Qoriah said, "He had earlier had sexual relations, and now he was sleeping it off."

   D. Rabbis say, "God had taken him and was showing him the whole world, saying to him, 'This is what an orchard looks like; this is an area suitable for sowing grain. So it is written: 'Through a land that no man had passed through, and where Adam had not dwelt' (Jer. 2:6)—that is, Adam had not lived there [but there were lands Adam had seen on his tour]."

2. A. ". . . of the fruit of the tree which is in the midst of the garden" (Gen. 3:3):

   B. That is in line with this verse: "Add not to his words, lest he reprove you, and you be found a liar" (Prov. 30:6). [God had said nothing about not touching the tree, but the woman said they were not to eat of the fruit of the tree or even to touch it.]

   C. R. Hiyya taught, "It is that one should not make the fence taller than the foundation, so that the fence will not fall down and wipe out the plants.

   D. "So the Holy One, blessed be he, had said, 'For on the day on

which you eat from it, you shall surely die' (Gen. 2:17). But that
is not what she then said to the snake. Rather: 'God said, "You
shall not eat from it *and you shall not touch it.*"' When the snake
saw that she was lying to him, he took her and pushed her
against the tree. He said to her, 'Have you now died? Just as you
did not die for touching it, so you will not die from eating it.'

E. "'Rather: "For God knows that when you eat of it, your eyes will
be opened and you will be like God"' (Gen. 3:5)."

XIX:IV

2. A. R. Joshua of Sikhnin in the name of R. Levi: "[The snake]
began to slander his creator, saying, 'From this tree did God eat
and then he created the world. Then he told you, "You shall not
eat of it" (Gen. 2:17), so that you should not create other
worlds. For everyone hates the competition.'"

B. R. Judah b. R. Simon said, "[This is what he said,] 'Whatever is
created in sequence after its fellow rules over its fellow. The
heaven came on the first day and the firmament on the second,
and does not the firmament bear the weight of heaven [so
serving it]? The firmament came on the second day and herbs
on the third, and does the firmament not provide water for
herbs? The herbs were created on the third day and the great
lights on the fourth, the lights on the fourth and the fowl on the
fifth.'"

C. R. Judah b. R. Simon said, "The splendor of a clean bird when
it flies through the heaven dims the orb of the sun."

D. [Continuing the discourse of B:] "'Yet you were created after
everything else, so you should rule over everything that came
before. Go ahead and eat before he creates other worlds, which
will in sequence rule over you.'

E. "That is in line with the following verse: 'And the woman saw
that it was good' (Gen. 3:6).

F. "What she saw was that the statement of the snake [was good]."

XIX:V

2. A. "She took of its fruit and ate" (Gen. 3:6):

B. Said R. Aibu, "She squeezed some grapes and gave him the
juice."

C. R. Simlai said, "She approached him fully prepared [with strong arguments], saying to him, 'What do you think? Is it that I am going to die, and that another woman will be created for you?' [That is not possible:] 'There is nothing new under the sun' (Eccl. 1:9).

D. "'Or perhaps you think that I shall die and you will live all by yourself? 'He did not create the world as a waste, he formed it to be inhabited' (Isa. 45:18)."

E. Rabbis say, "She began to moan and weep to him."

XIX:VII

2. A. Said R. Abba b. Kahana, "The word is not written 'move,' but rather 'walk,' bearing the sense that [the Presence of God] lept about and jumped upward.

B. "[The point is that God's presence lept upward from the earth on account of the events in the garden, as will now be explained:] The principal location of the Presence of God was [meant to be] among the creatures down here. When the first man sinned, the Presence of God moved up to the first firmament. When Cain sinned, it went up to the second firmament. When the generation of Enosh sinned, it went up to the third firmament. When the generation of the flood sinned, it went up to the fourth firmament. When the generation of the Dispersion [at the Tower of Babel] sinned, it went up to the fifth. On account of the Sodomites it went up to the sixth, and on account of the Egyptians in the time of Abraham it went up to the seventh.

C. "But, as a counterpart, there were seven righteous men who rose up: Abraham, Isaac, Jacob , Levi, Kahath, Amram, and Moses. They brought the Presence of God [by stages] down to earth.

D. "Abraham brought it from the seventh to the sixth, Isaac brought it from the sixth to the fifth, Jacob brought it from the fifth to the fourth, Levi brought it down from the forth to the third, Kahath brought it down from the third to the second, Amram brought it down from the second to the first. Moses brought it down to earth."

E. Said R. Isaac, "It is written: 'The righteous will inherit the land, and dwell therein forever' (Ps. 37:29). Now what will the wicked do? Are they going to fly in the air? But that the wicked did not make it possible for the Presence of God to take up residence on earth [is what the verse wishes to say]."

XIX:IX

1. A. "And the Lord God called to the man and said to him, 'Where are you?'" (Gen. 3:9):

   B. [The word for "where are you" yields consonants that bear the meaning] "How has this happened to you?"

   C. [God speaks:] "Yesterday it was in accord with my plan, and now it is in accord with the plan of the snake. Yesterday it was from one end of the world to the other [that you filled the earth], and now: 'Among the trees of the garden' (Gen. 3:8) [you hide out]."

2. A. R. Abbahu in the name of R. Yose b. Haninah: "It is written: 'But they are like a man [Adam]; they have transgressed the covenant' (Hos. 6:7).

   B. "'They are like a man': specifically, like the first man. [We shall now compare the story of the first man in Eden with the story of Israel in its land.]

   C. "'In the case of the first man, I brought him into the garden of Eden; I commanded him; he violated my commandment; I judged him to be sent away and driven out; but I mourned for him, saying "How . . ."' [which begins the book of Lamentations, hence stands for a lament, but which, as we just saw, also is written with the consonants that also yield 'Where are you'].

   D. "'I brought him into the garden of Eden.' As it is written: 'And the Lord God took the man and put him into the garden of Eden' (Gen. 2:15).

   E. "'I commanded him.' As it is written: 'And the Lord God commanded . . .' (Gen. 2:16).

   F. "'And he violated my commandment.' As it is written: 'Did you eat from the tree concerning which I commanded you?' (Gen. 3:11).

   G. "'I judged him to be sent away.' As it is written: 'And the Lord God sent him from the garden of Eden' (Gen. 3:23).

   H. "'And I judged him to be driven out.' 'And he drove out the man' (Gen. 3:24).

   I. "'But I mourned for him, saying, "How. . . ."'' 'And he said to

him, "Where are you?"' (Gen. 3:9), and the word for 'where are
you' is written 'How. . . .'

J. "'So too in the case of his descendants, [God continues to
speak,] I brought them into the Land of Israel; I commanded
them; they violated my commandment; I judged them to be
sent out and driven away but I mourned for them, saying,
"How. . . ."'"

K. "'I brought them into the Land of Israel.' 'And I brought you
into the land of Carmel' (Jer. 2:7).

L. "'I commanded them.' 'And you, command the children of
Israel' (Exod. 27:20). 'Command the children of Israel' (Lev.
24:2).

M. "'They violated my commandment.' 'And all Israel have violated your Torah' (Dan. 9:11).

N. "'I judged them to be sent out.' 'Send them away, out of my
sight and let them go forth' (Jer 15:1).

O. "'. . . and driven away.' 'From my house I shall drive them'
(Hos. 9:15).

P. "'But I mourned for them, saying, "How. . . ."'" 'How has the
city sat solitary, that was full of people' (Lam. 1:1)."

XIX:X

1. A. "And he said, 'I heard the sound of you in the garden, and I was
afraid, because I was naked, and I hid myself.' He said, 'Who
told you [that you were naked? Have you eaten of the tree of
which I commanded you not to eat?']" (Gen. 3:10-11):

B. Said R. Levi, "The matter may be compared to the case of a
woman who wanted to borrow a little yeast, who went in to the
house of the wife of a snake-charmer. She said to her, 'What
does your husband do with you? [How does he treat you?]'

C. "She said to her, 'Every sort of kindness does he do with me,
except for the case of one jug filled with snakes and scorpions, of
which he does not permit me to take charge.'

D. "She said to her, 'The reason is that that is where he has all his
valuables, and he is planning to marry another woman and to
hand them over to her.'

E. "What did the wife do? She put her hand into the jug [to find
out what was there]. The snakes and scorpions began to bite
her. When her husband got home, he heard her crying out. He
said to her, 'Could you have touched that jug?'

F. "So: 'Have you eaten of the tree of which I commanded you not to eat?' (Gen. 3:11)."

XIX:XI

1. A. "The man said, 'The woman whom you gave to be with me gave me fruit of the tree, and I ate'" (Gen. 3:12):
    B. There are four on whose pots the Holy One, blessed be he, knocked, only to find them filled with urine, and these are they: Adam, Cain, the wicked Balaam, and Hezekiah.
    C. Adam: "The man said, 'The woman whom you gave to be with me gave me fruit of the tree and I ate'" (Gen. 3:12).
    D. Cain: "And the Lord said to Cain, 'Where is Abel, your brother?'" (Gen. 4:9).
    E. The wicked Balaam: "And God came to Balaam and said, 'What men are these with you?'" (Num. 22:9)
    F. Hezekiah: "Then Isaiah the prophet came to king Hezekiah and said to him, 'What did these men say?'" (2 Kgs. 20:14).
    G. But Ezekiel turned out to be far more adept than any of these: "'Son of man, can these bones live?' And I said, 'O Lord God, you know'" (Ezek. 37:3).
    H. Said R. Hinena b. Pappa, "The matter may be compared to the case of a bird that was caught by a hunter. The hunter met someone who asked him, 'Is this bird alive or dead?'
    I. "He said to him, 'If you want, it is alive; but if you prefer, it is dead.' So: '"Will these bones live?" And he said, "Lord God, you know."'"

XX:I

1. A. "Then the Lord God said to the serpent, 'Because you have done this, cursed are you above all cattle, and above all wild animals'" (Gen. 3:14):
    B. "A slanderer shall not be established in the earth; the violent and wicked man shall be hunted with thrust upon thrust" (Ps. 140:11 [Hebrew v. 12]).
    C. Said R. Levi, "In the world to come the Holy One, blessed be he, will take the nations of the world and bring them down to Gehenna. He will say to them, 'Why did you impose fines upon my children.' They will say to him, 'Some of them slandered others among them.' The Holy One, blessed be he, will then

take these [Israelite slanderers] and those and bring them down
to Gehenna."

2. A. Another interpretation: "A slanderer" refers to the snake, who
        slandered his Creator.
    B. "Will not be established [standing upright] on earth": "Upon
        your belly you shall go" (Gen. 3:14).
    C. "The violent and wicked man shall be hunted": What is written
        is not "with a thrust" but "with thrust after thrust" [since not
        only the serpent was cursed]. What is written is "thrust after
        thrust," for man was cursed, woman was cursed, and the snake
        was cursed.
    D. "And the Lord God said to the serpent. . . ."

XX:II

1. A. "A contentious man sows strife, and a whisperer separates fa-
        miliar friends" (Prov. 16:28):
    B. "A contentious man" refers to the snake, who contended
        against the statement of his Creator.
    C. "And a whisperer" is one who whispered against his Creator,
        specifically, "You will certainly not die" (Gen. 3:4).
    D. "Separates familiar friends" is so called because he separated the
        world's friend [the Presence of God, which rose from the world].
    E. And because he separated the world's friend, he was cursed:
        "And the Lord God said to the snake. . . ."
2. A. ["The Lord God said to the serpent" (Gen. 3:14):] With man
        God entered into dialogue, with woman God entered into dia-
        logue, but with the snake God did not enter into dialogue.
    C. Rather, the Holy One, blessed be he, said, "This wicked snake
        is glib. If I say to him something, he will answer me.
    D. "Thus: 'You gave them a commandment, and I gave them a
        commandment. Why in the world did they forsake your com-
        mandment and follow my commandment?' "
    E. Instead, he simply confronted him and laid down the law for
        him: "And the Lord God said to the snake. . . ."

XX:V

1. A. "Upon your belly you shall go" (Gen. 3:14):
    B. When the Holy One, blessed be he, said to him, "Upon your
        belly you shall go," the ministering angels came down and cut

off his hands and feet. His roar went forth from one end of the world to the other.

    C. The destruction of the snake serves to teach a lesson concerning the fall of Babylonia and turns out to derive a lesson from that event: "Its cry is like that of the snake" (Jer. 46:22).

2. A. R. Yudan and R. Huna:

    B. One of them said, "You are the one who caused my creatures to walk along bent over [in grief caused by the advent into the world of death], so you too: 'Upon your belly you shall go' (Gen. 3:14)."

    C. Said R. Eleazar, "Even the curse of the Holy One, blessed be he, contains a blessing. If God had not said to him, 'On your belly you shall go' (Gen. 3:14), how could the snake flee to the wall to find refuge, or to a hole to be saved?"

3. A. "And dust you shall eat [all the days of your life]" (Gen. 3:14):

    B. Said R. Hilpai, "It is not any sort of dirt, but the snake digs down until it reaches rock or virgin soil, and he takes up the sinews of the earth and eats."

4. A. Said R. Levi, "In the age to come every creature will find its remedy, except for the snake and the Gibeonites.

    B. "The snake: 'And earth shall be the snake's food' (Isa. 65:25).

    C. "The Gibeonites: 'And they that serve the city out of all the tribes of Israel shall till it' (Ezek. 48:19). The sense is that all of the tribes of Israel will force them to till it."

5. A. R. Issi and R. Hoshiah in the name of R. Hiyya the Elder said, "There are four things [on the basis of Gen. 3:14, which the Holy One said to the snake]: Said the Holy One, blessed be he, to him, 'I made you to be king over all domesticated and wild beasts, but you did not want it: "Cursed are you above all cattle and above all wild animals" (Gen. 3:14).

    B. "'I made you to walk upright like a man, but you did not want it: "Upon your belly you shall go" (Gen. 3:14).

    C. "'I made you to eat the sort of food humans eat, but you did not want it: "And you shall eat dirt" (Gen. 3:14).

    D. "'You wanted to kill man and marry his wife: "I will put enmity between you and the woman, and between your seed and her seed" Gen. 3:15).'

    E. "So what turns out is that what he wanted was not given to him, and what he had was taken away from him.

    F. "And so we find in the case of Cain, Korah, Balaam, Doeg,

Gihazi, Ahitophel, Absalom, Adonijah, Uzziah, and Haman:
what they wanted was not given to them, and what they had
was taken away from them."

XX:IX

1. A. "In toil you shall eat of it all the days of your life" (Gen. 3:17):
   B. Said R. Issi, "Making a living is twice as hard as giving birth.
   C. "In connection with giving birth, it is written, 'In pain you will
      give birth to children' (Gen. 3:16), while 'in pain' written here
      [translated, 'toil'] bears the intensive sense of great pain: 'In toil
      you shall eat.'"
2. A. R. Eleazar and R. Samuel b. Nahman:
   B. R. Eleazar says, "The Scripture links redemption to making a
      living, and making a living to redemption.
   C. "Just as redemption is a matter of miracles, so making a living is
      a matter of miracles.
   D. "Just as making a living takes place every day, so redemption
      takes place every day."
   E. R. Samuel b. Nahman: "But making a living is greater than
      redemption, for redemption takes place through the agency of a
      divine messenger, while making a living takes place through
      the agency of the Holy One, blessed be he, himself.
   F. "Redemption takes place through the agency of a divine mes-
      senger: 'The angel who redeemed me from all evil' (Gen.
      48:16).
   G. "Making a living takes place through the agency of the Holy
      One, blessed be he, himself: 'You open up your hand and sus-
      tain every living thing with favor' (Ps. 145:16)."
   H. R. Joshua b. Levi said, "Making a living is more difficult than
      splitting the Red Sea: 'To him who divided the Red Sea in half'
      (Ps. 136:13) and 'who gives food to all flesh' (Ps. 136:25).
      [Freedman, p. 168, n. 2: The dividing of the Red Sea was for
      Israel only, whereas sustenance must be provided for all flesh.]"

XXI:V

2. A. ["Behold, the man has become like one of us" (Gen. 3:22)]:
      R. Judah b. Simon said, "['Like One of us' means] like the One
      of the world: 'Hear O Israel, the Lord our God, the Lord is one'
      (Deut. 6:4)."

B. Rabbis say, "['Like one of us' means] like Gabriel: 'And one man in the midst of them clothed in linen' (Ezek. 9:2), like a snail, whose garments are integral to itself."

C. R. Simeon b. Laqish said, "['Like one of us'] means, like Jonah: 'But as one was felling a beam' (2 Kgs. 6:5) [who was Jonah, hence the 'one' of the verse at hand is that 'one' to whom the cited verse refers]. Just as this one [Jonah] fled, so that one had also to flee. Just as this one did not long enjoy the honor that came to him, so that one did not long enjoy the honor that had come to him."

D. R. Berekhiah in the name of R. Hanina: "It was like Elijah. Just as this one [Elijah] never tasted the flavor of death, so that one never was supposed to taste the flavor of death."

E. The view of R. Berekhiah in the name of R. Hanan: "So long as man remained one and whole, [he was not meant to taste the flavor of death,] but once his rib was taken from him, then [he become one] 'knowing good and evil' (Gen. 3:22). [Freedman, p. 175, n. 1: The immediate effect of Eve's creation was that Adam should sin. He translates: Behold the man was as one, wholehearted in his obedience to God, but now that he has Eve, he has been enabled "to know good and evil."]"

"God Was Sorry . . . but Noah Found Grace"

God draws the necessary conclusion: the creation of man had erred. Man was incapable of good, thinking only of evil. So come the terrifying words: "God was sorry God made humanity." But strict justice and satisfying logic give way to mercy, expressed through grace. Our sages find in Noah that first step toward Abraham, then onward to Moses and Sinai, the redemption of humanity through the Torah. So the beginnings of the world, nature and history alike, point toward the ending of redemption and salvation. The story of the flood and of Noah set the stage, leading to deep reflection on God's sorrow, the divine pathos that matches God's condition with humanity's. The sages' power of exposition comes to full expression as they link detail to detail, tale to tale, finding once more how Scripture presents not (mere) narrative, but a set of enduring rules that show why things are the way they are. Scripture is a source not of history but of science: certain knowledge about the nature of human existence.

What forms the critical problem for the sages as they contemplate the story of the flood derives from their basically affirmative perspective on creation. How could God so have erred as to create sinful humanity? This question comes to expression—for the sages—when they read the verse that says that God was sorry that God had made humanity. A further question concerning God's justice emerges. The Scriptures are full of stories of the sinfulness of God's people. Yet God's people was preserved, at least in a remnant, while the entire generation of the flood was wiped out, save Noah. How then justify the mercy shown to Israel and the justice to the generation of the flood (and, in context, Sodom and Gomorroah)? So too why destroy the beasts? XXVIII:V and VI work out this problem at some length. Where you can point to God's sparing generations apparently as wicked as the one(s) whom God destroyed, whether the generation of the flood or Sodom, there is a reason. God recognized the merit of one or another, but found no merit in the generation of the flood. What is explained in the base verse, therefore, is the statement that God destroyed the generation of the flood "from the face of the earth," thus leaving no remnant. Then those who survived, even as a remnant, have to be compared to those who did not survive.

The complementary question is, why save Noah? Was it through his own merit, or was it an act of utter grace? Our sages take both positions. Noah was no better than the others. God saved Noah as an act of grace alone. Noah did have certain merit. God responded to that merit. The sages maintained that God responds to human merit, and furthermore that the merit of the early generations serves to protect and sustain their descendants. The merit of Noah consists in his admonishing his age, in obedience to God's message. But that merit was relative to the times. XXX:IX asks a legitimate question: is the language "in his generation" meant to limit the matter? By what standard Noah was found blameless therefore attracts attention. Noah was one thing, Abraham another. Noah walked with God, Abraham before God, because Noah was weak, Abraham strong. In an age of saints, Noah would have appeared a sinner. Noah's good deeds did not protect him from punishment, and the wicked all the more so will be punished, thus justifying the flood.

At issue is the justification of selecting Noah for survival, while all others perished. Noah stands in stark contrast with the others of his generation. The exegete turns to find reasons for singling out Noah. The sages wish to stress God's power, justice, and mercy, and this they accomplish by laying stress on absolute grace. Noah had done nothing to merit God's favor. It was pure grace. But the next passage contradicts that point: Noah was the grapecluster who produced good wine. The point of the intersecting verse is clear. But now Noah is saved not merely by an act of complete grace, but because of merit that he himself has attained. He is the grapecluster. XXIX:III then links the story of the salvation of Noah to the history of Israel. The grace shown to Noah derived from Israel. Noah on his own—that is, humanity—enjoyed salvation only because of Israel's merit. The proposition is striking and daring. God "found," that is, made an accidental discovery of a treasure, only three: Abraham, David, and Israel—that is, the beginning, the end, and the holy people that started with Abraham and found redemption through David. So once more, and in a stunning way, the story of creation reaches its fulfillment and resolution in the salvific history of Israel.

XXVII:VI

1. A. "And the Lord was sorry that he had made [man on the earth, and it grieved him to his heart]" (Gen. 6:6):
   B. R. Judah said, "[God said,] 'It was a blunder before me that I created him below [Freedman: out of earthly elements], for if I had made him of the elements of heaven he would never have rebelled against me.'"
   C. R. Nehemiah said, "[God said,] 'I take comfort in the fact that I created him below; for if I had created him above, just as he brought rebellion against me from the creatures below, so he would have led a rebellion against me among the creatures above.'"
   D. R. Aibu said, "'It is a blunder that I created in him the impulse to do evil; for if I had not created the impulse to do evil in him, he would never have rebelled against me.'"
   E. Said R. Levi, "'I am comforted that I made him from the earth [mortal, so he will go back to the dust].'"

2. A. "[And the Lord was sorry that he had made man on the earth,] and it grieved him to his heart" (Gen. 6:6):
   B. Said R. Berekhiah, "The matter may be compared to the case of a king who conducted his affairs through a trust officer and incurred a loss. To whom should he address his complaint? Is it not to the trust officer?
   C. "Accordingly: 'And it grieved him in his heart' (Gen. 6:6). [He blamed himself, that is, his own heart, for its incorrect impulse.]"

3. A. A Gentile asked R. Joshua b. Qorha, saying to him, "Do you not maintain that the Holy One, blessed be he, sees what is going to happen?"
   B. He said to him, "Indeed so."
   C. "But lo, it is written, 'And it grieved him in his heart' (Gen. 6:6)!"
   D. He said to him, "Did you ever have a son?"
   E. He said to him, "Yes."
   F. He said to him, "And what did you do?"
   G. He said to him, "I was happy, and I made everybody happy."
   H. He said to him, "But did you not know that in the end he would die?"

    I. He said to him, "'Rejoice in the time of joy, mourn in the time of mourning.'"

    J. He said to him, "And that is the way things are done before the Holy One, blessed be he."

    K. For R. Joshua b. Levi said, "For seven days the Holy One, blessed be he, went into mourning for his world before he brought the flood, as it is said: 'And it grieved him in his heart' (Gen. 6:5); and further it is said: 'For the king grieved for his son' (2 Sam. 19:2 [Hebrew v. 3])."

XXVIII:V

1. A. "From the face of the ground" (Gen. 6:7):

    B. Said R. Abba b. Kahana, "What was done by the ten tribes was not done by the generation of the flood.

    C. "With respect to the generation of the flood, it is written: 'And every imagination of the thoughts of his heart was only evil all day' (Gen. 6:5). With regard to the ten tribes: 'Woe to them that devise iniquity and work evil upon their beds' (Mic. 2:1), which is to say even by night. And how do we know that they did it by day as well? 'When the morning is light, they execute it' (Mic. 2:1).

    D. "Nonetheless, of those [of the generation of the flood] not a remnant was left, while of these [the ten tribes] a remnant was left.

    E. "It was on account of the merit of the righteous men and righteous women who were destined to emerge from [the ten tribes that a remnant was spared].

    F. "That is in line with this verse: 'And behold there shall be left a remnant therein that shall be brought forth, both sons and daughters' (Ezek. 14:22), that is, on account of the merit of the righteous men and righteous women who were destined to emerge from [the ten tribes a remnant was spared]."

2. A. Said R. Berekhiah, "What was done by the tribes of Judah and Benjamin was never done in Sodom.

    B. "In respect to Sodom, it is written: 'And yes, their sin is exceedingly grievous' (Gen. 18:20), but with regard to the tribes of Judah and Benjamin: 'The iniquity of the house of Israel and Judah is most exceedingly great' (Ezek. 9:9).

    C. "Nonetheless, of those [of the generation of the flood] not a remnant was left, while of these [the two tribes] a remnant was left.

    D. "As to Sodom, 'which was overthrown in a moment' (Lam. 4:6), they never put forth their hands to carry out religious duties, 'Hands therein accepted no duties' (Lam. 4:6), in line with what R. Tanhuma said, 'No hand joined another hand [to help one another].' [The people did not help one another to carry out their religious duties.]

    E. "But in regard to the others [of Judah and Benjamin], they extended hands to one another in carrying out religious duties: 'The hands of women full of compassion have sodden their own children and provided the mourner's meal' (Lam. 4:10)."

3. A. Said R. Hanan, "Things were done by the cities of the sea that were not done by the generation of the flood: 'Woe to the inhabitants of the seacoast, the nation of the Cherethites' (Zeph. 2:5), indicating by their name [consonants that bear the meaning of 'extirpation'] that they were suitable to be annihilated.

    B. "On account of what merit do they endure? It is on account of the merit of a singular Gentile, who fears heaven, that the Holy One, blessed be he, receives from their hand [that he spares them while having destroyed Sodom and the generation of the flood]. [There are some good among them.]"

    C. "The nation of the Cherethites" (Zeph. 2:5): Some explain the name in a positive sense, that is, "a nation that enters into a covenant [with God]."

XXVIII:VI

1. A. "Man and beast and creeping things and birds of the air" (Gen. 6:7):

    B. R. Yudan said, "The matter [of destroying the beasts and fowl] may be compared to the case of a king who handed his son over to a tutor, who misguided the boy and led him into bad ways. The king grew angry with his son and put him to death. Said the king, 'Is it not so that this one alone is responsible for leading my son into bad ways? My son has perished, and should this one survive?' Therefore: 'Man *and beast*' (Gen. 6:7). [How the beasts are responsible for man's sin is not specified. This will come up shortly. The beasts contributed to an excess of prosperity, on which the sin is blamed. But the passage as a whole would better explain wiping out a generation accused of bestiality.]"

C. R. Phineas said, "The matter may be compared to the case of a king who was marrying his son off and made a marriage canopy for him, which he plastered, painted, and decorated. The king grew angry with his son and killed him. He went into the marriage canopy and began to break down the rods, destroy the partitions, and tear the hangings. He said, 'My son has perished and should these remain?' Therefore: 'Man *and beast*' (Gen. 6:7). [But here why the king killed the son is not specified at all. Following is an attempted explanation of the destruction of the beasts, but that does not help us with the killing of the son in the present parable.]

D. "That [verse, concerning destroying the beasts and fowl too] is in line with this verse of Scripture: 'I will consume man and beast, and the stumbling blocks with the wicked' (Zeph. 1:3). [The beasts] were the ones that served as stumbling blocks for the wicked, for one would hunt a bird and say, 'Go, get fat, and then come back,' which the bird did. [Freedman, p. 228, n. 2: There was abundant prosperity, which led to evil.]"

XXVIII:VIII

1. A. ["Man and beast and creeping things and birds of the air" (Gen. 6:7):] [Explaining in a different way why the beasts as much as man were wiped out in the flood,] R. Azariah in the name of R. Judah: "Every species violated the rules of its kind in the generation of the flood, the dog with the wolf, the chicken with the peacock, thus 'For *all* flesh had corrupted their way' (Gen. 6:12) [and not just man]."

B. R. Luliani b. R. Tabari in the name of R. Isaac: "Even the earth itself committed adultery. People would sow wheat and get back rye grass [through hybridization], for the rye grass that we now have comes from the generation of the flood."

XXIX:II

1. A. R. Simon opened [discourse by citing the following verse of Scripture]: "'Thus says the Lord, "As when wine is found in the

cluster, one says, 'Do not destroy, it for a blessing is found in it'" (Isa. 65:8).

B. "There is this story. A certain pious man went out to his vine-yard and saw a grapecluster and said a blessing over it. He said, 'This grapecluster is worth my saying a blessing over it.'

C. "Thus: 'Thus says the Lord, "As when wine is found in the cluster . . .""."

XXIX:III

1. A. "And Noah found grace" (Gen. 6:8):

B. Said R. Simon, "There were three acts of finding on the part of the Holy One, blessed be he:

C. "'And you found [Abraham's] heart faithful before you' (Neh. 9:8).

D. "'I have found David, my servant' (Ps. 89:20 [Hebrew v. 21]).

E. "'I found Israel like grapes in the wilderness' (Hos. 9:10)."

F. His fellows said to R. Simon, "And is it not written, 'Noah found grace in the eyes of the Lord' (Gen. 6:8)?"

G. He said to them, "He found it, but the Holy One, blessed be he, did not find it."

H. Said R. Simon, "'He found grace in the wilderness' (Jer. 31:2) on account of the merit of the generation of the wilderness."

XXIX:IV

1. A. R. Huna and R. Phineas, R. Hanan and R. Hoshiah have not explained [what grace it was that Noah found].

B. R. Berekhiah said, "R. Yohanan, R. Simeon b. Laqish, and rabbis did explain it.

C. R. Yohanan said, "The matter may be compared to the case of someone who was going along the way and met someone and stuck by him. To what extent? To such an extent that he was bound to him in love. So here we find the word 'grace,' and elsewhere: 'And Joseph found grace in his sight' (Gen. 39:4). [Freedman: Thus Noah found as much favor in God's sight as Joseph in his master's.]"

D. R. Simeon b. Laqish said, "The matter may be compared to the case of someone who was going along the way and met someone and stuck by him. To what extent? To such an extent that he accepted the latter's authority as his ruler. So the word 'grace' is used here and in the following passage: 'And Esther obtained grace in the sight of all them that looked upon her' (Esth. 2:15)."

E. Rabbis said, "The matter may be compared to the case of someone who was going along the way and met someone and stuck by him. To what extent? To such an extent that he gave him his daughter in marriage. So the word 'grace' is used here and in the following passage: 'And I will pour upon the house of David and upon the inhabitants of Jerusalem the spirit of grace' (Zech. 12:10)."

F. To what extent [did Noah enjoy God's favor]? To the extent that he knew what animal had to be fed at two hours of the day, and which one at three hours in the night.

XXIX.V

1. A. Said R. Abbahu, "We know full well that the Holy One, blessed be he, does an act of kindness with later generations on account of the merit attained by the earlier generations. But how do we know that the Holy One, blessed be he, does an act of kindness with earlier generations on account of the merit to be attained by later generations?

   B. "As it is said, 'And Noah found grace' on account of the merit accruing to his generations to come, as it is written: 'These are the generations of Noah' (Gen. 6:9)."

XXX:VII

1. A. "[Noah was a righteous] man" (Gen. 6:9):

   B. Whenever Scripture speaks of "man," it refers to a righteous man who admonished [his age].

   C. For the entire one hundred twenty years before the flood, Noah went about planting cedars and cutting them down. So people said to him, "Why are you doing this?"

   D. He said to them, "The Master of the world told me that he is bringing a flood on the world."

   E. They said to him, "If a flood is coming, it will come only on the house of the father of that man [on you alone]."

   F. That is in line with the following verse of Scripture: "A contemptible brand in the thought of him who is at ease, a thing ready for them whose foot slips" (Job. 12:5).

2. A. Said R. Abba, "Said the Holy One, blessed be he, 'A single
herald stood up for me in the generation of the flood.' This is
Noah.

   B. "For hereabouts people say, '[Freedman:] Arouse him, stir him
up!' [Freedman, p. 235, n. 5: The word is made up of the same
consonants as the word in Job 12:5 translated 'brand,' so the
meaning is, 'arouse, stir up.']

   C. "[The cited verse refers to 'contemptible,'] for people ridiculed
him and called him a dirty old man.

   D. " 'In the thought of him who is at ease' teaches that they were as
hard as metal [Freedman: a play on the consonants of the word
for 'in the thought of'].

   E. " 'A thing ready for them whose foot slips' (Job. 12:5), for those
people were indeed ready for their foot to slip and break, breaking above and breaking below."

XXX:IX

1. A. "[Noah was a righteous man, blameless] in his generation"
(Gen. 6:9):

   B. R. Judah and R. Nehemiah:

   C. R. Judah said, "By the standard of his generation, he was indeed
righteous. But had he been in the generation of Moses or in the
generation of Samuel, he would hardly have been regarded as
righteous.

   D. "In the market of the blind, they call a one-eyed man far-
sighted, and the baby is a scholar.

   E. "The matter may be compared to the case of a man who had a
wine cellar. He opened the first keg and found it vinegar, the
second and found it vinegar. When he came to the third, he
found it turning. They said to him, 'It is turning.' He said to
them, 'Is there anything better here?' They told him, 'No.'

   F. "So too by the standard of his generation, he was a righteous
man. [But that is only by that standard.]"

   G. R. Nehemiah said, "Now if in the generation in which he lived
he was righteous, in the generation of Moses all the more so!

   H. "The matter may be compared to the case of a vial of perfume
lying tightly sealed in a cemetery, giving out a wonderful odor.
If it were located outside of the cemetery, how much the more
so!"

"Abram Believed the Lord"

We come to the end of the beginning: the tower of Babel, the advent of Abraham. Sages link these two events, seeing the one as counterpart and preparation for the other. Humanity could not fight its way upward into Heaven. God's grace reaches down to earth and raises up humanity, in the persons of Abraham and Sarah. But why did God not leave Abraham and Sarah in Babylonia? Why not have him do his work there? God had done the work, with the generation of the flood and of the Dispersion, and it had done no good. The latter returned to their own countries, so God had Abram leave Babylonia for the Land of Israel. That is the basic view expressed here. Linking Abram's call to the generation of the Dispersion not only ties the threads of the narrative. It also contrasts Israel's loyalty to the Land with the cosmopolitan character of the generation of the Dispersion, shown by its willingness to abandon its ancestral homeland.

Abraham and Sarah open the hopeful chapter in the history of humanity, leaving home and kindred for the land that God would show, abandoning the life of rebellion for the eternity of obedience. Sages' now-familiar quest for connections among biblical figures, their interest in the science of salvation, leads them to find in Abraham and Sarah the type and model of the righteous person. Even without the Torah, they carried out their religious duties—a point much in debate with Christianity, of course. But what is of special interest to the sages is the statement, "By you all the families of the earth shall bless themselves" (Gen. 12:3). How Abraham and Sarah formed a blessing for humanity defines a critical point of interest. For the sages, seeing Israel as Abraham's family in a genealogical as well as moral sense, took a keen interest in that very matter. Since the meaning of justification in Abraham's belief presents a matter of special interest, we close our brief encounter with Abraham by reviewing the sages' reading of that important passage.

We begin with the story of the Tower of Babel. The reason is that our sages here show their capacity in seeing connections between one story and the next. Scripture is remarkably silent about the deeds for which the generation of the Tower of Babel ("the generation of the Disper-

sion") are punished. True, Scripture makes the point that that generation was arrogant. But from that point we have silence. Sages solve this
problem at XXXVIII:VI by linking that generation to what is to come:
Abraham. They had a few words, but the words were against Abraham
and the Lord. We move immediately to the important story of Abraham
and idolatry. Our sages here take for granted that Abraham had a long
biography before those stunning words with which Gen. 12:1 introduces
Abraham. And here they fill the gap, beginning at XXXVIII:XIII. Then
comes the call to Abraham: the world is on fire, is there no one to care?
Then God responds: I care. The stress is that Abraham took the initiative. That was his greatness. And that justifies Abraham's willingness to
argue with God at Sodom (XXXIX:VI). Abraham of course is progenitor
of Israel, so we cannot find surprising our sages' effort to link the biography of Abraham to the history of Israel. We see a striking instance of that
approach at XLIV:V, where the sages insist on the uniqueness of the
covenant with Abraham. No one will take Abraham's place. No one will
push aside Abraham's and Sarah's children. Since, in the time of the
formation of Genesis Rabbah, Christians took that position, the reply
seems apt. The linkage of Abraham's deeds to the history of Israel (e.g.,
at XLIV:XV, which deals with Gen. 15:1ff., the covenant between the
parts) underlines that same point. The treatment of Abraham emphasizes his role as the founder of Israel. The sages stress Israel as the genealogical heirs and descendants of Abraham and Sarah, hence they find
in the recurrent theme of Abraham's not having a child a profound
motif. In the time of Genesis Rabbah's authorship, Christian theologians called into question the status of the Jews as "Israel," maintaining
that the Jews' had had salvation but not received it, so the status of
"Israel" now passed to those who did receive the salvation of Christ.
Sages' response was to underline the "Israelness" of the Jews as the
children "after the flesh" of Abraham, Isaac, and Jacob. That accounts
for the power, in their exegesis, of the theme of the heir.

The climax comes with the statement that Abraham trusted in God,
and God counted it to Abraham as righteousness. The exegetes want to
explain the costs of that act of trust: the things that made Abraham right
to fear. These encompassed, in particular, Israel's future history. The
special interest of the exegetes is in Israel's suffering later on, with the
particular stress on God's choosing subjugation to the nations as the
appropriate penalty for Israel's failures to come. In fact Abraham is made
party to the entire future history of Israel, even choosing, in dealing with

God, the penalty for their sin and their mode of atonement. So his faith
was despite and not because of the world, and that was a faith worthy of
justification. When Paul pointed to the salvific power of faith, foolish-
ness and scandal though the propositions of the faith may have appeared
to outsiders, he said no less than did our sages: faith despite the world,
and not because of it, is what is called for. The pertinence of the sages'
view to the life of Israel then and now—after the Holocaust—hardly has
to be spelled out.

XXXVIII:VI

1. A. "Now the whole earth had one language and few words" (Gen.
        11:1):
    B. R. Eleazar said, " 'Few words' means that while the deeds of the
        generation of the flood were spelled out, the deeds of the gener-
        ation of the Dispersion were not spelled out [and hence were
        covered by only a few words]."

2. A. "Few words": That phrase means that they addressed words
        against the two who are singular [using the same word as is
        translated 'few'], against the one of whom it is said "Abraham
        was one" (Ezek. 33:24) and against "The Lord, our God, the
        Lord is one" (Deut. 6:4).
    B. [They thus spoke against Abraham and against God.] They
        said, "This man Abraham is a barren mule, who will never have
        offspring."
    C. "Against 'The Lord our God, the Lord is one':" "He does not
        have the power to select the heavenly spheres for himself and
        hand over to us merely the lower world. So come, let us make a
        tower for ourselves and put an idol on top of it, and put a sword
        in its hand, so that it will appear as if it carries on warfare with
        him."

5. A. Said R. Eleazar, "Who is worse, one who says to the king,
        'Either you or I shall live in the palace,' or the one who says to
        him, 'Neither you nor I shall live in the palace'? It is the one
        who says, 'Either you or I shall live in the palace.'
    B. "So the generation of the flood said, 'What is the Almighty,
        that we should serve him' (Job 21:15).
    C. "But the generation of the Dispersion said, [against 'The Lord

our God, the Lord is one'], 'He does not have the power to select the heavenly spheres for himself and hand over to us merely the lower world. So come, let us make a tower for ourselves and put an idol on top of it, and put a sword in its hand, so that it will appear as if it carries on warfare with him.' [Thus: either you or I shall live in heaven.]

D. "Of the former not a remnant survived, while of the latter a remnant survived.

E. "Now as to the generation of the flood, because they were stuffed on the returns of thievery—'They remove the landmarks; they violently take away flocks and feed them' (Job 24:2)—not a remnant survived of them. But as to the others, because they [at least] loved one another—'Now the whole earth had one language and few words' (Gen. 11:1)—a remnant of them survived."

6. A. Rabbi said, "Great is peace. For even if Israel should worship idols, if there is peace among them, said the Holy One, blessed be he, it is as if I shall not exercise dominion over them [and punish them]. As it is said: 'Ephraim is united in idol worship, let him alone' (Hos. 4:17).

B. "But if they are torn by dissension, what is written concerning them? 'Their heart is divided, now shall they bear their guilt' (Hos. 10:2)."

XXXVIII:XIII

1. A. "Haran died in the presence of his father Terah in the land of his birth, in Ur of the Chaldaeans" (Gen. 11:28):

B. Said R. Hiyya [in explanation of how Haran died in his father's presence], "Terah was an idol manufacturer. Once he went off on a trip and put Abraham in charge of the store. Someone would come in and want to buy an idol. He would say to him, 'How old are you?'

C. "He said, 'Fifty years old.'

D. "He said, 'Woe to that man, who is fifty years old and is going to bow down to something a day old.' So the man would be ashamed and go his way.

E. "One time a woman came in with a bowl of flour, and said to him, 'Take this and offer it before them.'

F. "He went and took a stick, broke the idols, and put the stick in the hand of the biggest idol.

G. "When his father came back, he said to you, 'Why in the world have you been doing these things?'

H. "He said to him, 'How can I hide it from you? One time a woman came in with a bowl of flour, and said to me, "Take this and offer it before them." Then this idol said, "I'll eat first," and that idol said, "I'll eat first." One of them, the largest, got up and grabbed the stick and broke the others.'

I. "[Terah] said to him, 'Why are you making fun of me! Do those idols know anything [that such a thing could possibly happen]? [Obviously not!]'

J. "He said to him, 'And should your ears not hear what your mouth is saying?' He took him and handed him over to Nimrod.

K. "He said to him, 'Bow down to the fire.'

L. "He said to him, 'We really should bow down to water, which puts out fire.'

M. "He said to him, 'Bow down to water.'

N. "He said to him, 'We really should bow down to the clouds, which bear the water.'

O. "He said to him, 'Then let's bow down to the clouds.'

P. "He said to him, 'We really should bow down to the wind, which disperses the clouds.'

Q. "He said to him, 'Then let's bow down to the wind.'

R. "He said to him, 'We really should bow down to human beings, who can stand up to the wind.'

S. "He said to him, 'You're just playing word games with me. Let's bow down to the fire. So now, look, I am going to throw you into the fire, and let your God whom you worship come and save you from the fire.'

T. "Now Haran was standing there undecided. He said, 'What's the choice? If Abram wins, I'll say I'm on Abram's side, and if Nimrod wins, I'll say I'm on Nimrod's side. [So how can I lose?]'

U. "When Abram went down into the burning furnace and was saved, Nimrod said to him, 'On whose side are you?'

V. "He said to him, 'Abram's.'

W. "They took him and threw him into the fire, and his guts burned up and came out, and he died in the presence of his father.

X. "That is in line with the verse of Scripture: 'And Haran died in the presence of his father Terah' (Gen. 11:28)."

XXXIX:I

1. A. "Now the Lord said to Abram, 'Go [from your country and your kindred and your father's house to the land that I will show you']" (Gen. 12:1):

   B. R. Isaac opened [discourse by citing the following verse of Scripture:] "Hearken, O daughter, and consider and incline your ear; forget also your own people and your father's house" (Ps. 45:10 [Hebrew v. 11]).

   C. Said R. Isaac, "The matter may be compared to the case of someone who was going from one place to another when he saw a great house on fire. He said, 'Is it possible to say that such a great house has no one in charge?'

   D. "The owner of the house looked out and said to him, 'I am the one in charge of the house.'

   E. "Thus since Abraham, our father, [took the initiative and] said, 'Is it possible for the world to endure without someone in charge,' the Holy One, blessed be he, [responded and] looked out and said to him, 'I am the one in charge of the house, the Lord of all the world.'

   F. "'So shall the king desire your beauty' (Ps. 45:11 [Hebrew v. 12]), to show how splendid you are in this world.

   G. "'For he is your Lord, and do homage to him' (Ps. 45:11 [Hebrew v. 12]): 'Now the Lord said to Abram, Go . . .' (Gen. 12:1)."

XXXIX:IV

1. A. "Wisdom makes a wise man stronger than ten rulers" (Eccl. 7:19):

   B. The passage speaks of Abraham.

   C. ". . . Than ten . . . ": [He was stronger] than the ten generations that lived from Noah to Abraham.

   D. "Among all of them, I spoke only with you":

   E. "And the Lord said to Abram" (Gen. 12:1).

XXXIX:V

1. A. R. Azariah commenced discourse [by citing the following verse of Scripture] "'We would have healed Babylon, but she was not healed' (Jer. 51:9).

B. "'We would have healed Babylon' refers to the generation of Enosh.

C. "'But she was not healed' refers to the generation of the flood.

D. "'Forsake her' refers to the generation of the Dispersion.

E. "'. . . and let us go every one to his own country' (Jer. 51:9):

F. "Thus: 'Now the Lord said to Abram, "Go from your country and your kindred . . . to the land that I will show you"' (Gen. 12:1)."

XXXIX:VI

1. A. R. Azariah in the name of R. Aha commenced [discourse by citing the following verse of Scripture:] "You have loved righteousness and hated wickedness" (Ps. 45:7 [Hebrew v. 8]).

B. R. Azariah in the name of R. Aha interpreted the verse to speak of our father, Abraham: "When our father, Abraham, stood to seek mercy for the Sodomites, what is written there? 'Far be it from you to do such a thing' (Gen. 18:25)."

C. Said R. Aha, "[Abraham said to God,] 'You bound yourself by an oath not to bring a flood upon the world. Are you now going to act deceitfully against the clear intent of that oath? True enough, you are not going to bring a flood of water, but you are going to bring a flood of fire. If so you will not carry out the oath!'"

D. Said R. Levi, "'Will not the judge of all the earth do justly?' (Gen. 18:25). 'If you want to have a world, there can be no justice; and if justice is what you want, there can be no world. You are holding the rope at both ends—you want a world and you want justice. If you don't give in a bit, the world can never stand.'

E. "Said the Holy One, blessed be he, to him, 'Abraham, "You have loved righteousness and hated wickedness. Therefore God, your God, has anointed you with the oil of gladness above your fellows." (Ps. 45:7 [Hebrew v. 8]).

F. "'From Noah to you there are ten generations [that is, that lived from Noah to Abraham.

G. "'Among all of them, I spoke only with you.'"

H. "And the Lord said to Abram, ['Go from your country and your kindred and your father's house to the land that I will show you']" (Gen. 12:1).

XXXIX:IX

1. A. Said R. Levi, "'Go, go' (Gen. 12:1) is repeated twice [once in
the present context, the other at Gen. 22:1, in going to offer up
Isaac at Mount Moriah].

   B. "We do not know which of them is more precious, the first or
the second."

2. A. Said R. Yohanan, "'Go from your country' (Gen. 12:1), refers
to your hyparchy.

   B. "'From your birthplace' refers to your neighborhood.

   C. "'From your father's house' refers literally to the house of your
father.

   D. "To the land that I will show you': But why did he not inform
him [in advance where that would be]?

   E. "It was so as to make it still more precious in his view and to give
him a reward for each step that he took [in perfect faith and
reliance on God]."

   F. That is the view of R. Yohanan, for R. Yohanan said, "'And he
said, "Take your son"' (Gen. 22:2).

   G. "'Which son?' 'Your only son.'

   H. "'This one is the only son of his mother, and that one is the only
son of his mother.'

   I. "'Whom you have loved' (Gen. 22:2).

   J. "'This one I love, and that one I love. Are there boundaries
within one's heart?'

   K. "So he said to him, 'Isaac' (Gen. 22:2).

   L. "And why did he not tell him to begin with whom he wanted?

   M. "It was so as to make it still more precious in his view and to give
him a reward for each statement that he made [in perfect obedience to and reliance on God]."

3. A. For R. Huna said in the name of R. Eliezer, "He whom the Holy
One, blessed be he, puts in doubt and holds in suspense—
namely, the righteous—he then informs, explaining his reasoning.

   B. "Thus: 'To the land that I will show you' (Gen. 12:1). 'On one
of the mountains which I shall tell you' (Gen. 22:2). 'And make
to it the proclamation that I shall tell you' (Jonah 3:2). 'Arise,
go forth to the plain, and there I will speak with you' (Ezek.
3:22)."

XXXIX:X

1. A. R. Berekhiah b. R. Simon in the name of R. Nehemiah: "The matter may be compared to the case of a king who was traveling from place to place, and a pearl fell out of his crown. The king stopped there and held up his retinue there, collected sand in heaps and brought sieves. He had the first pile sifted and did not find the pearl. So he did with the second and did not find it. But in the third heap he found it. People said, 'The king has found his pearl.'

    B. "So said the Holy One, blessed be he, to Abraham, 'Why did I have to spell out the descent of Shem, Arpachshad, Shelah, Eber, Peleg, Reu, Serug, Nahor, and Terah? Was it not entirely for you?'

    C. "'And he *found* his heart faithful before you' (Neh. 9:8). [Freedman, p. 319, n. 2: He was the pearl that God found.]

    D. "So said the Holy One, blessed be he, to David, 'Why did I have to spell out the descent of Perez, Hezron, Ram, Amminadab, Nahshon, Salmon, Boaz, Obed, and Jesse? Was it not entirely for you?'

    E. "Thus: 'I have *found* David my servant; with my holy oil have I anointed him' (Ps. 89:20 [Hebrew v. 21])."

XXXIX:XI

1. A. "And I will make of you a great nation" (Gen. 12:2):

    B. [Abram] said to him, "And from Noah have you not raised up seventy nations?"

    C. He said to him, "From you I shall raise up that nation of whom it is written: 'For what great nation is there that has God so near to them' (Deut. 4:7)." [The reference, in both passages, is to a great nation, not merely to a nation.]

2. A. Said R. Berekhiah, "What is written is not 'I will give you' or 'I will set you,' but 'I will make of you,' meaning 'once I create you in a completely new act of creation, you will be fruitful and multiply.'"

3. A. R. Levi b. Ahyatah, R. Abba: "In the present passage there are three references to greatness and four references to blessings.

    B. "In this way God gave Abram the good news that there will be three patriarchs and four matriarchs."

4. A. Said R. Berekhiah, "[Reference to Abram's having many chil-
dren] is because traveling causes three things. It diminishes the
act of procreation, one's financial resources, and one's repute
[since one is far from people who know him]. [So God had to say
to him,] 'I shall make you a great nation [despite the rigors of
travel].'

   B. "Since it diminishes the act of procreation: 'I shall make you a
great nation' (Gen. 12:2).

   C. "Since it diminishes one's financial resources: 'I shall bless you'
(Gen. 21:2).

   D. "Since it diminishes one's repute: 'I will make your name great'
(Gen. 12:2).

   E. "And even though people say, 'From house to house a move
costs a shirt, from place to place a move costs a life; in your case,
however, you will lose neither your life nor your money.'"

5. A. R. Berekhiah in the name of R. Helbo: "[The promise that God
will make Abram great] refers to the fact that his coinage had
circulated in the world.

   B. "There were four whose coinage circulated in the world.

   C. "Abraham: 'And I will make you' (Gen. 12:2). And what image
appeared on his coinage? An old man and an old woman on the
obverse side, a boy and a girl on the reverse [Abraham and
Sarah, Isaac and Rebekah].

   D. "Joshua: 'So the Lord was with Joshua, and his fame was in all
the land' (Josh. 6:27). That is, his coinage circulated in the
world. And what image appeared on his coinage? An ox on the
obverse, a wild-ox on the reverse: 'His firstling bullock, majesty
is his, and his horns are the horns of a wild ox' (Deut 33:17).
[Joshua descended from Joseph.]

   E. "David: 'And the fame of David went out into all lands' (1 Chr.
14:17). That is, his coinage circulated in the world. And what
image appeared on his coinage? A staff and a wallet on the
obverse, a tower on the reverse: 'Your neck is like the tower of
David, built with turrets' (Cant. 4:4).

   F. "Mordecai: 'For Mordecai was great in the king's house, and his
fame went forth throughout all the provinces' (Esth. 9:4). That
is, his coinage circulated in the world. And what image appeared on his coinage? Sackcloth and ashes on the obverse, a
golden crown on the reverse."

6. A. Said R. Isaac, "[God said to Abraham,] 'I shall provide a bless-ing for you in the Eighteen Benedictions,' but you do not know whether 'mine' comes first or 'yours' comes first."

   B. Said R. Aha in the name of R. Zeira, "[He told him,] 'Yours comes before mine,' since people say first, '. . . the shield of Abraham,' and only afterward they say, '. . . who resurrects the dead' [thus referring first to Abraham, then to God]."

8. A. [Commenting on Gen. 12:2: "So that you will be a bless-ing,"] said R. Levi, "No one ever haggled with Abraham about the price of a cow without being blessed, and no one ever gave a price to Abraham to sell him a cow without being blessed.

   B. "Abraham would pray for barren women until they conceived, for the sick and they would be healed."

   C. R. Huna said, "It was not the end of the matter that Abraham would have to go to the sick person; but if the sick person merely laid eyes on him, he got better."

   D. Said R. Haninah, "Even ships that sailed on the ocean would be saved on account of the merit of Abraham."

   E. But were they not carrying wine used for libations [and so serv-ing idolatry]?

   F. [He replied,] "'Vinegar cheapens wine'—wherever Gentile wine [used for libations to idols] is abundant, Israelite wine also is sold at a cheap price."

   G. Said R. Isaac, "God treated Job the same way: 'You have blessed the work of his hands' (Job 1:10). No one took a penny from Job and had to get another penny from him [since the original act of charity sufficed to bring the pauper prosperity]."

9. A. "And you will be a blessing" (Gen. 12:2):

   B. [Since the word may be read "pool of water," what it means is "Just as a pool of water removes the cultic uncleanness of an unclean person, so you will bring near to God those who are far from him."

10. A. Said R. Berekhiah, "Since the Scripture states 'I will bless you,' why does it go on to state 'You will be a blessing'?

    B. "He said to him, 'Up to this point I had to give a blessing to my world. From now on, lo, the power of bestowing a blessing is handed over to you. To the person whom you wish to give a blessing, give a blessing.'"

XLIV:V

2. A. "After these things" (Gen. 15:1): There were some second thoughts.

  B. Who had second thoughts? Abraham did. He said before the Holy One, blessed be he, "Lord of the ages, you made a covenant with Noah that you would not wipe out his children. I went and acquired a treasure of religious deeds and good deeds greater than his, so the covenant made with me has set aside the covenant made with him. Now is it possible that someone else will come along and accumulate religious deeds and good deeds greater than mine and so set aside the covenant that was made with me on account of the covenant to be made with him?"

  C. Said the Holy One, blessed be he, "Out of Noah I did not raise up shields for the righteous, but from you I shall raise up shields for the righteous. And not only so, but when your children will fall into sin and evil deeds, I shall see a single righteous man among them who can say to the attribute of justice, 'Enough.' Him I shall take and make into the atonement for them all."

XLIV:VII

1. A. "Fear not, Abram" (Gen. 15:1):

  B. On what account was he afraid?

  C. R. Berekhiah said, "He was afraid of Shem [for he had killed his descendants, Chedorlaomer and his sons], as it is said: 'The isles saw and feared' (Isa. 41:5).

  D. "Just as islands are distinct in the sea, so Abraham and Shem were distinguished in the world.

  E. "'. . . and were afraid': This one [Abraham] feared that one [Shem], and that one feared this one.

  F. "This one [Abraham] feared that one, thinking, 'Perhaps he has a gripe against me, because I killed his descendants.'

  G. "That one [Shem] feared this one, thinking, 'Perhaps he has a gripe against me, because I produced wicked descendants.'

  H. "'The ends of the earth' (Isa. 41:5): This one lived at one end of the world, and that one lived at the other end of the world.

  I. "'They drew near and came' (Isa. 41:5): This one drew near that one, and that one drew near this one.

J. " 'They helped each one his neighbor' (Isa. 41:6): This one helped that one, and that one helped this one.

K. "This one helped that one by means of blessings: 'And he blessed him and said, "Blessed be Abram"' (Gen. 14:19).

L. "And that one helped this one by means of gifts: 'And he gave him a tenth of all' (Gen. 14:20).

M. " 'So the carpenter encouraged' (Isa. 41:7) refers to Shem, who made the ark.

N. " 'The refiner' refers to Abraham, whom the Holy One, blessed be he, refined in the fiery furnace.

O. " 'And he that smoothes with the hammer him that smites the anvil' (Isa. 41:7): He smoothed with the hammer and beat all of those who pass through the world into a single path.

P. " 'Saying of the join, "It is good"' (Isa. 41:7) refers to the nations of the world, who say, 'It is better to cleave to the God of Abraham and not to the idolatry of Nimrod.'

Q. " 'And he strengthens it with nails' (Isa. 41:7): Abraham strengthened Shem through the practice of religious duties and good deeds, so that 'he shall not be moved' (Isa. 41:7), meaning Abraham."

XLIV:VIII

1. A. "But Abram said, 'O Lord, God, what will you give me, [for I continue childless, and the heir of my house is Eliezer of Damascus]?' " (Gen. 15:2):

B. Said R. Jonathan, "There were three who were allowed to ask: Solomon, Ahaz, and the King Messiah.

C. "Solomon: 'Ask what I shall give you' (1 Kgs. 3:5).

D. "Ahaz: 'Ask a sign for yourself' (Isa. 7:11).

E. "The king messiah: 'Ask of me' (Ps. 2:8)."

F. R. Berekiah and R. Ahi in the name of R. Samuel b. Nahman: "We may produce two more, based on lore: Abraham and Jacob.

G. "Abraham: 'What will you give me?' He could never have said, 'What will you give me?' unless God had already said to him, 'Ask.'

H. "Jacob: 'And of all that you shall give me' (Gen. 28:22). He could never have said, 'Of all that you shall give me' (Gen. 28:22) unless he had already said to him, 'Ask.' "

XLIV:XIII

1. A. "And he believed the Lord, and he reckoned it to him as righteousness. And he said to him, 'I am the Lord who brought you from Ur of the Chaldeans to give you this land to possess'" (Gen. 15:6-7):
    B. R. Eliezer b. Jacob: "Michael went down and saved Abraham from the furnace."
    C. Rabbis say, "The Holy One, blessed be he, himself saved him, in line with this verse: 'I am the Lord who brought you from the furnace [Ur] of the Chaldeans.'
    D. "And when was it that Michael [not God in person] went down? It was in the case of Hananiah, Mishael, and Azariah."

XLIV:XIV

1. A. "But he said, 'O Lord God, how am I to know that I shall possess it?'" (Gen. 15:8):
    B. R. Hama b. Haninah said, "It was not as though he were complaining, but he said to him, 'On account of what merit [shall I know it? That is, how have I the honor of being so informed?]'
    C. "He said to him, 'It is on account of the merit of the sacrifice of atonement that I shall hand over to your descendants.'"

XLIV:XV

1. A. Another matter: "Bring me a heifer three years old, [a she-goat three years old, a ram three years old, a turtledove, and a young pigeon]" (Gen. 15:9):
    B. "Bring me a heifer three years old" refers to Babylonia, which produced three [kings important in Israel's history], Nebuchadnezzar, Evil-merodach, and Belshazzar.
    C. ". . . a she-goat three years old" refers to Media, which also produced three kings, Cyrus, Darius, and Ahasuerus.
    D. ". . . a ram three years old" refers to Greece.
    E. R. Eleazar and R. Yohanan:
    F. R. Eleazar said, "Greece conquered every point on the compass except for the east."
    G. R. Yohanan said to him, "And indeed so, for is it not written: 'I saw the ram pushing westward and northward and southward, and no beasts could stand before him' (Dan. 8:4)?"

H. That indeed is the view of R. Eleazar, for the verse at hand does not refer to the east.

I. ". . . a turtledove, and a young pigeon" (Gen. 15:9) refers to Edom. It was a turtledove that would rob.

2. A. "And he brought him all these" (Gen. 15:10):

B. R. Judah said, "He showed him the princes of the nations."

C. R. Nehemiah said, "It was the princes of Israel that he showed him."

D. In the view of R. Judah, [the statement, "He laid each half over against the other" indicates that] he set the throne of one opposite the throne of another. [Freedman, p. 371, n. 2: He showed him the hostility of the nations toward each other, in contrast with which the bird, symbolizing Israel, was not to be divided but united.]

E. In the view of R. Nehemiah, [laying each half over against the other symbolized the fact that] there [in Jerusalem] the great Sanhedrin of Israel [seated in semicircles, so each half could see the other] was in session and laying down the laws of Israel.

3. A. "But he did not cut the birds in two" (Gen. 15:10):

B. R. Abba b. Kahana in the name of R. Levi: "The Holy One, blessed be he, showed him that whoever stands against the wave is swept away by the wave, and whoever does not stand against the wave is not swept away by the wave."

XLIV:XVII

4. A. "[And it came to pass, as the sun was going down,] lo, a deep sleep fell on Abram, and lo, a dread and great darkness fell upon him" (Gen. 15:12):

B. ". . . lo, a dread" refers to Babylonia, as it is written: "Then was Nebuchadnezzar filled with fury" (Dan. 3:19).

C. ". . . and darkness" refers to Media, which darkened the eyes of Israel by making it necessary for the Israelites to fast and conduct public mourning.

D. ". . . great . . ." refers to Greece.

E. R. Simon said, "The kingdom of Greece set up one hundred and twenty commanders, one hundred and twenty hyparchs, and one hundred and twenty generals."

F. Rabbis said, "It was sixty of each, as it is written: 'Serpents, fiery serpents, and scorpions' (Deut. 8:15). Just as the scorpion produces sixty eggs at a time, so the kingdom of Greece set up sixty at a time."

G. ". . . fell upon him" refers to Edom, as it is written: "The earth quakes at the noise of their fall" (Jer. 49:21).

H. Some reverse matters:

I. ". . . fell upon him" refers to Babylonia, since it is written: "Fallen, fallen is Babylonia" (Isa. 21:9).

J. ". . . great . . ." refers to Media, in line with this verse: "King Ahasuerus did make great" (Esth. 3:1).

K. ". . . and darkness" refers to Greece, which darkened the eyes of Israel by its harsh decrees.

L. ". . . lo, a dread" refers to Edom, as it is written: "After this I saw . . . , a fourth beast, dreadful and terrible" (Dan. 7:7).

XLIV:XVIII

1. A. "Then the Lord said to Abram, 'Know of a certainty [that your descendants will be sojourners in a land that is not theirs, and they will be slaves there, and they will be oppressed for four hundred years; but I will bring judgment on the nation which they serve, and afterward they shall come out with great possessions]'" (Gen. 15:13-14):

B. "Know" that I shall scatter them.

C. "Of a certainty" that I shall bring them back together again.

D. "Know" that I shall put them out as a pledge [in expiation of their sins].

E. "Of a certainty" that I shall redeem them.

F. "Know" that I shall make them slaves.

G. "Of a certainty" that I shall free them.

2. A. ". . . that your descendants will be sojourners in a land that is not theirs, and they will be slaves there, and they will be oppressed for four hundred years":

B. It is four hundred years from the point at which you will produce a descendant. [The Israelites will not serve as slaves for four hundred years, but that figure refers to the passage of time from Isaac's birth.]

C. Said R. Yudan, "The condition of being outsiders, the servitude, the oppression in a land that was not theirs all together would last for four hundred years—that was the requisite term."

XLIV:XXI

2. A. ". . . Behold, a smoking fire pot and a flaming torch passed between these pieces" (Gen. 15:17):

   B. Simeon b. Abba in the name of R. Yohanan: "He showed him four things: Gehenna, the [four] kingdoms, the giving of the Torah, and the sanctuary. He said to him, 'So long as your descendants are occupied with these latter two, they will be saved from the former two. If they abandon two of them, they will be judged by the other two.'

   C. "He said to him, 'What is your preference? Do you want your children to go down into Gehenna or to be subjugated to the four kingdoms?'"

   D. R. Hinena b. Pappa said, "Abraham chose for himself the subjugation to the four kingdoms."

   E. R. Yudan and R. Idi and R. Hama b. Hanina: "Abraham chose for himself Gehenna, but the Holy One, blessed be he, chose the subjugation to the four kingdoms for him."

   F. That [statement of R. Hinena b. Papa] is in line with the following: "How should one chase a thousand, and two put ten thousand to flight, except their rock had given them over" (Deut. 32:30). That statement refers to Abraham.

   G. "But the Lord delivered them up" (Deut. 32:30) teaches that God then approved what he had chosen.

3. A. R. Huna in the name of R. Aha: "Now Abraham sat and puzzled all that day, saying, 'Which should I choose?'

   B. "Said the Holy One, blessed be he, to him, 'Choose without delay.' That is in line with this verse: 'On that day the Lord made a covenant with Abram' (Gen. 15:18)."

   C. This brings us to the dispute of R. Hinena b. Pappa with R. Yudan and R. Idi and R. Hama b. Haninah.

   D. R. Hinena b. Pappa said, "Abraham chose for himself the subjugation to the four kingdoms."

   E. R. Yudan and R. Idi and R. Hama b. Haninah said in the name of a single sage in the name of Rabbi: "The Holy One, blessed be he, chose the subjugation to the four kingdoms for him, in line with the following verse of Scripture: 'You have caused men to ride over our heads' (Ps. 66:12). That is to say, you have made ride over our heads various nations, and it is as though 'we went through fire and through water' (Ps. 66:12)."

F. R. Joshua said, "Also the splitting of the Red Sea he showed
him, as it is written: 'That passed between these pieces' (Gen.
15:17), along the lines of the verse 'O give thanks to him who
divided the Red Sea in two' [in which the same word, the letters
for 'pieces,' occurs as 'in two'] (Ps. 136:13)."

PART TWO

LEVITICUS

Introduction to Leviticus as Read in Leviticus Rabbah

At the center of Leviticus Rabbah and the faith of its framers we find a simple proposition: Israel is God's special love. That love is shown in a simple way. Israel's present condition of subordination—remember, we are in the fourth century C.E., just as with Genesis Rabbah—derives from its own deeds. It follows that God cares, so Israel may look forward to redemption on God's part in response to Israel's own regeneration through repentance. The authorship of Leviticus Rabbah brought to the book of Leviticus a mode of thought, a deeply philosophical and scientific quest, and an acute problem of history and society. In their search for the rules of Israel's life and salvation, they found answers not in the one-time events of history but in paradigmatic facts, social laws of salvation. It was in the mind and imagination of the already philosophical authors of Leviticus Rabbah that Scripture came to serve—as did nature, as did everyday life and its parables, all together—to reveal laws everywhere and always valid—if people would only keep them. The recurrent message of the book of Leviticus derived by the framers of Leviticus Rabbah may be stated in a single paragraph.

God loves Israel, so he gave them the Torah, which defines their life and governs their welfare. Israel is alone in its category (sui generis), so what is a virtue to Israel is a vice to the nations, life-giving to Israel but poison to the Gentiles. True, Israel sins, but God forgives that sin, having punished the nation on account of it. Such a process has yet to come to an end, but it will culminate in Israel's complete regeneration.

Meanwhile, Israel's assurance of God's love lies in the many expressions of special concern, for even the humblest and most ordinary aspects of the national life: the food the nation eats, the sexual practices by which it procreates. These life-sustaining, life-transmitting activities draw God's special interest, as a mark of his general love for Israel. Israel then is supposed to achieve its life in conformity with the marks of God's love. These indications, moreover, signify also the character of Israel's difficulty, namely, subordination to the nations in general, but to the fourth kingdom (Rome) in particular. Both food laws and skin diseases stand for the nations.

Yet another category of sin exists, also collective and generative of collective punishment, and that is social. The moral character of Israel's life, the treatment of people by one another, the practice of gossip and small-scale thuggery—these too draw down divine penalty. The nation's fate therefore corresponds to its moral condition. The moral condition, however, emerges not only from the current generation. Israel's richest hope lies in the merit of the ancestors, thus in the scriptural record of the merits attained by the founders of the nation, those who originally brought it into being and gave it life.

The world to come upon the nation is so portrayed as to restate these same propositions. Merit overcomes sin, and doing religious duties or supererogatory acts of kindness will win merit for the nation that does them. Israel will be saved at the end of time, and the age, or world, to follow will be exactly the opposite of this one. Much that we find in the account of Israel's national life, worked out through the definition of the liminal relationships, recurs in slightly altered form in the picture of the world to come.

One further theme is commonplace, namely, the meaning of Israel's history. In this context, it is not Israel's history in the fourth century, the time of the formation of our document, but Israel's history solely in scriptural times, down through the return to Zion.

And that is the key to appreciating—and therefore learning the lessons of—this profound reading of a book of the Bible that would not, on first glance, yield the profoundly theological picture I have portrayed. The one-time events of the generation of the flood, Sodom and Gomorrah, the patriarchs and the sojourn in Egypt, the exodus, the revelation of the Torah at Sinai, the golden calf, the Davidic monarchy and the building of the Temple, Sennacherib, Hezekiah, and the destruction of northern Israel, Nebuchadnezzar and the destruction of the Temple in 586, the life of Israel in Babylonian captivity, Daniel and his associates, Mordecai and Haman each occur over and over again. These events turn out to serve as paradigms of sin and atonement, steadfastness and divine intervention, and equivalent lessons. We find, in fact, a fairly standard repertoire of scriptural heroes or villains, on the one side, and conventional lists of Israel's enemies and their actions and downfall, on the other. The boastful, for instance, include the generation of the flood, Sodom and Gomorrah, Pharaoh, Sisera, Sennacherib, Nebuchadnezzar, and the wicked empire (Rome)—contrasted to Israel, "despised and humble in this world." The four kingdoms recur again and again, always ending with Rome, with the repeated message that after Rome will come Israel. But Israel has to make this happen through its faith and submission to God's will. Lists of enemies ring the changes on Cain, the Sodomites, Pharaoh, Sennacherib, Nebuchadnezzar, Haman.

These lists of events of ancient Israel's history through the power of repetition are meant to make a single enormous point or prove a social law of history. The catalogues of exemplary heroes and historical events serve a further purpose. They provide a model of how contemporary events are to be absorbed into the biblical paradigm. And that is the key to the relevance of Leviticus Rabbah to Christian readers. Our sages show how to identify the pattern of scriptural truth, as laid out in events, with the disorderly and unpatterned happenings of the day. They derive from Scripture those rules of history as God has laid out the rules that tell us, for our own day, what things mean and what can happen.

This they do by searching for the rules that scriptural events follow. Since biblical events exemplify recurrent happenings—sin and redemption, forgiveness and atonement—they lose their one-time character. At the same time and in the same way, current events find a place within the ancient, but eternally present, paradigmatic scheme. So no new historical events, other than exemplary episodes in lives of heroes, demand narration because, through what is said about the past, what was happening in the times of the framers of Leviticus Rabbah would also come under consideration. This mode of dealing with biblical history and contemporary events produces two reciprocal effects. The first is to treat biblical stories not as one-time events but as models, to remove them from the framework of ongoing, unique patterns of history and sequences of events and to turn them into accounts of things that happen all the time. The second is that contemporary events too lose all of their specificity and enter the framework of a paradigm or pattern of the real meaning of existence. *Scripture's history happens every day, because every day produces re-enactment of Scripture's account.*

The Christian reader must find this message familiar. But the place in which our sages locate it is surprising. This too provides a model of what the faithful exegete can find in Scripture. The message of Leviticus Rabbah attaches itself to the book of Leviticus, as if that book had come from prophecy and addressed the issue of salvation. But it came from the priesthood and spoke of sanctification. In the very setting of sanctification we find the promise of salvation. In the topics of the cult and the priesthood, to which the book of Leviticus is devoted, we uncover the national and social issues of the moral life and redemptive hope of Israel. The repeated comparison and contrast of priesthood and prophecy, sanctification and salvation, turn out to produce a complement, which comes to most perfect union in the text at hand. Let me proceed to spell out the message to the age at hand.

Are we lost for good to the fourth empire, now-Christian Rome? No, we may yet be saved.

Has God rejected us forever? No, aided by the merit of the patriarchs and matriarchs and of the Torah and religious duties, we gain God's love.

What must we do to be saved? We must do nothing; we must be something: sanctified.

That status we gain through keeping the rules that make Israel holy. So salvation is through sanctification, all embodied in Leviticus read as rules for the holy people.

The Messiah will come not because of what a pagan emperor does, nor, indeed, because of Jewish action either, but because of Israel's own moral condition. When Israel enters the right relationship with God, then God will respond to Israel's condition by restoring things to their proper balance. Israel cannot—but need not—so act as to force the coming of the Messiah. Israel can so attain the condition of sanctification, by forming a moral and holy community, that God's response will follow the established prophecy of Moses and the prophets.

So the basic doctrine of Leviticus Rabbah is the metamorphosis of Leviticus. Instead of holy caste, the priesthood, we deal with holy people. Instead of holy place, we deal with holy community, in its holy Land. The deepest exchange between reality and inner vision, therefore, comes at the very surface: the rereading of Leviticus in terms of a different set of realities from those to which the book, on the surface, relates. No other biblical book would have served so well; it had to be Leviticus. Only through what the framers did on that particular book could they deliver their astonishing message and vision.

The complementary points of stress in Leviticus Rabbah—the age to come will come, but Israel must reform itself beforehand—address that context defined by Julian, on the one side, and by the new anti-Judaic Christian policy of the later fourth and fifth centuries, on the other. The repeated reference to Esau and Edom and how they mark the last monarchy before that of God through Israel underlines the same point. These truly form the worst of the four kingdoms. But they also come at the end. If only we shape up, so will history. As I said, that same message will hardly have surprised earlier generations and it would be repeated afresh later on. But it is the message of our document, and it does address this context in particular. We therefore grasp an astonishing correspondence between how people are thinking, what they wish to say, and the literary context—rereading a particular book of Scripture in terms of a set of values different from those expressed in that book—in which they deliver their message. Given the mode of thought, the crisis that demanded reflection, the message found congruent to the crisis, we must find entirely logical the choice of Leviticus and the treatment accorded to it. So the logic and the doctrine prove remarkably to accord with the society and politics that produced and received Leviticus Rabbah.

People who seek the rules that diverse facts follow in our own day are philosophers, on the one side, and scientists, on the other. They are the ones who regard the one-time as exemplary, who want to know why a specific thing is the way it is, meaning who ask what rule governs. What we have in Leviticus Rabbah, therefore, is the result of the mode of thought not of prophets or historians, but of philosophers and scientists. The framers propose not to lay down, but to *discover*, rules governing Israel's life. That too forms a model for the contemporary Christian exegete—and why not! If we believe Scripture contains the record of God's perspective on humanity, then we have to approach Scripture in the mode of thought of the philosopher or the scientist and ask, What are the rules yielded by the examples at hand?

As we find the rules of nature by identifying and classifying facts of natural life, so we find rules of society by identifying and classifying the facts of Israel's social life. In both modes of inquiry we make sense of things by bringing together like specimens and finding out whether they form a species, then bringing together like species and finding out whether they form a genus—in all, classifying data and identifying the rules that make possible the classification. That sort of thinking lies at the deepest level of list-making—so characteristic of our sages in Leviticus Rabbah—which is, as I said, work of offering a proposition and facts (for social rules) as much as a genus and its species (for rules of nature). Once discovered, the social rules of Israel's national life of course yield explicit statements, such as that God hates the arrogant and loves the humble. The readily assembled syllogism follows.

If one is arrogant, God will hate him; and if he is humble, God will love him.

The logical status of statements such as these, in context, is as secure and unassailable as the logical status of statements about physics, ethics, or politics, as these emerge in philosophical thought. What differentiates the statements is not their logical status—as sound, scientific philosophy—but only their subject matter, on the one side, and distinctive rhetoric, on the other.

The meaning of these facts for our appreciation of Leviticus Rabbah is clear. We have to turn to the book not to understand what it says about a given verse in the book of Leviticus. Leviticus Rabbah is anything but an exegetical exercise. We err if we are taken in by the powerful rhetoric of our document, which resorts so ubiquitously to the citation of biblical verses and, more important, to the construction, out of diverse verses, of a point transcendent of the cited verses. At hand is not an exegetical composition at all, nor even verses of Scripture read as a corpus of prooftexts. We have, rather, a statement that stands by itself, separate from Scripture, and that makes its points only secondarily along the way by evoking verses of Scripture to express and exemplify those same points. We miss the main point if we posit that Scripture plays a definitive or even central role in providing the program and agenda for the framers of Leviticus Rabbah. Their program is wholly their own. But of course, Scripture then serves their purposes very well indeed. The constant invocation of scriptural verses compares with the place of the classics or of Scripture in the speech and writing of gentlefolk of an earlier age, in which the mark of elegance was perpetual allusion to classical writers. No Christian author of the age would have found alien the aesthetic at hand. So while the constant introduction of verses of Scripture provides the wherewithal of speech, these verses serve only as do the colors of the painter. The painter cannot paint without the oils. But the colors do not make the painting. The painter does.

This approach to the reading of Scripture is one we are not used to. In general people ask about the original meaning, meaning the sense of a passage when it was first written. Leviticus Rabbah's authorship teaches us a different way of seeing Scripture, namely, as if Scripture spoke to us, not only long ago. They could not imagine that Scripture's purpose was fulfilled only long ago, with nothing to say here and now. Bringing their troubled hearts to the Torah, they took for granted that the Torah spoke about times past, but as if it addressed the age at hand. Perhaps that is a natural mode of thought for the Jews of this period (and not then alone), so long used to calling themselves God's first love, yet now seeing others with greater worldly reason claiming that same advantaged relationship. In the politics of the world, the people that remembered its origins along with the very creation of the world and founding of humanity, that recalled how it alone served—and serves—the one and only God for more than three hundred years had confronted a quite different existence. The radical disjuncture between the way things were and the way Scripture said things were supposed to be—and in actuality would some day become—surely imposed an unbearable tension. It was one thing for the slave born to slavery to endure. It was another for the free person sold into slavery to accept that same condition. The vanquished people, the nation that had lost its city and its Temple, and that had, moreover, produced another nation from its midst to take over its Scripture and much else could not bear too much reality. That defeated people will then have found refuge in a mode of thought that trained vision to see matters other than as the eyes perceived them. Among the diverse ways by which the weak and subordinated accommodate to their circumstance, the one of iron-willed pretense in life is most likely to yield the mode of thought at hand: things never are, because they cannot be, what they seem.

Reading one thing in terms of something else, the builders of the document systematically adopted for themselves the reality of the Scripture, its history and doctrines. They transformed that history from a sequence of one-time events, leading from one place to some other, into an ever-present mythic world. No longer was there one Moses, one David, one set of happenings of a distinctive and never-to-be-repeated character. Now whatever happens, of which the thinkers propose to take account, must enter and be absorbed into that established and ubiquitous pattern and structure founded in Scripture. It is not that biblical history repeats itself. Rather, biblical history no longer constitutes history as a story of things that happened once, long ago, and pointed to some one moment in the future. Rather, it becomes an account of things that happen every day. And the result of the new vision was a re-imagining of the social world envisioned by the document at hand, meaning the everyday world of Israel in its Land in that difficult time. For what the sages now proposed was a reconstruction of existence along the lines of the ancient design of Scripture as they read it. What that meant was that, from a sequence of one-time and linear events, everything that happened was turned into a repetition of known and already experienced paradigms, hence, once more, a mythic being. The source and core of the myth, of course, derive from Scripture—Scripture reread, renewed, reconstructed along with the society that revered Scripture.

The mode of thought that dictated the issues and the logic of the document, telling the thinkers to see one thing in terms of something else, taught the framers of the document to see Scripture in a new way, just as they saw their own circumstance afresh, rejecting their world in favor of Scripture's, reliving Scripture's world in their own terms. That is why they did not write history, an account of what was happening and what it meant. It was not that they did not recognize or appreciate important changes and trends reshaping their nation's life. They could not deny that reality. In their apocalyptic reading of the dietary and leprosy laws, they made explicit their close encounter with the history of the world as they knew it. But they had another mode of responding to history. It was to treat history as if it were already known and readily understood. Whatever happened had already happened. Scripture dictated the contents of history, laying forth the structures of time, the rules that prevailed and were made known in events. Self-evidently, these same thinkers projected into Scripture's day the realities of their own, turning Moses and David into rabbis, for example. But that is how people think in that mythic, enchanted world in which, to begin with, reality blends with dream, and hope projects onto future and past alike how people want things to be. So once more, as with Genesis Rabbah, we find at the center of our sages' reading of Scripture the message of hope. Judaism can offer Christianity, in this troubled age of reconciliation, nothing more than hope. But, on the other side of the Holocaust, that is no small gift.

God Loves the Humble: Israel's Great Leaders are Humble

Our sages' principal message, with which by now we are familiar, is that the greatest virtue is humility. One's relationship to God must be acceptance and self-abnegation. Abraham is the first example of that fact, David the next, and Moses, important because Leviticus 1:1 starts, "He called. . . ," is another. We know that Moses was favored because God called Moses in particular. This leads to the contrast between God's address to Moses—direct and personal—and God's address to lesser mortals. The merit of Moses in particular was his modesty and humility. The great rabbi, Hillel, likewise points to modesty as a source of pride (paradoxically). The latter point then joins the former, God spoke to Moses out of the bush, the most humble of shrubbery, and God revealed himself to Moses in recognition of his humility. So the main point is that it is the humble person who is called upon to undertake leadership.

I:IV

1.   A. R. Abin in the name of R. Berekhiah the Elder opened [discourse by citing the following verse]: "'Of old you spoke in a vision to your faithful one, saying, "I have set the crown upon one who is mighty, I have exalted one chosen from the people"'" (Ps. 89:20).

   B. "[The Psalmist] speaks of Abraham, with whom [God] spoke both in word and in vision.

   C. "That is in line with the following verse of Scripture: 'After these words the word of God came to Abram in a vision, saying . . .' (Gen. 15:1).

   D. "'. . . to your faithful one'—'You will show truth to Jacob, faithfulness to Abraham' (Mic. 7:20).

   E. "'. . . saying, "I have set the crown upon one who is mighty"— for [Abraham] slew four kings in a single night.'

F. "That is in line with the following verse of Scripture: 'And he divided himself against them by night . . . and smote them' (Gen. 14:15)."

2. A. Said R. Phineas, "And is there a case of someone who pursues people already slain?

B. "For it is written, 'He smote them and he [then] pursued them' (Gen. 14:15)!

C. "But [the usage at hand] teaches that the Holy One, blessed be he, did the pursuing, and Abraham did the slaying.

3. A. [Abin continues,] " 'I have exalted one chosen from the people' (Ps. 89:20).

B. " 'It is you, Lord, God, who chose Abram and took him out of Ur in Chaldea' (Neh. 9:7)."

4. A. ["I have exalted one chosen from the people" (Ps. 89:20)] speaks of David, with whom God spoke both in speech and in vision.

B. That is in line with the following verse of Scripture: "In accord with all these words and in accord with this entire vision, so did Nathan speak to David" (2 Sam. 7:17).

C. "To your faithful one" (Ps. 89:20) [refers] to David, [in line with the following verse:] "Keep my soul, for I am faithful" (Ps. 86:2).

D. ". . . saying, 'I have set the crown upon one who is mighty' " (Ps. 89:20)—

5. A. ["Of old you spoke in a vision to your faithful one . . ."] speaks of Moses, with whom [God] spoke in both speech and vision, in line with the following verse of Scripture: "With him do I speak mouth to mouth [in a vision and not in dark speeches]" (Num. 12:8).

B. "To your faithful one"—for [Moses] came from the tribe of Levi, the one concerning which it is written, "Let your Thummim and Urim be with your faithful one" (Deut. 33:8).

C. ". . . saying, 'I have set the crown upon one who is mighty' "—

D. the cited passage is to be read in accord with that which R. Tanhum b. R. Hanilai said, "Under ordinary circumstances a burden which is too heavy for one person is light for two, or too heavy for two is light for four. But is it possible to suppose that a burden that is too weighty for six hundred thousand can be light for a single individual? Now the entire people of Israel were

standing before Mount Sinai and saying, 'If we hear the voice of
the Lord our God any more, then we shall die' (Deut. 5:22).
But, for his part, Moses heard the voice of God himself and
lived."

E. You may know that that is indeed the case, for among them all,
the act of speech [of the Lord] called only to Moses, in line with
that verse which states, "And [God] called to Moses" (Lev. 1:1).

F. "I have exalted one chosen from the people" (Ps. 89:20)—"Had
not Moses, whom he chose, stood in the breach before him to
turn his wrath from destroying them" [he would have destroyed
Israel] (Ps. 106:23).

I:V

1. A. R. Joshua of Sikhnin in the name of R. Levi opened [discourse
by citing the following] verse: "'For it is better to be told,
"Come up here," than to be put lower in the presence of the
prince' (Prov. 25:7)."

B. R. Aqiba repeated [the following tradition] in the name of R.
Simeon b. Azzai, "Take a place two or three lower and sit down,
so that people may tell you, 'Come up,' but do not go up [be-
yond your station] lest people say to you, 'Go down.' It is better
for people to say to you, 'Come up, come up,' than that they say
to you, 'Go down, go down.'"

C. And so did Hillel say, "When I am degraded, I am exalted, and
when I am exalted, I am degraded."

D. What is the pertinent biblical verse? "He who raises himself is
to be made to sit down, he who lowers himself is to be [raised so
that he is] seen" (Ps. 113:5).

E. So too you find that, when the Holy One, blessed be he, revealed himself to Moses from the midst of the bush, Moses hid
his face from him.

F. That is in line with the following verse of Scripture: "Moses hid
his face" (Ex. 3:6).

2. A. Said to him the Holy One, blessed be he, "And now, go (LKH),
I am sending you to Pharaoh" (Ex. 3:10).

B. Said R. Eleazar, "[Taking the word 'Go,' LK, not as the impera-
tive, but to mean, 'to you,' and spelled LKH, with an H at the
end, I may observe that] it would have been sufficient to write,

'You (LK),' [without adding] an H at the end of the word. [Why then did Scripture add the H?] To indicate to you, 'If you are not the one who will redeem them, no one else is going to redeem them.'

C. "At the Red Sea, Moses stood aside. Said to him the Holy One, blessed be he, 'Now you, raise your rod and stretch out your hand [over the sea and divide it]' (Ex. 14:16).

D. "This is to say, 'If you do not split the sea, no one else is going to split it.'

E. "At Sinai Moses stood aside. Said to him the Holy One, blessed be he, 'Come up to the Lord, you and Aaron' (Ex. 24:1).

F. "This is to say, 'If you do not come up, no one else is going to come up.'

G. "At the [revelation of the instructions governing sacrifices at] the tent of meeting, [Moses] stood to the side. Said to him the Holy One, blessed be he, How long are you going to humble yourself? For the times demand only you.'

H. "You must recognize that that is the case, for among them all, the speech of God called only to Moses, as it is written, 'And [God] called to Moses' (Lev. 1:1)."

Who Is the True Prophet?

The true prophet is Moses. The nations have prophets, but they are of lesser standing. This point is made through the interesting contrast between Moses and Balaam, who is taken to be the paradigm of the Gentile prophet. The contrast between Israel's prophets and the nations' prophets then is drawn. God speaks to Israel's prophets directly, but is far from those of the nations. God speaks openly to Israel's prophets, but to the nations' prophets only in private. The entire relationship is different and diminished. The nations' prophets see their vision through a glass, darkly—through that dirty mirror to which Paul referred in another context—but Israel's prophets see their vision openly and clearly.

I:XII

1. A. Said R. Isaac, "Before the tent of meeting was set up, prophecy was common among the nations of the world. Once the tent of meeting was set up, prophecy disappeared from among them. That is in line with the following verse of Scripture: 'I held it [the holy spirit, producing], and would not let it go [until I had brought it . . . into the chamber of her that conceived me]' (Cant. 3:4)."
    B. They said to him, "Lo, Balaam [later on] practiced prophecy!"
    C. He said to them, "He did so for the good of Israel: 'Who has counted the dust of Jacob?' (Num. 23:10). 'No one has seen iniquity in Jacob' (Num. 23:21). 'For there is no enchantment with Jacob' (Num. 23:23). 'How goodly are your tents, O Jacob' (Num. 24:5). 'There shall go forth a star out of Jacob' (Num. 24:17). 'And out of Jacob shall one have dominion' (Num. 24:19)."

I:XIII

1. A. What is the difference between the prophets of Israel and those of the nations [= Genesis Rabbah LII:V]?

B. R. Hama b. Hanina and R. Issachar of Kefar Mandi:

C. R. Hama b. Hanina said, "The Holy One, blessed be he, is revealed to the prophets of the nations of the world only in partial speech, in line with the following verse of Scripture: 'And God called [Hebrew *wyqr*, rather than *wyqr'* as at Lev. 1:1] Balaam' (Num. 23:16). On the other hand, [he reveals himself] to the prophets of Israel in full and complete speech, as it is said: 'And [the Lord] called (*wyqr'*) to Moses' (Lev. 1:1)."

D. Said R. Issachar of Kefar Mandi, "Should that [prophecy, even in partial form] be [paid to them as their] wage? [Surely not, in fact there is no form of speech to Gentile prophets, who are frauds]. [The connotation of] the language, 'And [God] called (Hebrew *wyqr*) to Balaam' (Num. 23:16) is solely uncleanness. That is in line with the usage in the following verse of Scripture: 'That is not clean, by that which happens (*mqrh*) by night' (Deut. 23:10 [Hebrew v. 11]). [So the root is the same, with the result that *yqr* at Num. 23:16 does not bear the meaning of God's calling to Balaam. God rather declares Balaam unclean.]

E. "But the prophets of Israel [are addressed] in language of holiness, purity, clarity, in language used by the ministering angels to praise God. That is in line with the following verse of Scripture: 'And they called (Hebrew *qr'*) one to another and said' (Isa. 6:3)."

2. A. Said R. Eleazar b. Menahem, "It is written: 'The Lord is far from the wicked, but the prayer of the righteous does he hear' (Prov. 15:29).

B. "'The Lord is far from the wicked' refers to the prophets of the nations of the world.

C. "'But the prayer of the righteous does he hear' refers to the prophets of Israel.

D. "You [furthermore] find that the Holy One, blessed be he, appears to the prophets of the nations of the world only like a man who comes from some distant place.

E. "That is in line with the following verse of Scripture: 'From a distant land they have come to me, from Babylonia' (Isa. 39:3).

F. "But in the case of the prophets of Israel [he is always] near at hand: 'And he [forthwith] appeared [not having come from a great distance]' (Gen. 18:1), 'and [the Lord] called' (Lev. 1:1)."

3. A. Said R. Yose b. Biba, "The Holy One, blessed be he, is revealed to the prophets of the nations of the world only by night, when

people leave one another: 'When men branch off, from the visions of the night, when deep sleep falls on men' (Job 4:13), 'Then a word came secretly to me' (Job 4:12). [Job is counted among the prophets of the Gentiles.]"

4. A. R. Hinena b. Pappa and rabbis [= Genesis Rabbah LXXIV:VII]:

B. R. Hinena b. Pappa said, "The matter may be compared to a king who, with his friend, is in a hall, with a curtain hanging down between them. When [the king] speaks to his friend, he turns back the curtain and speaks with his friend."

C. And rabbis say, "[The matter may be compared] to a king who has a wife and a concubine. When he walks about with his wife, he does so in full public view. When he walks about with his concubine, he does so discreetly. So, too, the Holy One, blessed be he, is revealed to the prophets of the nations of the world only at night, in line with that which is written: 'And God came to Abimelech in a dream by night' (Gen. 20:3). 'And God came to Laban, the Aramean, in a dream by night' (Gen. 31:24). 'And God came to Balaam at night' (Num. 22:20).

D. "To the prophets of Israel, however, [he comes] by day: '[And the Lord appeared to Abraham . . .] as he sat at the door of his tent in the heat of the day' (Gen. 18:1). 'And it came to pass by day that the Lord spoke to Moses in the land of Egypt' (Exod. 6:28). 'On the day on which he commanded the children of Israel' (Lev. 7:38). 'These are the generations of Aaron and Moses. God spoke to Moses by day on Mount Sinai' (Num. 3:1)."

I:XIV

1. A. What is the difference between Moses and all the other [Israelite] prophets?

B. R. Judah b. R. Ilai and rabbis:

C. R. Judah said, "All the other prophets saw [their visions] through nine mirrors [darkly], in line with the following verse of Scripture: 'And the appearance of the vision which I saw was like the vision that I saw when I came to destroy the city; and the visions were like the vision that I saw by the River Chebar, and I fell on my face' (Ezek. 43:3) [with the Hebrew root r'h occurring once in the plural, hence two, and seven other times in the singular, nine in all].

D. "But Moses saw [his vision] through a single mirror: 'in [one vision] and not in dark speeches' (Num. 12:8)."

E. Rabbis said, "All other [Israelite] prophets saw [their visions] through a dirty mirror. That is in line with the following verse of Scripture: 'And I have multiplied visions, and by the ministry of the angels I have used similitudes' (Hos. 12:11).

F. "But Moses saw [his vision] through a polished mirror: 'And the image of God does he behold' (Num. 12:8)."

2. A. R. Phineas in the name of R. Hoshiah: "[The matter may be compared] to a king who makes his appearance to his courtier in his informal garb [as an intimate].

B. "For in this world the Indwelling Presence makes its appearance only to individuals [one by one], while concerning the age to come, what does Scripture say? 'The glory of the Lord shall be revealed, and all flesh shall see [it together, for the mouth of the Lord has spoken]' (Isa. 40:5)."

How God Shows Love

Christians and other Gentiles see the Judaic holy way of life, with its dietary laws and other rules of everyday conduct, as a burden. But Judaism teaches that these are marks of God's special love for Israel, along with the Torah. Accordingly, our sages wished to stress, in their reading of Leviticus, how the cultic and other ritual laws of this particular biblical book—of such slight interest to the world at large—in fact testify to God's grace and love, to that covenantal nomism to which E. P. Sanders in his *Paul and Palestinian Judaism* (Philadelphia: Fortress, 1977) calls attention. Here we have an explicit statement of that fact. Indeed, when Leviticus begins, "Speak to the children of Israel," our sages take as a mark of God's speaking to Israel the substance of the message: God cares, even for what Israel eats, how it sustains life. The Torah is the first mark of grace, the substance of the Torah—the rules for the conduct of life— the second. The point of the passage, however, has to do with Israel's particular relationship to God: Israel cleaves to God, declares God to be king, and accepts God's dominion. None of these ideas has bearing upon the issues of Lev. 1:2.

II:IV

1. A. "Speak to the children of Israel" (Lev. 1:2).
    B. R. Yudan in the name of R. Samuel b. R. Nehemiah [Pesiqta de R. Kahana ḥSeqalim 15:2-17]: "The matter may be compared to the case of a king who had an undergarment, concerning which he instructed his servant, saying to him, 'Fold it, shake it out, and be careful about it!'
    C. "He said to him, 'My lord, O king, among all the undergarments that you have, [why] do you give me such instructions only about this one?'
    D. "He said to him, 'It is because this is the one that I keep closest to my body.'
    E. "So too did Moses say before the Holy One, blessed be he, Lord

of the Universe: 'Among the seventy distinct nations that you have in your world, [why] do you give me instructions only concerning Israel? [For instance,] "Command the children of Israel" [Num. 28:2], "Say to the children of Israel" [Exod. 33:5], "Speak to the children of Israel"' [Lev. 1:2].

F. "He said to him, 'The reason is that they stick close to me, in line with the following verse of Scripture: "For as the undergarment cleaves to the loins of a man, so have I caused to cleave unto me the whole house of Israel"' (Jer. 13:11)."

G. Said R. Abin, "[The matter may be compared] to a king who had a purple cloak, concerning which he instructed his servant, saying, 'Fold it, shake it out, and be careful about it!'

H. "He said to him, 'My Lord, O king, among all the purple cloaks that you have, [why] do you give me such instructions only about this one?'

I. "He said to him, 'That is the one that I wore on my coronation day.'

J. "So too did Moses say before the Holy One, blessed be he, Lord of the Universe: 'Among the seventy distinct nations that you have in your world, [why] do you give instructions to me only concerning Israel? [For instance,] "Say to the children of Israel," "Command the children of Israel," "Speak to the children of Israel.""'

K. "He said to him, 'They are the ones who at the [Red] Sea declared me to be king, saying, "The Lord will be king" (Exod. 15:18).'"

L. Said R. Berekhiah, "[The matter may be compared] to an elder, who had a hood [signifying his office as elder], concerning which he instructed his disciple, saying to him, 'Fold it, shake it out, and be careful about it!'

M. "He said to him, 'My lord, elder, among all the hoods that you have, [why] do you give me such instructions only about this one?'

N. "He said to him, 'It is because that is the one that I wore on the day on which I was officially named an elder.'

O. "So too did Moses say before the Holy One, blessed be he, Lord of the Universe: 'Among the seventy distinct nations that you have in your world, [why] do you give instructions to me only concerning Israel?'

P. "He said to him, '[It is because] they accepted my dominion on them at Mount Sinai, saying, "Whatever the Lord has spoken we shall do and we shall hear"' (Exod. 24:7)."

2. A. Said R. Yudan, "Now take note of how the Holy One, blessed be he, cherishes Israel.

B. "For he makes mention of them five times in a single verse of Scripture, in line with the following verse: 'And I have given the Levites as a gift to Aaron and his sons [from among the people of Israel, to do the service for the people of Israel at the tent of meeting, and to make atonement for the people of Israel, that there may be no plague among the people of Israel in case the people of Israel should come near the sanctuary]' (Num. 8:19)."

II:V

1. A. Said R. Simeon b. Yohai, "[The matter may be compared] to a king who had an only son. Every day he would give instructions to his steward, saying to him, 'Make sure my son eats, make sure my son drinks, make sure my son goes to school, make sure my son comes home from school.'

B. "So every day the Holy One, blessed be he, gave instructions to Moses, saying, 'Command the children of Israel,' 'Say to the children of Israel,' 'Speak to the children of Israel.'"

2. A. Said R. Judah b. R. Simon, "[The matter may be compared] to a person who was sitting and making a crown for the king. Someone passed by and said to him, 'What are you doing?'

B. "He replied, 'Making a crown for the king.'

C. "He said to him, 'Whatever [precious stones] that you can affix [to the crown] you should affix, put on emeralds, put on jewels, put on pearls. For that crown is going to be put on the head of the king.'

D. "So too did the Holy One, blessed be he, say to Moses, 'In whatever way you can praise Israel, give that praise; if you can magnify them, do it; if you can adorn them, do it. Why? Because through [Israel] I am going to be glorified.' [That is] in line with the following verse of Scripture: 'And he said to me, "You are my servant, Israel, in whom I will be glorified"' (Isa. 49:3)."

II:VI

1. A. R. Joshua of Sikhnin in the name of R. Levi: "Even the Scriptures paid honor to Israel.
   B. "That is in line with the following verse of Scripture: 'When any man of you brings an offering' [Lev. 1:2].
   C. "Now when [Scripture] proceeds to yet another [but less praiseworthy] topic, [how does it phrase matters?] 'When a man of you has on the flesh of his skin' is not written, but rather, 'When man will have on the flesh of his skin is rising' (Lev. 13:2)."
   D. R. Samuel b. R. Nehemiah made two points [in this same manner]:
   E. "It is written: 'But there shall be no needy among you' [Deut. 15:4].
   F. "Now when [Scripture] proceeds to yet another [but less praiseworthy] topic, [how does it phrase matters?]
   G. " 'For there shall be no needy in your midst' is not written here, but rather, '. . . from the midst of the land' (Deut. 15:11)."
   H. R. Samuel b. R. Nehemiah made yet another point [in the same manner]:
   I. "It is written: 'These shall stand to bless the people on Mount Gerizim' [Deut. 27:12].
   J. "Now when [Scripture] proceeds to yet another [but less praiseworthy] topic, [how does it phrase matters?]
   K. " 'These will stand to curse the people' is not written here, but rather, '. . . these will stand concerning (Hebrew *l*) the curse' (Deut. 27:13)."
2. A. R. Berekhiah, R. Helbo, and R. Ami in the name of R. Ilai: "Not only so, but when punishment comes into the world, the righteous overcome it, in line with that which is written: 'These shall stand against (*l*) the curse' (Deut. 27:13)."

God Loves the Poor

Our sages studied the offerings listed in Leviticus and looked for a key as to why situations called for a given beast or other type of sacrifice. They sought meaning in these details, and the meaning they found proves instructive for the conduct of life. The first point we see is that the animals that Israel offers themselves provide a model. They cannot be stolen. They themselves may not be predatory, but must be beasts of a peaceful character. Adam's offering provides the paradigm for the offerings of Israel later on. Then Adam's situation—master of all things, owner of everything—serves to provide the base for the homily that people should not offer what they do not own. God really owns everything, so people may offer only thanksgiving offerings. Since at issue in most of the offerings of the present passage of Leviticus is not thanksgiving offerings but sin offerings of various sorts, perhaps the sense of the exegete was to contrast truly worthwhile offerings with those at hand. But, as it is, the point is not so elevated. It just indicates that people must offer what is theirs, and not what they have acquired, for example, by oppressing the poor. This point is made in a number of ways. First, the sages emphasize that a meagre offering ("widow's mite") is acceptable. Second, they say not only is it acceptable, but, because of the greater personal sacrifice involved, it takes precedence even over the offering of a king. God wants the sacrifice of a contrite heart. The priest should understand that the woman's paltry sacrifice is all she has, and perhaps more than she can afford.

II:VII

1. A. Said R. Berekhiah, "Said the Holy One, blessed be he, to this man (Adam) [to whom Scripture refers, 'When any man (Adam) of you brings an offering . . .' (Lev. 1:2)], 'Man, let your offering be like the offering of the first man.'
   B. "Just as the first man had everything under his dominion and so did not bring an offering that had been acquired by robbery or

violence, so you, in whose dominion all things [do not fall], should offer nothing acquired by robbery or violence, and, if you conform, 'It will please the Lord more than an ox, [or a bull with horns and hoofs]' (Ps. 69:31 [Hebrew v. 32]). [In context: 'I will praise the name of God with a song; I will magnify him with thanksgiving. This will please the Lord more than an ox. . . . Let the oppressed see it and be glad. . . . For the Lord hears the needy, and does not despise his own that are in bonds' (Ps. 69:30-33 [Hebrew vv. 31-34]).]"

III:IV

1. A. ["When anyone brings a cereal offering" (Lev. 1:2).] Now what is written just after this statement?

    B. "And he shall take away its crop with the feathers [and cast it beside the altar on the east side, in the place for ashes; and he shall tear it by its wings, but shall not divide it asunder. And the priest shall burn it on the altar upon the wood that is on the altar; it is a burnt offering, an offering by fire, a pleasing odor to the Lord]" (Lev. 1:16-17).

    C. Said R. Tanhum b. R. Hanilai, "A bird such as this flies about and swoops all over the place and eats everywhere, so what it eats constitutes stolen property and comes by violence. Said the Holy One, blessed be he, 'Since this crop [of the bird] is filled with the result of thievery and violence, let it not be offered up on the altar.'

    D. "That is why it is said, 'And he shall take away its crop with the feathers. . . .'

    E. "By contrast, a domestic animal is raised at the crib of its owner and so does not eat whatever it finds anywhere, things that are stolen or come by violence. Therefore one may offer up the entire beast.

    F. "That is why it is said, 'And the priest shall offer the whole [of the burnt offering of the flock or herd]' (Lev. 1:13)."

2. A. Since a person steals and gains through violence, come and see how much bother and effort [are necessary] before [food] comes out from it: from mouth to gullet, from gullet to stomach, from stomach to second stomach, from second stomach to maw, from maw to intestines, from the small winding intestine to the

large winding intestine, from the large winding intestine to the
mucal sieve, from mucal sieve to rectum, from rectum to anus,
from anus outside.

B. So take note of how much bother and effort [are necessary]
before its food exudes from it.

III:V

1. A. "And he shall tear it by its wings but shall not divide it asunder,
[and the priest shall burn it on the altar, upon the wood that is
on the fire; it is a burnt offering, an offering by fire, a pleasing
odor to the Lord]" (Lev. 1:17).

B. Said R. Yohanan, "If an ordinary fellow should smell the odor of
the burning wings, it would turn his stomach, and yet you say,
'And the priest shall burn it on the altar' (Lev. 1:17).

C. "Why go to all this trouble? It is so that the altar may be
ornamented by the offering of [even] a poor man [who cannot
afford a beast (Lev. 1:10), but can afford a bird (Lev. 1:14)]."

2. A. King Agrippas wanted to offer a thousand bird offerings on a
single day. He sent a message to the priest, "Let no one beside
me make an offering on this day."

B. A poor man came, with two birds in his hand, and said to [the
priest], "Offer these for me."

C. [The priest] said to him, "The king ordered me not to permit
anyone but him to make an offering today."

D. [The poor man] said to him, "My lord, priest, I catch four birds
every day, two which I offer, and two which I use for a living. If
you do not offer these two up, you cut my living in half."

E. The priest took them and offered them up.

F. In a dream King Agrippas foresaw [this message], "A poor man's
offering came before yours."

G. He sent a message to the priest, "Didn't I tell you not to let
anyone but me make an offering that day?"

H. He sent words to him, "My lord, king, a poor man came, with
two birds in his hand and said to me, 'Offer these for me.' I said
to him, 'The king ordered me not to permit anyone but him to
make an offering today.' He said to me, 'I catch four birds every
day, two which I offer, and two which I use for a living. If you do
not offer these two up, you cut my living in half.' Now should I
not have offered them up?!"

    I. He said to him, "You did things right."

3. A. The story is told: People were leading an ox to be offered, but it would not be led. A poor man came with a bundle of endive in his hand, and held it out to the beast, which ate it. [The ox] sneezed and expelled a needle, and it then allowed itself to be led on to be offered. [If the needle had not been expelled, it would have caused an internal perforation, resulting in a blemish invalidating the animal for sacrificial purposes.]

    B. The owner of the ox saw a message in his dream: "The offering of a poor man came before yours."

4. A. The story is told: A woman brought a handful of fine flour [for a cereal offering, in line with Lev. 2:1]. But the priest ridiculed her and said, "See what these women are bringing as their offerings! In such a paltry thing what is there to eat? And what is there to offer up?"

    B. The priest saw a message in his dream: "Do not ridicule her on such an account, for it is as if she was offering up her own soul."

    C. Now is it not a matter of an argument a fortiori? If concerning someone who doesn't offer up a living soul [of a beast] Scripture uses the word, "Soul": "[When any soul (RSV: one) brings a cereal offering,] if someone brings a [contrite] soul, how much the more is it as if this one has offered her own soul."

III:VI

1. A. "[When any one brings a cereal offering as an offering to the Lord, his offering shall be of fine flour; he shall pour oil upon it and put frankincense on it,] and bring it to Aaron's sons, the priests" (Lev. 2:1-2).

    B. R. Hiyya taught, "[That is the case] even if they are many. [Even if many priests have to be involved with the paltry offering, for example, in measuring the flour, pouring on the oil, kneading it, putting on the frankincense, taking the handful, and the like, each priest must do his part, to show respect for the offering even of a poor man."

    C. Said R. Yohanan [citing a prooftext for the foregoing proposition], " 'In the multitude of people is the king's glory' (Prov. 14:28)."

2. A. "And he shall take from it a handful of fine flour and oil, [with all of its frankincense, and the priest shall burn this as its memo-

rial portion upon the altar, an offering by fire, a pleasing odor to
the Lord. And what is left of the cereal offering shall be for
Aaron and his sons]" (Lev. 2:2-3).

B. ". . . Of the fine flour": And not the whole of the fine flour.

C. ". . . Of the oil": And not the whole of the oil.

D. Lo, [there was the case of] one [who] brought his cereal offering
from Gaul or Spain or those distant parts, and saw the priest
taking [and offering only] a handful and eating the remainder.
He said, "Woe is me for all the trouble I went to, [merely] so
that this one should eat."

E. People made him feel better, telling him, "Now if this [priest],
who has gone to the trouble of merely taking two steps, between
the hall and the altar (Joel 2:17) gains merit to allow him to eat
[the meal offering remnant], you, who went to all this trouble,
how much the more so [should you gain merit from this offering
of yours]!"

F. Moreover, "And what is left of the cereal offering shall be for
Aaron and his sons" (Lev. 2:3). [Not only does the officiating
priest gain possession of the remainder, but he can pass on the
right to his sons. The one who has brought the offering all the
more so gains the right to pass on the merit of his deed to his
children after him.]

3. A. [In Aramaic:] R. Hananiah b. R. Aha went to a certain place
and found the following verse at the head of the order [of the
reading of the Pentateuch in the synagogue on that Sabbath]:
"And what is left of the cereal offering shall be for Aaron and his
sons" (Lev. 2:3).

B. With what verse did he commence the discourse in that regard?

C. "From men beneath your hand, O Lord, from men whose portion [in life is of the world, may their belly be filled with what
you have stored up for them; may their children have more than
enough; and may they leave something over to their babes]"
(Ps. 17:14).

D. [Understanding Hebrew *mmtym*, 'men,' as *m(h) mtym*, 'who are
(mighty) men,' he proceeded:] "Who are mighty men? They
are the ones who took their portion from beneath your hand,
O Lord.

E. "And who might such a one be? It is the tribe of Levi.

F. " 'From men whose portion in life is of the world': These are the ones who did not take a share in the land [but rather got their support from the leftovers of God's altar and agricultural dues].

G. "'Their portion in life': This refers to the Holy Things of the sanctuary.

H. "'May their belly be filled with what you have stored up for them': This refers to the Holy Things separated in the provinces [from the crops, that is, the priestly rations of various kinds supplied by the farmers].

I. "'May their children have more than enough': 'Every male among the children of Aaron may eat of it' (Lev. 6:18 [Hebrew v. 11]).

J. "'And may they leave something over to their babes': 'And what is left of the cereal offering shall be for Aaron and his sons' (Lev. 2:3)."

4. A. Aaron imparted merit [to eat Holy Things] to his sons, whether valid or invalid [for service at the altar, for blemished priests also may eat priestly rations].

5. A. So Scripture states: "My covenant with him was a covenant of life and peace, and I gave them [to him, that he might fear, and he feared me, he stood in awe of my name. True instruction was in his mouth, and no wrong was found on his lips. He walked with me in peace and uprightness, and he turned many from iniquity. For the lips of a priest should seek instruction from his mouth, for he is a messenger of the Lord of hosts]" (Mal. 2:5-7).

B. "My covenant with him was a covenant of life and peace," for he pursued the interests of peace in Israel.

C. "And I gave them to him, that he might fear, and he feared me," for he accepted upon himself the discipline of the teachings of the Torah in a spirit of fear, awe, trembling, and quaking.

6. A. What is the meaning of the following clause: "He stood in awe of my name"?

B. They say: When Moses poured out the anointing oil on Aaron's head, he trembled and fell backward, exclaiming "Woe is me! I might well have committed sacrilege against the anointing oil [in using it in this way]!"

C. The Holy Spirit answered him, "'Behold, how good and pleasant it is when brothers dwell in unity! (Ps. 133:1) [It is like the precious oil upon the head, running down upon the beard, upon

the beard of Aaron, running down on the collar of his robes!] It
is like the dew of Hermon, which falls on the mountains of
Zion! [For there the Lord has commanded the blessing, life for
evermore]' (Ps. 133:2-3).

D. "Just as sacrilege does not apply to dew, so sacrilege does not
apply to anointing oil."

7. A. "It is like the precious oil upon the head, running down upon
the beard, upon the beard of Aaron" (Ps. 133:2).

B. Now did Aaron have two beards, that the cited verse should
make reference to the word "beard" two times, "the beard," "the
beard of Aaron"?

C. But: When Moses saw the anointing oil running down the
beard of Aaron, he rejoiced as if it ran down his own beard.

D. As it is written: "True instruction [Torah] was in his mouth"
(Mal. 2:6). [The oil that had flowed down on the mouth and
beard of Aaron represented true Torah.]

8. A. "[True instruction (Torah) was in his mouth], and no wrong
was found on his lips. He walked with me in peace and uprightness, [and he turned many from iniquity]" (Mal. 2:6).

B. "True instruction was in his mouth," for he never called what
was unclean clean, or what was clean, unclean.

C. "And no wrong was found on his lips," for he never declared
prohibited what was permitted, nor did he declare permitted
what was forbidden.

D. "He walked with me in peace and uprightness," for he never
entertained misgivings about the ways of the Omnipresent, just
as Abraham never entertained misgivings.

E. "And he turned many from iniquity," for he turned sinners back
to the study of the Torah.

F. And Scripture says, "Sincerely do they love you" (Cant. 1:4).

G. What is written at the end of the passage? "For the lips of a priest
should seek instruction from his mouth, for he is a messenger of
the Lord of hosts" (Mal. 2:7).

The Soul Bears Responsibility for Sin

A critical issue facing the faithful is the nature of sin, and responsibility for sin. Our sages make explicit, in their reading of Lev. 4:1 ("When a soul sins unwittingly") that the soul bears responsibility for sin. All of the physical parts of the body are at the soul's disposal. The soul makes the difference: we are what we do, and we are responsible for what we do. IV:IV.1 makes this point. The paradox is that, with the authority exercised by the soul over the rest of the body, there can be unwitting sin at all. But the point is that when a person sins, it is the soul that bears responsibility. The whole human being is represented by the soul, as in the parable of IV:V. We have two sizable parables, in which the answer to the question of why the soul and body are equally culpable is dramatically presented in colloquy.

IV:IV

1. A. Ten things serve the soul, and these are they: gullet for food, windpipe for [making] sound, liver for anger, bile for envy, lungs for absorbing fluid, first stomach for grinding food, spleen for laughter, maw for sleep, kidneys for counsel, heart for understanding, [and] the tongue concludes.
   B. But the soul is above them all.
   C. Said the Holy One, blessed be he, to it [that is, the soul], "I set you above them all, yet you go and sin, steal and grab."
   D. "When a soul sins unwittingly . . ." (Lev. 4:1). [Does a soul ever sin unwittingly?]

IV:V

1. A. "Speak to the children of Israel, 'A soul . . .'" ["If any one sins unwittingly in any of the things which the Lord has commanded not to be done"] (Lev. 4:1):

    B. Why [does Scripture make explicit reference to] a soul, [rather than speaking of "a man"]?

    C. [The intent is to] punish the soul.

2. A. R. Ishmael taught, "[The matter of the soul's and body's guilt for sin may be] compared to the case of a king, who had an orchard, in which were excellent early figs. So he set up two guards to keep watch [over the orchard], one lame, one blind. He told them, 'Keep watch over the early figs.' He left them there and went his way.

    B. "The lame guard said to the blind one, 'I spy some wonderful figs.'

    C. "The other said, 'Come on, let's eat.'

    D. "The lame one said, 'Now, can I walk around?'

    E. "The blind one said, 'And can I see a thing?'

    F. "What did they do? The lame one rode on the blind one, and they picked the figs and ate them. Then they went back and each one took his original place.

    G. "After a while the king came back and said to them, 'Where are my figs?'

    H. "The blind one said to him, 'Can I see a thing?'

    I. "The lame one said, 'And can I walk around?'

    J. "Since the king was smart, what did he do? He had the lame one climb onto the blind one, and he judged the two of them as a single defendant. He said to them, 'This is how you did it when you went and ate the figs.'

    K. "So in time to come, the Holy One will say to the soul, 'Why did you sin before me?'

    L. "And the soul will say before him, 'Lord of the age[s], am I the one that sinned before you? It is the body that sinned. From the day that I left it, have I committed a single sin?'

    M. "So the [Holy One] will say to the body, 'Why did you sin?'

    N. "And it will say before him, 'Lord of the ages, it is the soul that committed the sin. From the day on which it left me, have I not been cast down before you like a shard on a garbage dump?'

    O. "What will the Holy One, blessed be he, do? He will put the soul back into the body and judge them as a single defendant.

    P. "That is in line with the following verse of Scripture: 'He calls to the heavens above and to the earth, that he may judge his people' (Ps. 50:4).

Q. " 'He calls to the heavens': To produce the soul.

R. " 'And to the earth': To bring forth the body.

S. "And then: 'To judge with him' [all together, reading as if it read not Hebrew *'amo* but *'imo*]."

3. A. R. Hiyya taught, "[The matter of the soul's guilt for sin may be compared] to the case of a priest who had two wives, one the daughter of a priest, the other the daughter of an Israelite.

B. "He gave them a piece of dough in the status of heave offering [which was to be kept in conditions of cultic cleanness], but they rendered it cultically unclean.

C. "He went and remonstrated with the daughter of the priest, but he left the daughter of the Israelite alone.

D. "She said to him, 'Our lord, priest, you gave it to both of us simultaneously. Why do you remonstrate with me and leave that one alone?'

E. "He said to her, 'You are a priest's daughter and experienced [on account of growing up] in your father's house [in dealing with the rules of cultic cleanness], but that one is an Israelite's daughter and not experienced from her upbringing in her father's house.

F. " 'Therefore I remonstrate with you.'

G. "So in time to come, the Holy One, blessed be he, will say to the soul, 'Why have you sinned before me?'

H. "And the soul will say before him, 'Lord of the age[s], the body and I sinned simultaneously. Why then are you remonstrating with me but leaving that one alone?'

I. "He will then say to the soul, 'You come from the upper world, a place in which people do not sin, while the body comes from the lower world, a place in which people sin. Therefore I remonstrate with you.'"

The Human Soul Is Like God's Soul

We know that our sages' principal question is what it means for humanity to be "in our image, after our likeness," a question answered for Christians by Christ on the cross. Our sages speculate along parallel lines, by drawing the comparison between the soul of a human being and the soul of God. The person is like the world. Just as the soul fills the body, so God fills the world. That is why the soul must praise God. And further, the extended comparison of the human soul to God evokes the soul's natural duty to praise God.

IV:VII

1.   A. R. Yohanan and R. Joshua b. Levi:
    B. R. Yohanan said, "Five times is the word 'soul' written here [Ps. 103], [that is] five times for the five scrolls of the Torah."
    C. R. Joshua b. Levi said, "Five times the word 'soul' is written here, for the five ages which a person sees.
    D. "'Bless the Lord, O my soul, and all that is within me, bless his holy name!' [Ps. 103:1].
    E. "That is when a babe is still in his mother's womb.
    F. "'Bless the Lord, O my soul, and forget not all his benefits' [Ps. 103:2].
    G. "That is when a babe leaves his mother's womb: 'Do not forget the goodness which I have bestowed upon you.'
    H. "'Bless the Lord, O my soul, in all the places of his dominion' [Ps. 103:22].
    I. "This a person says when he gains his full growth and goes forth to make a living.
    J. "'Bless the Lord, O my soul. O Lord my God, you are very great! You are clothed in majesty' [Ps. 104:1].
    K. "This a person says when he leaves [this life] for his eternal home.

L. "And, finally, one for the world to come: 'Let sinners be consumed from the earth and let the wicked be no more! Bless the
Lord, O my soul! Hallelujah!'"

2. A. R. Samuel b. R. Nehamiah in the name of R. Nathan said
[Babylonian Talmud *Berakoth* 9b], "David had written 120
psalms, and in none of them did he conclude, 'Hallelujah,'
until he saw the downfall of the evil, as it is said: 'Let sinners be
consumed from the earth' (Ps. 104:35)."

IV:VIII

1. A. Why did the soul of David praise the Holy One, blessed be he?

B. David said, "Just as the soul fills the body, so the Holy One,
blessed be he, fills the whole world, as it is written: "'Do I not fill
the entire heaven and earth?" says the Lord' (Jer. 23:24). So let
the soul, which fills the body, come and praise the Holy One,
blessed be he, who fills the world.

C. "The soul supports the body, the Holy One [blessed be he]
supports the world, for it is written: 'Even to your old age I am
he, and to gray hairs [I will carry you]' (Isa. 46:4). So let the
soul, which supports the body, come and praise the Holy One,
blessed be he, who supports the world.

D. "The soul outlasts the body, and the Holy One, blessed be he,
outlasts the world: 'They will perish, but you do endure; they
will all wear out like a garment. [You change them like a garment and they pass away, but you are the same, and your years
have no end]' (Ps. 102:26-27). So let the soul, which outlasts
the body, come and praise the Holy One, blessed be he, who
outlasts the world.

E. "The soul in the body does not eat, and as to the Holy One,
blessed be he, there is no eating so far as he is concerned, as it is
written: 'If I were hungry, I would not tell you, for the world and
all that is in it is mine' (Ps. 50:12). Let the soul in the body,
which does not eat, come and praise the Holy One, blessed be
he, before whom there is no eating.

F. "The soul is singular in the body, and the Holy One, blessed be
he, is singular in his world, as it is said: 'Hear, O Israel, the Lord
our God is a singular Lord' (Deut. 6:4). Let the soul, which is
singular in the body, come and praise the Holy One, blessed be
he, who is singular in his world.

G. "The soul is pure in the body, and the Holy One, blessed be he, is pure in his world: 'You who are of eyes too pure to behold evil' (Hab 1:13). Let the soul, which is pure in the body, come and praise the Holy One, blessed be he, who is pure in his world.

H. "The soul sees but is not seen, and the Holy One, blessed be he, sees but is not seen, as it is written: '[Am I a God at hand says the Lord, and not a God afar off?] Can a man hide himself in secret places so that I cannot see him? says the Lord. Do I not fill heaven [and earth? says the Lord]' (Jer. 23:23-24). Let the soul, which sees but is not seen, come and praise the Holy One, blessed be he, who sees but is not seen.

I. "The soul does not sleep in the body, and the Holy One, blessed be he, is not subject to sleep, as it is said: 'Lo, the Guardian of Israel neither slumbers nor sleeps' (Ps. 121:4). Let the soul, which does not sleep in the body, come and praise the Holy One, blessed be he, who is not subject to sleep: 'Lo, he slumbers not nor sleeps.'"

God Punishes for Just Cause

From the responsibility of the soul for sin and the duty of the soul to praise God, we move on to God's justice. Our sages viewed a world in which the wicked prosper and the good suffer, and they wondered at the ways of the just God. They recognized that, when the wicked prosper, it is only for a time, and it is only for this world. But they asked why God gave tranquillity to the wicked. Then they explained that, when God ultimately inflicted just punishment for sin, the wicked had no complaint. The other half of the equation of just punishment invoked the metaphor of "the hiding of the face." When our sages wished to speak of God's punishment, they said that God "hid his face," on which account humanity suffered. We know that metaphor in the priestly blessing: "May the Lord lift up his face to you," meaning the opposite, then, of "the hiding of the face." The deeper meaning is that to have God's attention is to enjoy God's love. God is love. We review the list of sinners—Sodom and Gomorrah, the ten tribes of northern Israel—and specify the tranquillity that each enjoyed, then the penalty that each ultimately received. And we know—the point is self-evident—that the sinners of the day may enjoy tranquillity but will ultimately suffer their just reward.

The context of this message itself is interesting. The passage of Leviticus subject to explanation deals with the unwitting sin of the anointed priest (Lev. 4:1ff.). When ordinary people commit an unwitting sin, it involves the common life. The same penalty applies to both. God cares equally for the high and the low. What then is the primary intent of the exegete? It is to emphasize the equality of anointed priest and ordinary Israelites. The expiation demanded of the one is no greater than that of the other. Considering the importance of the anointed priest, the ceremony by which he attains office, the sanctity attached to his labor, we cannot miss the polemic. What the anointed priest does unwittingly will usually involve some aspect of the cult. When the community commits a sin unwittingly, it will not involve the cult but some aspect of the collective life of the people. The one is no more consequential than the other; the same penalty pertains to both. So the people and the priest stand on the same plane before God.

The further meaning of the verse of Job then cannot be missed. When God hides his face, in consequence of which the people suffer, it is for just cause. No one can complain; he is long-suffering but in the end exacts his penalties. And these will cover not unwitting sin, such as Leviticus knows, but deliberate sin, as with the generation of the flood, Sodom, and the ten tribes.

V:II

1. A. "When he is quiet, who can condemn" (Job 34:29).
   B. When he gave tranquillity to the Sodomites, who could come and condemn them?
   C. What sort of tranquillity did he give them?
   D. "As for the earth, out of it comes bread, but underneath it is turned up as by fire. Its stones are the place of sapphires, and it has dust of gold" (Job 28:5-6).
2. A. "That path no bird of prey knows, and the falcon's eye has not seen it" (Job 28:7).
   B. R. Levi in the name of R. Yohanan b. Shahina: "The falcon [*bar hadayya*-bird] spots its prey at a distance of eighteen miles."
   C. And how much is its portion [of food]?
   D. R. Meir said, "[A mere] two handbreadths."
   E. R. Judah said, "One handbreadth."
   F. R. Yose said, "Two or three fingerbreadths."
   G. [In Aramaic:] And when it stood on the trees of Sodom, it could not see the ground because of the density of [the foliage of] the trees.
3. A. "When he hides his face, who can set him right?":
   B. When he hides his face from them, who comes to say to him, "You did not do rightly"?
   C. And when did he hide his face from them?
   D. When he made brimstone and fire rain down on them.
   E. That is in line with the following verse of Scripture: "Then the Lord made brimstone and fire rain on Sodom and Gomorrah" (Gen. 19:24).

V:III

1. A. "When he is quiet, who can condemn? When he hides his face, who can set him right?" (Job 34:29).

    B. When he gave tranquillity to the ten tribes, who could come and condemn them?

    C. What sort of tranquillity did he give them? "Woe to those who are at ease in Zion, and to those who feel secure on the mountain of Samaria, the notable men of the first of the nations, to whom the house of Israel come" (Amos 6:1).

2. A. "Woe to those who are at ease in Zion" refers to the tribes of Judah and Benjamin.

    B. "Those who feel secure on the mountain of Samaria" refers to the ten tribes.

    C. "The notable men of the first of the nations" derive from the two noteworthy names, Shem and Eber.

    D. When the nations of the world eat and drink, they pass the time in nonsense talk, saying, "Who is a sage, like Balaam! Who is a hero, like Goliath! Who is rich, like Haman!"

    E. And the Israelites come after them and say to them, "Was not Ahitophel a sage, Samson a hero, Korah rich?"

3. A. "Pass over to Calneh and see; [and thence go to Hamath the great; then go down to Gath of the Philistines. Are they better than these kingdoms? Or is their territory greater than your territory?]" (Amos 6:2).

    B. [Calneh] refers to Ctesiphon.

    C. "Hamath the great" refers to Hamath of Antioch.

    D. "Then go down to Gath of the Philistines" refers to the mounds of the Philistines.

    E. "Are they better than these kingdoms? Or is their territory greater than your territory?"

    F. "O you who put far away the evil day" (Amos 6:3) [refers to] the day on which they would go into exile.

4. A. "And bring near the seat of violence?" (Amos 6:3). This refers to Esau.

    B. "Did you bring yourselves near to sit next to violence": This refers to Esau.

    C. That is in line with the following verse of Scripture: "For the violence done to your brother Jacob, [shame shall cover you]" (Obad. 10).

5. A. "[Woe to] those who lie upon beds of ivory" (Amos 6:4): On beds made of the elephant's tusk.

    B. "And stink on their couches" (Amos 6:4): Who do stinking transgressions on their beds.

C. "Who eat lambs from the flock [and calves from the midst of the stall]" (Amos 6:4).

D. They say: When one of them wanted to eat a kid of the flock, he would have the whole flock brought before him, and he would stand over it and slaughter it.

E. When he wanted to eat a calf, he would bring the entire herd of calves before him and stand over it and slaughter it.

6. A. "Who sing idle songs to the sound of the harp [and like David invent for themselves instruments of music]" (Amos 6:5).

B. [They would say that] David provided them with musical instruments.

7. A. "Who drink wine in bowls" (Amos 6:6).

B. Rab, R. Yohanan, and rabbis:

C. Rab said, "It is a very large bowl" [using the Greek text of the Bible].

D. R. Yohanan said, "It was in small cups."

E. Rabbis say, "It was in cups with saucers attached."

F. Whence did the wine they drink come?

G. R. Aibu in the name of R. Hanina said, "It was wine from Pelugta, for the wine would entice (Hebrew *pth*) the body."

H. And rabbis in the name of R. Hanina said, "It was from Pelugta's [separation], since, because of their wine drinking, the ten tribes were enticed [from God] and consequently sent into exile."

8. A. "And anoint themselves with the finest oils" (Amos 6:6).

B. R. Judah b. R. Ezekiel said, "This refers to oil of unripe olives, which removes hair and smooths the body."

C. R. Hanina said, "This refers to oil of myrrh and cinnamon."

9. A. And [in spite of] all this glory: "They are not grieved over the ruin of Joseph" (Amos 6:6).

B. "Therefore they shall now be the first of those to go into exile, [and the revelry of those who stretch themselves shall pass away]" (Amos 6:7).

C. What is the meaning of "the revelry of those who stretch themselves"?

D. Said R. Aibu, "They had thirteen public baths, one for each of the tribes, and one additional one for all of them together.

E. "And all of them were destroyed, and only this one [that had served all of them] survived."

    F. "This shows how much lewdness was done with them."

10. A. "When he hides his face, who can set him right?" (Job 34:29).

    B. When he hid his face from them, who then could come and say to him, "You did not do right"?

    C. How did he hide his face from them? By bringing against them Sennacherib, the king of Assyria.

    D. That is in line with the following verse of Scripture: "In the fourteenth year of King Hezekiah, Sennacherib, king of Assyria, came up [against all the fortified cities of Judah and took them] (2 Kgs. 18:13; Isa. 36:1)."

11. A. What is the meaning of, "and took them"?

    B. Said R. Abba b. Kahana, "Three divine decrees were sealed on that day.

    C. "The decree against the ten tribes was sealed, for them to fall into the hand of Sennacherib; the decree against Sennacherib was sealed, for him to fall into the hand of Hezekiah; and the decree of Shebna was sealed, to be smitten with leprosy."

12. A. "Whether it be a nation [or a man]" (Job 34:29). This refers to Sennacherib, as it is said: "For a nation has come up upon my land" (Joel 1:6).

    B. ". . . Or a man" (Job 34:29). This refers to Israel: "For you, my sheep, the sheep of my pasture, are a man" (Ezek. 34:31).

    C. "Together" (Job 34:29). This refers to King Uzziah, who was smitten with leprosy.

    D. That is in line with the following verse of Scripture: "And Uzziah the King was a leper until the day he died" (2 Chr. 26:21).

13. A. ". . . Whether it be a nation or a man together" (Job 34:29): Now the justice of the Holy One, blessed be he, is not like man's justice.

    B. A mortal judge may show favor to a community, but he will never show favor to an individual.

    C. But the Holy One, blessed be he, is not so. Rather: "If it is the anointed priest who sins, [thus bringing guilt on the people,] then let him offer [for the sin which he has committed] a young bull [without blemish to the Lord as a sin offering]" (Lev. 4:3-4).

    D. "[If the whole congregation of Israel commits a sin unwittingly, and the thing is hidden from the eyes of the assembly, and they

do any one of the things which the Lord has commanded not to
be done and are guilty, when the sin which they have committed becomes known,] the assembly shall offer a young bull for a
sin offering" (Lev. 4:13-14). [God exacts the same penalty from
an individual and from the community and does not distinguish
the one from the other. The anointed priest and the community
both become subject to liability for the same offering, a young
bull.]

Prayer Requires Care

Our sages of course knew that God hears and answers prayer. They therefore put much thought into the appropriate way in which to say one's prayers. They drew the contrast between the one who prays thoughtlessly and casually and the one who prays with all his or her heart. In the parable that follows, they lay out the difference as they conceive it. David, the psalmist, then is shown to provide the model of the right way of praying.

V:VIII

1. A. R. Simeon b. Yohai taught, "How masterful are the Israelites, for they know how to find favor with their Creator."

    B. Said R. Yudan [in Aramaic], "It is like the case of Samaritan [beggars]. The Samaritan [beggars] are clever at beginning. One of them goes to a housewife, saying to her, 'Do you have an onion? Give it to me.' After she gives it to him, he says to her, 'Is there such a thing as an onion without bread?' After she gives him [bread], he says to her, 'Is there such a thing as food without drink?' So, all in all, he gets to eat and drink."

    C. Said R. Aha [in Aramaic], "There is a woman who knows how to borrow things, and there is a woman who does not. The one who knows how to borrow goes over to her neighbor. The door is open, but she knocks [anyhow]. Then she says to her neighbor, 'Greetings, good neighbor. How're you doing? How's your husband doing? How're your kids doing? Can I come in? [By the way], would you have such-and-such a utensil? Would you lend it to me?' [The neighboring housewife] says to her, 'Yes, of course.'

    D. "But the one who does not know how to borrow goes over to her neighbor. The door is closed, so she just opens it. She says [to the neighboring housewife], 'Do you have such-and-such a utensil? Would you lend it to me?' [The neighboring housewife] says to her, 'No.'"

E. Said R. Huna [in Aramaic], "There is a tenant farmer who knows how to borrow things, and there is a tenant farmer who does not know how to borrow. The one who knows how to borrow combs his hair, brushes off his clothes, puts on a good face, and then goes over to the overseer of his work to borrow from him. [The overseer] says to him, 'How's the land doing?' He says to him, 'May you have the merit of being fully satisfied with its [wonderful] produce.' 'How are the oxen doing?' He says to him, 'May you have the merit of being fully satisfied with their fat.' 'How are the goats doing?' 'May you have the merit of being fully satisfied with their young.' 'And what would you like?' Then he says, 'Now if you might have an extra ten denars, would you give them to me?' The overseer replies, 'If you want, take twenty.'

F. "But the one who does not know how to borrow leaves his hair a mess, his clothes filthy, his face gloomy. He too goes over to the overseer to borrow from him. The overseer says to him, 'How's the land doing?' He replies, 'I hope it will produce at least what [in seed] we put into it.' 'How are the oxen doing?' 'They're scrawny.' 'How are the goats doing?' 'They're scrawny, too.' 'And what do you want?' 'Now if you might have an extra ten denars, would you give them to me?' The overseer replies, 'Go, pay me back what you already owe me!'"

G. Said R. Huna, "David was one of the good tenant farmers. To begin with, he starts a psalm with praise [of God], saying, 'The heavens declare the glory of God, and the firmament shows his handiwork' (Ps. 19:1 [Hebrew v. 2]). The heaven says to him, 'Perhaps you need something?' 'The firmament shows his handiwork.' The firmament says to him, 'Perhaps you need something?'

H. "And so he would continue to sing: 'Day unto day utters speech, and night to night reveals knowledge' (Ps. 19:2 [Hebrew v. 3]).

I. "Said to him the Holy One, blessed be he, 'What do you want?'

J. "He said before him, 'Who can discern errors?' (Ps. 19:12 [Hebrew v. 13]).

K. "'What sort of unwitting sin have I done before you!'

L. "[God] said to him, 'Lo, this one is remitted, and that one is forgiven you.'

M. "'And cleanse me of hidden sins' (Ps. 19:12 [Hebrew v. 13]): '. . . From the secret sins that I have done before you.'

N. "He said to him, 'Lo, this one is remitted, and that one is forgiven to you.'

O. "'Keep back your servant also from deliberate ones' (Ps. 19:13 [Hebrew v. 14]). This refers to transgressions done in full knowledge.

P. "'That they may not have dominion over me. Then I shall be faultless' (Ps. 19:13 [Hebrew v. 14]). This refers to the most powerful of transgressions.

Q. "'And I shall be clear of great transgression' (Ps. 19:13 [Hebrew v. 14])."

R. Said R. Levi, "David said before the Holy One, blessed be he, 'Lord of the age[s], you are a great God, and, as for me, my sins are great too. It will take a great God to remit and forgive great sins: "For your name's sake, O Lord, pardon my sin, for [your name] is great"'" (Ps. 25:11).

The Righteous Person Must Bear Witness

Beyond the responsibility for sin and the power of prayer, the sages imposed on the faithful a further, critical duty. It is to bear witness. We are responsible not only for what we do, but for what lies in our power to prevent. This message comes to us in a parable related to Lev. 5:1, concerning bearing witness when called upon.

VI:II

1. A. "The partner of a thief hates his own life. He hears the curse [of Lev. 5:1] but discloses nothing" (Prov. 29:24).
   B. The governor of Caesarea would [merely] flog the thieves, but he would execute the fences. The citizens ridiculed him, saying to him, "Do things right! [Kill the thieves too.]"
   C. He went and made a proclamation through the city, saying, "Everybody to the central square."
   D. He brought weasels and put pieces of food before them, but he stopped up the holes [where the weasels would hide their food]. The weasels took the pieces of food, brought them to their holes, and, finding the holes stopped up, brought the pieces of food back to the original place.
   E. This then showed that everything was the fences' fault.
   F. Now, lo, [we have illustrated the matter of Prov. 29:24 on the basis of what the government did.] How can we show the same matter by means of an illustrative case?
   G. Reuben stole from Simeon, and Levi knew about it. [Reuben] said to him, "If you don't squeal on me, we'll go halves."
   H. Later this man [Levi] went to synagogue and heard the voice of the reader [of the Torah passage of the day] saying, "[If anyone sins in that he hears a public adjuration to testify,] and though he is a witness, whether he has seen or come to know the

matter, [yet does not speak, he shall bear his iniquity]" (Lev. 5:1).

I. What should he do? Will he keep silence? But the Torah has already made its decree: ". . . Whether he has seen or come to know. . . ."

Israel's Faith and Israel's Fate

What we see in Leviticus Rabbah is consistent with what we have already observed in Genesis Rabbah: how the sages absorb events into their system of classification. But the sages do more than relate what happens in world empires to the life of Israel. They also show how the everyday affairs of ordinary people symbolize, through action and restraint, the politics of world empires. As a result, the sages relate ordinary everyday life to the greatest concerns of the state. Individuals make history through the thoughts they think and the rules they lay down—and even the food they eat symbolizes large and deep considerations. The protracted passage that follows shows us how the sages explain Israel's history and Israel's way of life as part of a single pattern of meaning. That means that what happens to Israel in politics and what the individual eats for breakfast (so to speak) bear a profound interrelationship. That is an amazing conception, but one that vastly strengthens the religious life by integrating all details into one vast picture—a life of obedience to God's will, humility before the majesty of God. A measure of patience is needed to follow the argument. First we link the four monarchies to Eden. But then we show how the rules governing the beasts Israel may offer on the altar and eat on its table relate to world history. What is important is the negative: the beasts that are excluded. These turn out to stand for the nations of the world, the great empires. Genesis Rabbah has already prepared us for that conception. But—in the majestic and patient passage that follows—we must come to Moses to understand the tight link between history and everyday life. We deal, then, with Deut. 14:7, "the camel, rock badger, hare," which Israel may not eat or offer on the altar. We turn, further, to the pig (Lev. 11:7). Rome is compared to the pig, which looks to be suitable, since it has a cloven hoof, but is invalid, because it does not chew the cud. (Jerome in his commentary to Leviticus makes the same point concerning Israel.) The work on Lev. 4-8 bears its own points of interest. It forms a model for the finding in Scripture of pertinent symbols for one's own time and circumstance, an approach to the reading of the Bible that surely proves relevant in our own time.

Let me briefly review the message of the construction as a whole. This comes in two parts, first the explicit and then the implicit. As to the former, the first claim is that God had told the prophets what would happen to Israel at the hands of the pagan kingdoms, Babylonia, Media, Greece, and Rome. These are further represented by Nebuchadnezzar, Haman, and Alexander for Greece, and Edom or Esau, interchangeably, for Rome. The same vision came from Adam, Abraham, Daniel, and Moses. The same policy toward Israel—oppression, destruction, enslavement, and alienation from the true God—emerged from all four. How does Rome stand out? First, it was made fruitful through the prayer of Isaac in behalf of Esau. Second, Edom is represented by the fourth and final beast. Rome is related through Esau, as Babylonia, Media, and Greece are not. The fourth beast was seen in a vision separate from the first three. It was worst of all and outweighed the rest. In the apocalypticizing of the animals of Lev. 11:4-8/Deut. 14:7 (the camel, rock badger, hare, and pig), the pig, standing for Rome, again emerges as different from the others and more threatening than the rest. Just as the pig pretends to be a clean beast by showing the cloven hoof but in fact is an unclean one, so Rome pretends to be just but in fact governs by thuggery. Edom does not pretend to praise God but only blasphemes; it does not exalt the righteous but kills them. These symbols concede nothing to Christian monotheism and biblicism. Of greatest importance, while all the other beasts bring further ones in their wake, the pig does not: "It does not bring another kingdom after it." It will restore the crown to the one who will truly deserve it, Israel. Esau will be judged by Zion (so Obad. 21). Now, how has the symbolization delivered an implicit message? It is in the treatment of Rome as distinct, but essentially equivalent to the former kingdoms. This seems to me a stunning way of saying that the now-Christian empire in no way requires differentiation from its pagan predecessors. Nothing has changed, except matters have become worse. Beyond Rome, standing in a straight line with the others, lies the true shift in history, the rule of Israel and the cessation of the dominion of the (pagan) nations. We remember that Leviticus Rabbah came to closure, it is generally agreed, around 400 C.E., that is, approximately a century after the Roman Empire in the east had begun to become Christian and half a century after the last attempt to rebuild the Temple in Jerusalem had failed—a tumultuous age indeed. Accordingly, we have had the chance to see how distinctive and striking are the ways in which, in the text at hand, the symbols of animals that stand for the four successive empires of humanity and point towards the messianic time serve for the framers' message. The lesson on how to transform Scripture from a merely historical document of an ancient people into a model for God's perspective on the world today derives not so much from what our sages say as from how they reach their conclusions.

XIII:V

1. A. Said R. Ishmael b. R. Nehemiah, "All the prophets foresaw what the pagan kingdoms would do [to Israel].

    B. "The first man foresaw what the pagan kingdoms would do [to Israel].

    C. "That is in line with the following verse of Scripture: 'A river flowed out of Eden [to water the garden, and there it divided and became four rivers]' (Gen. 2:10). [The four rivers stand for the four kingdoms, Babylonia, Media, Greece, and Rome]."

2. A. R. Tanhuma said it, [and] R. Menahema [in the name of] R. Joshua b. Levi: "The Holy One, blessed be he, will give the cup of reeling to the nations of the world to drink in the world to come.

    B. "That is in line with the following verse of Scripture: 'A river flowed out of Eden' (Gen 2:10), the place from which justice (Hebrew *dyn*) goes forth."

3. A. "[There it divided] and became four rivers" (Gen 2:10): This refers to the four kingdoms.

    B. "The name of the first is Pishon (Hebrew *pswn*); [it is the one which flows around the whole land of Havilah, where there is gold; and the gold of that land is good; bdellium and onyx stone are there]" (Gen. 2:11-12).

    C. This refers to Babylonia, on account [of the reference to Babylonia in the following verse:] "And their [the Babylonians'] horsemen spread themselves (Hebrew *psw*)" (Hab. 1:8).

    D. [It is further] on account of [Nebuchadnezzar's being] a dwarf, shorter than ordinary men by a handbreadth.

    E. ["It is the one which flows around the whole land of Havilah"] (Gen. 2:11).

    F. This [reference to the river's flowing around the whole land] speaks of Nebuchadnezzar, the wicked man, who came up and surrounded the entire Land of Israel, which places its hope in the Holy One, blessed be he.

G. That is in line with the following verse of Scripture: "Hope in God, for I shall again praise him" (Ps. 42:5 [Hebrew v. 6]).

H. "Where there is gold" (Gen. 2:11): This refers to the words of Torah, "which are more to be desired than gold, more than much fine gold" (Ps. 19:10 [Hebrew v. 11]).

I. "And the gold of that land is good" (Gen. 2:12).

J. This teaches that there is no Torah like the Torah that is taught in the Land of Israel, and there is no wisdom like the wisdom that is taught in the Land of Israel.

K. "Bdellium and onyx stone are there" (Gen. 2:12): Scripture, Mishnah, Talmud, and lore.

4. A. "The name of the second river is Gihon; [it is the one which flows around the whole land of Cush]" (Gen. 2:13).

B. This refers to Media, which produced Haman, that wicked man, who spit out venom like a serpent.

C. It is on account of the verse: "On your belly will you go" (Gen. 3:14).

D. "It is the one which flows around the whole land of Cush" (Gen. 2:13).

E. [We know that this refers to Media, because it is said:] "Who rules from India to Cush" (Esth. 1:1).

5. A. "And the name of the third river is Tigris (Hebrew hdql), [which flows east of Assyria]" (Gen. 2:14).

B. This refers to Greece [Syria], which was sharp (Hebrew hd) and speedy (ql) in making its decrees, saying to Israel, "Write on the horn of an ox that you have no portion in the God of Israel."

C. "Which flows east (Hebrew qdmt) of Assyria" (Gen. 2:14).

D. Said R. Huna, "In three aspects the kingdom of Greece was in advance (Hebrew qdmh) of the present evil kingdom [Rome]: in respect to ship-building, the arrangement of camp vigils, and language."

E. Said R. Huna, "Any and every kingdom may be called 'Assyria' (Hebrew ashur), on account of all of their making themselves powerful at Israel's expense."

F. Said R. Yose b. R. Hanina, "Any and every kingdom may be called Nineveh (Hebrew nnwh), on account of their adorning (nwy) themselves at Israel's expense."

G. Said R. Yose b. R. Hanina, "Any and every kingdom may be called Egypt (Hebrew msrym), on account of their oppressing (msyrym) Israel."

6. A. "And the fourth river is the Euphrates (Hebrew *prt*)" (Gen. 2:14).

    B. This refers to Edom [Rome], since it was fruitful (Hebrew *prt*), and multiplied through the prayer of the elder [Isaac at Gen. 27:39].

    C. Another interpretation: It was because it was fruitful and multiplied, and so cramped his world.

    D. Another explanation: Because it was fruitful and multiplied and cramped his son.

    E. Another explanation: Because it was fruitful and multiplied and cramped his house.

    F. Another explanation: "Parat"—because in the end, "I am going to exact a penalty from it."

    G. That is in line with the following verse of Scripture: "I have trodden (Hebrew *pwrh*) the winepress alone" (Isa. 63:3).

7. A. [Genesis Rabbah XLII:II] Abraham foresaw what the evil kingdoms would do [to Israel].

    B. "[As the sun was going down,] a deep sleep fell on Abram; and lo, a dread and great darkness fell upon him]" (Gen. 15:12).

    C. "Dread" (Hebrew *'ymh*) refers to Babylonia, on account of the statement, "Then Nebuchadnezzer was full of fury (*hmh*)" (Dan. 3:19).

    D. "Darkness" refers to Media, which brought darkness to Israel through its decrees: "to destroy, to slay, and to wipe out all the Jews" (Esth. 7:4).

    E. "Great" refers to Greece.

    F. Said R. Judah b. R. Simon, "The verse teaches that the kingdom of Greece set up 127 governors, 127 hyparchs, and 127 commanders."

    G. And rabbis say, "They were 60 in each category."

    H. R. Berekhiah and R. Hanan in support of this position taken by rabbis: "'Who led you through the great terrible wilderness, with its fiery serpents and scorpions and thirsty ground where there was no water]' (Deut. 8:15).

    I. "Just as the scorpion produces eggs by sixties, so the kingdom of Greece would set up its administration in groups of sixty."

    J. "Fell on him" (Gen. 15:12).

    K. This refers to Edom, on account of the following verse: "The earth quakes at the noise of their [Edom's] fall" (Jer. 49:21).

    L. There are those who reverse matters.

    M. "Fear" refers to Edom, on account of the following verse: "And this I saw, a fourth beast, fearful, and terrible" (Dan. 7:7).

    N. "Darkness" refers to Greece, which brought gloom through its decrees. For they said to Israel, "Write on the horn of an ox that you have no portion in the God of Israel."

    O. "Great" refers to Media, on account of the verse: "King Ahasuerus made Haman [the Median] great" (Esth. 3:1).

    P. "Fell on him" refers to Babylonia, on account of the following verse: "Fallen, fallen is Babylonia" (Isa. 21:9).

8. A. Daniel foresaw what the evil kingdoms would do [to Israel].

    B. "Daniel said, I saw in my vision by night, and behold, the four winds of heaven were stirring up the great sea. And four great beasts came up out of the sea, [different from one another. The first was like a lion and had eagles' wings. Then as I looked, its wings were plucked off. . . . And behold, another beast, a second one, like a bear. . . . After this I looked, and lo, another, like a leopard. . . . After this I saw in the night visions, and behold, a fourth beast, terrible and dreadful and exceedingly strong; and it had great iron teeth]" (Dan. 7:2-7).

    C. If you enjoy sufficient merit, it will emerge from the sea, but if not, it will come out of the forest.

    D. The animal that comes up from the sea is not violent, but the one that comes up out of the forest is violent.

    E. Along these same lines: "The boar out of the wood ravages it" (Ps. 80:13 [Hebrew v. 14]).

    F. If you enjoy sufficient merit, it will come from the river, and if not, from the forest.

    G. The animal that comes up from the river is not violent, but the one that comes up out of the forest is violent.

    H. "Different from one another" (Dan. 7:3).

    I. Differing from [hating] one another.

    J. This teaches that every nation that rules in the world hates Israel and reduces them to slavery.

    K. "The first was like a lion [and had eagles' wings]" (Dan. 7:4).

    L. This refers to Babylonia.

    M. Jeremiah saw [Babylonia] as a lion. Then he went and saw it as an eagle.

N. He saw it as a lion: "A lion has come up from his thicket" (Jer. 4:7).

O. And [as an eagle:] "Behold, he shall come up and swoop down as the eagle" (Jer. 49:22).

P. People said to Daniel, "What do you see?"

Q. He said to them, "I see the face like that of a lion and wings like those of an eagle: 'The first was like a lion and had eagles' wings. Then, as I looked, its wings were plucked off, and it was lifted up from the ground [and made to stand upon two feet like a man and the heart of a man was given to it]' (Dan. 7:4).

R. R. Eleazar and R. Ishmael b. R. Nehemiah:

S. R. Eleazar said, "While the entire lion was smitten, its heart was not smitten.

T. "That is in line with the following statement: 'And the heart of a man was given to it' (Dan. 7:4)."

U. And R. Ishmael b. R. Nehemiah said, "Even its heart was smitten, for it is written: 'Let his heart be changed from a man's' (Dan. 4:16 [Aramaic v. 13])."

X. "And behold, another beast, a second one, like a bear. [It was raised up one side; it had three ribs in its mouth between its teeth, and it was told, 'Arise, devour much flesh']" (Dan. 7:5).

Y. This refers to Media.

Z. Said R. Yohanan, "It is like a bear."

AA. It is written: "similar to a wolf" (Aramaic *db*); thus, "And a wolf was there."

BB. That is in accord with the view of R. Yohanan, for R. Yohanan said, "'Therefore a lion out of the forest [slays them]' (Jer. 5:6): This refers to Babylonia.

CC. "'A wolf of the desert spoils them' (Jer. 5:6) refers to Media.

DD. "'A leopard watches over their cities' (Jer. 5:6) refers to Greece.

EE. "'Whoever goes out from them will be savaged' (Jer. 5:6) refers to Edom.

FF. "Why so? 'Because their transgressions are many, and their backslidings still more' (Jer. 5:6)."

GG. "After this, I looked, and lo, another, like a leopard [with four wings of a bird on its back; and the beast had four heads; and dominion was given to it]" (Dan. 7:6).

HH. This [leopard] refers to Greece, which persisted impudently in making harsh decrees, saying to Israel, "Write on the horn of an ox that you have no share in the God of Israel."

II. "After this I saw in the night visions, and behold, a fourth beast, terrible and dreadful and exceedingly strong; [and it had great iron teeth; it devoured and broke in pieces and stamped the residue with its feet. It was different from all the beasts that were before it; and it had ten horns]" (Dan. 7:7).

JJ. This refers to Edom [Rome].

KK. Daniel saw the first three visions on one night, and this one he saw on another night. Now why was that the case?

LL. R. Yohanan and R. Simeon b. Laqish:

MM. R. Yohanan said, "It is because the fourth beast weighed as much as the first three."

NN. And R. Simeon b. Laqish said, "It outweighed them."

OO. R. Yohanan objected to R. Simeon b. Laqish, "'Prophesy, therefore, son of man; clap your hands [and let the sword come down twice, yea thrice. The sword for those to be slain; it is the sword for the great slaughter, which encompasses them]' (Ezek. 21:14-15 [Hebrew vv. 19-20]). [So the single sword of Rome weighs against the three others]."

PP. And R. Simeon b. Laqish, how does he interpret the same passage? He notes that [the threefold sword] is doubled (Ezek. 21:14 [Hebrew v. 19]), [thus outweighs the three swords, equally twice their strength].

9. A. Moses foresaw what the evil kingdoms would do [to Israel].

B. "The camel, rock badger, and hare" (Deut. 14:7). [Compare: "Nevertheless, among those that chew the cud or part the hoof, you shall not eat these: the camel, because it chews the cud but does not part the hoof, is unclean to you. The rock badger, because it chews the cud but does not part the hoof, is unclean to you. And the hare, because it chews the cud but does not part the hoof, is unclean to you, and the pig, because it parts the hoof and is cloven-footed, but does not chew the cud, is unclean to you" (Lev. 11:4-7).]

C. "The camel (Hebrew *gml*)" refers to Babylonia, [in line with the following verse of Scripture: "O daughter of Babylonia, you who are to be devastated!] Happy will be he who requites (*gml*) you, with what you have done to us" (Ps. 137:8).

D. "The rock badger" (Deut. 14:7): This refers to Media.

E. Rabbis and R. Judah b. R. Simon:

F. Rabbis say, "Just as the rock badger exhibits traits of unclean-ness and traits of cleanness, so the kingdom of Media produced both a righteous man and a wicked one."

G. Said R. Judah b. R. Simon, "The last Darius was Esther's son. He was clean on his mother's side and unclean on his father's side."

H. "The hare" (Deut 14:7): This refers to Greece. The mother of King Ptolemy was named "Hare" [Greek *lagos*].

I. "The pig" (Deut. 14:7): This refers to Edom [Rome].

J. Moses made mention of the first three in a single verse and the final one in a verse by itself [(Deut. 14:7-8)]. Why so?

K. R. Yohanan and R. Simeon b. Laqish:

L. R. Yohanan said, "It is because [the pig] is equivalent to the other three."

M. And R. Simeon b. Laqish said, "It is because it outweighs them."

N. R. Yohanan objected to R. Simeon b. Laqish, "'Prophesy, therefore, son of man, clap your hands [and let the sword come down twice, yea thrice]' (Ezek. 21:14 [Hebrew v. 19])."

O. And how does R. Simeon b. Laqish interpret the same passage? He notes that [the threefold sword] is doubled (Ezek. 21:14 [Hebrew v. 19]).

10. A. [Genesis Rabbah LXV:I:] R. Phineas and R. Hilqiah in the name of R. Simon: "Among all the prophets, only two of them revealed [the true evil of Rome], Asaph and Moses.

B. "Asaph said, 'The pig out of the wood ravages it' (Ps. 80:13 [Hebrew v. 14]).

C. "Moses said, 'And the pig, [because it parts the hoof and is cloven-footed but does not chew the cud]' (Lev. 11:7).

D. "Why is [Rome] compared to a pig?

E. "It is to teach you the following: Just as, when a pig crouches and produces its hooves, it is as if to say, 'See how I am clean [since I have a cloven hoof],' so this evil kingdom takes pride, seizes by violence, and steals, and then gives the appearance of establishing a tribunal for justice."

F. There was the case of a ruler in Caesarea, who put thieves, adulterers, and sorcerers to death, while at the same time telling his counsellor, "That same man [I] did all these three things on a single night."

11. A. Another interpretation: "The camel" (Lev. 11:4).

   B. This refers to Babylonia.

   C. "Because it chews the cud [but does not part the hoof]" (Lev. 11:4).

   D. For it brings forth praises [with its throat] of the Holy One, blessed be he. [The Hebrew words for "chew the cud" (literally, "bring up cud") are now understood to mean "give praise." Hebrew *grh* is connected with *grwn*, "throat," hence, "bring forth (sounds of praise through) the throat."]

   E. R. Berekhiah and R. Helbo in the name of R. Ishmael b. R. Nahman: "Whatever [praise of God] David [in writing a psalm] treated singly [item by item], that wicked man [Nebuchadnezzar] lumped together in a single verse.

   F. " 'Now I, Nebuchadnezzar, praise and extol and honor the King of heaven; for all his works are right and his ways are just; and those who walk in pride he is able to abase' (Dan. 4:37 [Aramaic v. 34]).

   G. " 'Praise': 'O Jerusalem, praise the Lord' (Ps. 147:12).

   H. " 'Extol': 'I shall extol you, O Lord, for you have brought me low' (Ps. 30:1 [Hebrew v. 2]).

   I. " 'Honor the king of heaven': 'The Lord reigns; let the peoples tremble! He sits enthroned upon the cherubim; let the earth quake' (Ps. 99:1).

   J. " 'For all his works are right': 'For the sake of thy steadfast love and thy faithfulness' (Ps. 115:1).

   K. " 'And his ways are just': 'He will judge the peoples with equity' (Ps. 96:10).

   L. " 'And those who walk in pride': 'The Lord reigns; he is robed in majesty; the Lord is robed, he is girded with strength' (Ps. 93:1).

   M. " 'He is able to abase': 'All the horns of the wicked he will cut off' (Ps. 75:10 [Hebrew v. 11])."

   N. "The rock badger" (Lev. 11:5): This refers to Media.

   O. "For it chews the cud": For it gives praise to the Holy One, blessed be he: "Thus says Cyrus, king of Persia, 'All the kingdoms of the earth has the Lord, the God of the heaven, given me'" (Ezra 1:2).

   P. "The hare": This refers to Greece.

   Q. "For it chews the cud": For it gives praise to the Holy One, blessed be he.

   R. Alexander the Macedonian, when he saw Simeon the Righteous, said, "Blessed be the God of Simeon the Righteous."

S. "The pig" (Lev. 11:7): This refers to Edom.

T. "For it does not chew the cud": For it does not give praise to the Holy One, blessed be he.

U. And it is not enough that it does not give praise, but it blasphemes and swears violently, saying, "Whom do I have in heaven, and with you I want nothing on earth" (Ps. 73:25).

12. A. Another interpretation [of Hebrew *grh*, 'cud,' now with reference to *gr*, 'stranger']:

B. "The camel" (Lev. 11:4): This refers to Babylonia.

C. "For it chews the cud [now: brings up the stranger]": For it exalts righteous men: "And Daniel was in the gate of the king" (Dan. 2:49).

D. "The rock badger" (Lev. 11:5): This refers to Media.

E. "For it brings up the stranger": For it exalts righteous men: "Mordecai sat at the gate of the king" (Esth. 2:19).

F. "The hare" (Lev. 11:6): This refers to Greece.

G. "For it brings up the stranger": For it exalts the righteous.

H. When Alexander of Macedonia saw Simeon the Righteous, he would rise up on his feet. They said to him, "Can't you see the Jew, that you stand up before this Jew?"

I. He said to them, "When I go forth to battle, I see something like this man's visage, and I conquer."

J. "The pig" (Lev. 11:7): This refers to Rome.

K. "But it does not bring up the stranger": For it does not exalt the righteous.

L. And it is not enough that it does not exalt them, but it kills them.

M. That is in line with the following verse of Scripture: "I was angry with my people, I profaned my heritage; I gave them into your hand, you showed them no mercy; on the aged you made your yoke exceedingly heavy" (Isa. 47:6).

N. This refers to R. Aqiba and his colleagues.

13. A. Another interpretation [now treating "bring up the cud" (Hebrew *gr*) as "bring along in its train" (*grr*)]:

B. "The camel" (Lev. 11:4): This refers to Babylonia.

C. "Which brings along in its train": For it brought along another kingdom after it.

D. "The rock badger" (Lev. 11:5): This refers to Media.

E. "Which brings along in its train": For it brought along another kingdom after it.

F. "The hare" (Lev. 11:6): This refers to Greece.

G. "Which brings along in its train": For it brought along another kingdom after it.

H. "The pig" (Lev. 11:7): This refers to Rome.

I. "Which does not bring along in its train": For it did not bring along another kingdom after it.

J. And why is it then called "pig" (Hebrew *hzyr*)? For it restores (*mhzrt*) the crown to the one who truly should have it [namely, Israel, whose dominion will begin when the rule of Rome ends].

K. That is in line with the following verse of Scripture: "And saviors will come up on Mount Zion to judge the Mountain of Esau [Rome], and the kingdom will then belong to the Lord" (Obad. 21).

PART THREE

NUMBERS

Introduction to Numbers as Read in Sifré to Numbers

We have now examined how our sages read in light of events of their own day two quite divergent biblical books, Genesis, a narrative, and Leviticus, a handbook for the priesthood. In both pentateuchal books, as our sages interpreted them, we are able to see an important trait with which, in our own day, we are able to identify. It is the power of our sages to bring to Scripture the public and communal issues of the time—source of their most profound anguish—and to find in Scripture not merely reassurance but a well-founded faith—a faith that, in its way, rested on the most secure scientific thinking of the day. When we turn to how our sages read the book of Numbers, as illustrated in Sifré to Numbers (a work of the third or fourth century—we do not know exactly when it was compiled), we review the familiar approaches. We see how our sages derived from the book of Numbers lessons of critical relevance to their own day. But we see something more, and to understand what that is, I must take a sizable detour. For we now enter into the inner life, the private issues, of the sages themselves. One of the passages we shall review goes over the ground of an intensely debated theological issue particular to our sages and their day. Yet as soon as I have spelled it out, the reader will understand how remarkably current the issue remains: the character and standing of Scripture, weighed against the power of human reason. So, in our terms, we shall consider the issue (as they phrased it) of reason versus faith.

In looking at how these same sages read the book of Numbers we find an example of yet another approach to Scripture. Here our sages read Scripture in an appeal for assistance in settling issues heatedly debated among the sages themselves. So we come across a more private, a more inward-looking set of questions, those that troubled the waters of the sages' own world. This approach too presents a familiar face to us. For Scripture is there not only for the world outside, but—far more—for the faithful within, the church and the synagogue as the faithful work out the issues of the faith. That self-evident fact allows us to appreciate our sages' way of asking Scripture for evidence on an issue that troubled them very profoundly. It was the status and standing of the Mishnah, a second-century philosophical law-code that the sages knew as the foundation document of the life of Israel, the Jewish people. When theologians today take up biblical passages in working out correct theology, they show us what, in the setting of late antiquity, the Judaic sages also illustrate.

To explain the inward-facing issue at hand, I must point to a particular trait of the Mishnah that will surprise readers today. Since we have already encountered a sizable sample of our sages' writing, we realize how constant and persistent was their appeal to Scripture. They lavishly cited verses of Scripture at every turn. But that paramount trait of the compilations of scriptural exegeses does not, overall, characterize the Mishnah. Rather, the authors of that document cite Scripture only sparingly and, in general, make their statements in their own terms, not buttressed by scriptural prooftexts. This characteristic way of laying down the law led to the question of the authority and the standing of the Mishnah and its statement of Israel's polity. For the Jewish people had long framed rules in line with scriptural prooftexts, and some found surprising the failure of the Mishnah's authors to do so.

One formulation of the issue concerns us here, because it is at the center of our sages' reading of the book of Numbers. I will frame matters as a set of contradictory propositions.

(1) All truth derives from Scripture. Therefore no statement (e.g., of a rule of law or theology) can be valid unless it rests upon the authority and foundation of a statement of Scripture. The truth derives from exegesis of Scripture, which is the sole source of reliable and ultimately valid theology and law.

(2) Reason serves as a source of truth, in addition to Scripture. The human mind, guided by the givens of Scripture, may through appropriate logic reach reliable and valid conclusions.

This argument, drawing us deep into the inner intellectual life of the sages themselves, will not prove unfamiliar—even in its own terms—to contemporary religious people. The conflicts of faith and reason, of religion and science, form counterparts, in terms of our own day, to what was at issue. For when religious thinkers maintained, as some did in antiquity, that Scripture was the sole reliable source of truth, they took a position not distant from religious thinkers of our own time who turn to Scripture for truth about topics covered also in science, philosophy, and history. So too, when religious thinkers held—as did many of our sages—that human logic serves as well as Scripture to provide truth, they appealed to the notion that the human mind, in God's likeness, after God's image, served too. In our own time religious scientists, philosophers, and historians point to the power of science, philosophy, and history to bring us to an appreciation of the greatness of God, Creator of the world and providential ruler of human history.

The argument therefore centers on issues that are not entirely alien to us. But the terms of the argument, in detail, will prove somewhat less immediately accessible than in the instance of the earlier compilations of scriptural exegesis. Sifré to Numbers is more technical, on the one side, and less open and public in its messages, on the other. Yet there is a key to the lock. It is in the recurrent rhetorical patterns of discourse. If we see how the framers of the document repeatedly formulated their ideas, we shall find ready access to what was on their minds. I characterize the formal traits of Sifré to Numbers, which may be reduced to two, as a commentary. First is the exegesis of a verse in the book of Numbers in terms of the theme or problems of that verse, hence, "intrinsic exegesis." Second is the exegesis of a verse in Numbers in terms of a theme or polemic not particular to that verse, hence, "extrinsic exegesis." That simple classification will allow us to see what is on the minds of the authorship of this reworking of the book of Numbers. In our sample of the document, we shall see concrete instances of these modes of reading verses of Scripture.

The forms of extrinsic exegesis. The implicit message of the external category proves simple to define, since the several extrinsic classifications turn out to form a cogent polemic. The recurrent polemic of external exegesis may be stated as follows.

(1) *The syllogistic composition.* As we know from our reading of Genesis Rabbah and Leviticus Rabbah, Scripture supplies hard facts, which, properly classified, generate syllogisms. By collecting and classifying facts of Scripture, therefore, we may produce firm laws of history, society, and Israel's everyday life. The diverse compositions in which verses from various books of the Scriptures are compiled in a list of evidence for a given proposition—whatever the character or purpose of that proposition—make that one point. And given their power and cogency, they make the point stick.

(2) *The fallability of reason unguided by scriptural exegesis.* Scripture alone supplies reliable basis for speculation. Laws cannot be generated by reason or logic unguided by Scripture. Efforts at classification and contrastive-analogical exegesis, in which Scripture does not supply the solution to all problems, prove few and far between (and always in Ishmael's name, for whatever that is worth). This polemic forms the obverse of the point above.

So when extrinsic issues intervene in the exegetical process, they coalesce to make a single point. The recurrent and implicit message of the forms of external exegesis may be stated as follows.

Scripture stands paramount; logic, reason, and analytical processes of classification and differentiation are secondary. Reason not built on scriptural foundations yields uncertain results. The Mishnah itself demands scriptural bases.

The forms of intrinsic exegesis. What about the polemic present in the intrinsic exegetical exercises? This clearly does not allow for ready characterization. At least three intrinsic exegetical exercises focus on the use of logic (specifically, the logic of classification, comparison and contrast of species of a genus) in the explanation of the meaning of verses of the book of Numbers. The internal dialectical mode, moving from point to point as logic dictates, underlines the main point already stated: logic produces possibilities, and Scripture chooses among them. Again, the question, Why is this passage stated? commonly produces an answer generated by further verses of Scripture (for example, This matter is stated here to clarify what otherwise would be confusion left in the wake of other verses). So Scripture produces problems of confusion and duplication, and Scripture—and not logic, not differentiation, not classification—solves those problems.

To state matters simply:

Scripture is complete, harmonious, perfect (in contemporary language, Scripture is inerrant). Logic not only does not generate truth beyond the limits of Scripture but also plays no important role in the harmonization of difficulties yielded by what appear to be duplications or disharmonies.

These forms of internal exegesis then make the same point as do the extrinsic ones: Scripture is inerrant.

Yet one more formal pattern exists, the single most profuse category of exegesis: (1) a verse of Scripture or a clause is cited, followed by (2) a brief statement of the meaning at hand. Here I see no unifying polemic in favor of, or against, a given proposition. The most common form also proves the least pointed: X bears this meaning, Y bears that meaning; or, as we have seen, citation of verse X, followed by ["what this means is"]. . . . Whether simple or elaborate, the upshot is the same. And yet, I argue, this simple form bears the most profound statement of all.

This may be explained by asking a question: What can be at issue when no polemic expressed in the formal traits of syntax and logic finds its way to the surface? What do I do when I merely clarify a phrase? Or, to frame the question more logically: What premises must validate my

intervention, that is, my willingness to undertake to explain the meaning
of a verse of Scripture? These seem to me propositions that must serve to
justify the labor of intrinsic exegesis as we have seen its results here.

(1) My independent judgment bears weight and produces meaning. I—that is,
my mind—therefore may join in the process.

(2) God's revelation to Moses at Sinai requires my intervention. I have the
role, and the right, to say what that revelation means.

(3) What validates my entry into the process of revelation is the correspondence between the logic of my mind and the logic of the document. Only if I
think in accord with the logic of the revealed Torah can my thought processes
join issue in clarifying what is at hand: the unfolding of God's will in the Torah. If
the Torah does not make statements in accord with a syntax and a grammar that I
know, I cannot so understand the Torah as to explain its meaning. But if I can
join in the discourse of the Torah, it is because I speak the same language of
thought: syntax and grammar at the deepest levels of my intellect.

(4) Then to state matters affirmatively and finally: Since a shared logic of
syntax and grammar joins my mind to the mind of God as revealed in the Torah, I
can say what a sentence of the Torah means. So I too can amplify, clarify,
expand, revise, rework—that is to say, create a commentary. It follows that the
intrinsic exegetical forms stand for a single proposition.

*While Scripture stands paramount, and logic, reason, and analytical pro-
cesses of classification and differentiation secondary, nonetheless, the human
mind joins God's mind when a person receives and sets forth the Torah.*

The purpose of the authorship of Sifré to Numbers may be stated in a
few words. Beyond all concrete propositions, the document as a whole
through its fixed and recurrent formal preferences or literary structures
makes two complementary points.

(1) Reason unaided by Scripture produces uncertain propositions.
(2) Reason operating within the limits of Scripture produces truth.

To whom do these moderate and balanced propositions matter? The
sages in particular, I think. The polemic addresses arguments internal to
their circles. If we contrast the polemic of our document about the
balance between revelation and reason, Torah and logic, with the polemic of another canonical document (that is, another document within
the oral Torah) about some other topic altogether, the contrast will tell.
Then and only then shall we see the choices people faced. In that way we
shall appreciate the particular choice the authorship at hand has made.
With the perspective provided by an exercise of comparison, we shall see

how truly remarkable a document we have in Sifré to Numbers. By itself the book supplies facts. Seen in context, the book makes points. So we require a context of comparison.

Having characterized the position, based on the formal rhetoric, of Sifré to Numbers, I turn to the description of another document of the same general venue, a canonical document produced by the sages some time before the closure of the Talmud of Babylonia in about 600 c.e. but after the formation of the Mishnah in about 200, thus a document emerging around 400, in the time of the Talmud of the Land of Israel and perhaps of Sifré to Numbers. It is, of course, Genesis Rabbah, because we are familiar with the traits of literature and theology of that document. We therefore compare two pieces of writing of approximately the same period (plus or minus a hundred years).

To briefly review the overall characterization of Genesis Rabbah presented earlier, its authorship focuses its discourse on the proposition that the book of Genesis speaks to the life and historical condition of Israel, the Jewish people. The entire narrative of Genesis is so formed as to point toward the sacred history of Israel: its slavery and redemption, its coming Temple in Jerusalem, its exile and salvation at the end of time. The powerful message of Genesis in the pages of Genesis Rabbah proclaims that the world's creation commenced a single, straight line of events, leading in the end to the salvation of Israel and through Israel all humanity. If I had to point to the single most important proposition of Genesis Rabbah, it is that in the story of the beginnings of creation, humanity, and Israel we find the message of the meaning and end of the life of the Jewish people. The deeds of the founders supply signals for the children about what is going to come in the future. If the sages could announce a single syllogism and argue it systematically, that is the proposition on which they would insist.

We now ask ourselves a simple question: Is the message of Sifré to Numbers the same as that of Genesis Rabbah (or of Leviticus Rabbah, for that matter)? The answer is obvious. No, these are different books. They make different points in answering different questions. In plan and in program they yield more contrasts than comparisons. Why does that fact matter to my argument? Since these are different books, which do use different forms to deliver different messages, it must follow that there is nothing routine or given or to be predicted about the point that the authorship of Sifré to Numbers wishes to make. It is not a point that is simply "there to be made." It is a striking and original point. When the sages who produced Genesis Rabbah read Genesis, they made a different point from the one at hand.

So contrasting the one composition with the other shows us that each composition bears its own distinctive traits—traits of mind, traits of plan, traits of program. Once we characterize the persistent polemic of Sifré to Numbers and then compare that polemic to the characteristic point of argument of Genesis Rabbah (and, as it happens, Leviticus Rabbah as well), we see that our document has chosen forms to advance its own distinctive, substantive argument. Its exegetical program points, explicitly in extrinsic exegesis, implicitly in intrinsic exegesis, to a single point, and that point is made on every page.

Inner-directed, facing issues of the interior life of the community vis-à-vis revelation and the sanctification of the life of the nation, Sifré to Numbers is centered on issues urgent to the sages themselves. For to whom are the debates about the relationship between Torah and logic, reason and revelation, going to make a difference, if not to the intellectuals of the textual community at hand? Within the same classification scheme, Genesis Rabbah and Leviticus Rabbah appear outer-directed, addressing issues of history and salvation, taking up critical concerns of the public life of the nation vis-à-vis history and the world beyond. Sifré to Numbers addresses sanctification; Genesis Rabbah and Leviticus Rabbah, salvation.

The documents, we now see, do not merely assemble this and that, forming a hodgepodge of things people happen to have said. In the case of each document we can answer the question: Why this, not that? Genesis Rabbah, Leviticus Rabbah, and Sifré to Numbers are not compilations but compositions; seen as a group, therefore, (to state matters negatively) they are not essentially the same, lacking all viewpoint, serving a single undifferentiated task of collecting and arranging whatever was at hand. Quite to the contrary, Genesis Rabbah, Leviticus Rabbah, and Sifré to Numbers emerge as rich in differences from one another and sharply defined each through its distinctive viewpoints and particular polemics, on the one side, and formal and aesthetic qualities, on the other. And yet Genesis Rabbah, Leviticus Rabbah, and Sifré to Numbers comprise separate books that all together make a single statement.

The Power of Sin

Sin is a two-sided matter. On the one side, the human being is responsible for it. On the other, God forgives sin, so that sin does not permanently estrange God from humanity or humanity from God. In the context of the stories of Numbers that concern cultic cleanness and uncleanness, this point is made in a very specific way. Even though Israel becomes unclean, God is still within the camp. Nonetheless, sin does have the power to place a barrier between humanity and God, and that barrier must be taken away. We take up a polemic: Israel is beloved, even though Israel sins. I:X.1 introduces the theological evaluation of the theme at hand, uncleanness. While Israelites are subject to uncleanness, that marks God's love for them: God loves them even though they may become unclean. This point is made by a series of facts: prooftexts. Nothing, then, is particular to our passage. We have moved on to a general theme and expressed it as a syllogism proved by a list of facts. I:X.2 goes on to another proposition independent of the present context but, of course, relevant to it. It is that uncleanness marks sin, and the fact that Israelites can become unclean indicates that they commit sin. Joined to I:X.1, the larger proposition is powerful: while Israel sins, God still dwells among them. I:X.3 completes the matter. Because of sin Israel loses its faith in God. The mark of regeneration then is their capacity to relate to God. Two further points are made. First, the Israelites obeyed God. Second, even the sinners among them, affected by uncleanness, submitted without complaint to God's will.

I:X

1. A. " '[You shall put out both male and female, putting them outside the camp, that they may not defile their camp,] in the midst of which I dwell.' [And the people of Israel did so and drove them outside the camp; as the Lord said to Moses, so the people of Israel did]" (Num. 5:3-4).

   B. So beloved is Israel that even though they may become unclean, the Presence of God remains among them.

    C. And so Scripture states: ". . . Who dwells with them in the midst of their uncleanness" (Lev. 16:16).

    D. And further: ". . . By making my sanctuary unclean, which [nonetheless] is in their midst " (Lev. 15:31).

    E. And it further says: ". . . That they may not defile their camp, in the midst of which I dwell" (Num. 5:3-4).

    F. And it further says: "You shall not defile the land in which you live, in the midst of which I dwell; for I the Lord dwell in the midst of the people of Israel" (Num. 35:34).

2. A. R. Yose the Galilean says, "Come and take note of how great is the power of sin. For before the people had laid hands on transgression, people afflicted with flux and lepers were not located among them, but after they had laid hands on transgression, people afflicted with flux and lepers did find a place among them.

    B. "Accordingly, we learn that these three events took place on one and the same day: [transgression, the presence of those afflicted with flux, the development of leprosy among the people]."

3. A. R. Simeon b. Yohai says, "Come and take note of how great is the power of sin. For before the people had laid hands on transgression, what is stated in their regard?

    B. " 'Now the appearance of the glory of the Lord was like a devouring fire on the top of the mountain in the sight of the people of Israel' (Exod. 24:17).

    C. "Nonetheless, the people did not fear nor were they afraid.

    D. "But once they had laid hands on transgression, what is said in their regard?

    E. " 'And when Aaron and all the people of Israel saw Moses, behold, the skin of his face shone, and they were afraid to come near him' (Exod. 34:30)."

I:XI

1. A. " '[You shall put out both male and female, putting them outside the camp, that they may not defile their camp, in the midst of which I dwell.' And the people of Israel did so and drove them outside the camp; as the Lord said to Moses,] so the people of Israel did" (Num. 5:3-4):

      B. This statement, [". . . And the people of Israel did so,"] serves to recount praise for the Israelites, for just as Moses instructed them, so did they do.

2. A. Scripture states: ". . . As the Lord said to Moses, so the people of Israel did."

      B. What this teaches is that even the unclean people did not register opposition [but accepted the decree without complaint].

The Power of Reason

We come to an example of that rather unfamiliar issue, whether truth may come from human reason or solely from Scripture. In what follows the focus is upon an issue that applies to all exegeses: Is exegesis necessary at all, or can logic, independent of the evidence of scriptural verses, reach firm and reliable conclusions? The formal indicator is the presence of the question, in one of several versions: Is it not a matter of logic? That is the never-failing formal indicator. From that clause we invariably move on to a set of arguments of a highly formalized character on taxonomic classification: What is like, or unlike? What is like follows a given rule, what is unlike follows the opposite rule, and it is for us to see whether the likenesses or unlikenesses prevail.

The issue before us takes second place to the interest in the mode of argument. It has to do with whether one may offer two species offerings of animal sacrifices at one and the same time. The alternative is that each type of sacrifice has to be brought entirely by itself, not in conjunction with some other. What we see is how this issue is worked out in two ways. First, we look for the answer to the question by employing our powers of reasoning (for example, by comparison and contrast, or by analogy and the contrary to analogy). Then we resort to Scripture. Issi b. Aqabia's proof, CVII:III.3, is that only Scripture can give reliable guidance as to the law. The issue again is whether the beasts for the specified offerings encompass both sheep and goats, or whether one may bring two sheep or two goats. The exercise presents the usual frustrations, since each analogy is shown to be inadequate. In consequence, argument by analogy alone does not suffice, and only a clear exegesis of Scripture settles the question.

As we see, there is no interest only in the explanation of the cited verses or even of their topic. The real issue—the generative and precipitating intellectual program of the pericope—lies elsewhere. It is whether or not logic alone suffices. That issue is extrinsic to the passage at hand. But it occurs throughout our document and forms one of its recurrent formal choices. The interest of the contemporary reader focuses not only upon the rather general example of how, in olden times, the rabbis worked out their issues. It is also a good instance of a mode of reasoning, in response to Scripture, that people may employ today: looking for analogies and contrasts. That appeal to Scripture for insight into today's issues, after all, assumes that Scripture not only applies. It also turns today's life into an analogy for the eternal patterns provided by Scripture. Is our case like theirs? If it is, then we logically invoke Scripture's rule or principle, and, if not, we invoke the opposite of that rule or principle. This mode of creative reasoning within the framework of Scripture is still open to us.

CVII:III

3. A. Issi b. Aqabia says, "'. . . To the Lord from the herd or from the flock . . . to make a pleasing odor to the Lord' means from this species by itself or from that species by itself.

   B. "You say that it means from this species by itself or from that species by itself.

   C. "But perhaps one may bring both simultaneously?

   D. "For there is an argument a fortiori: Now if the lambs brought for the Pentecost offering (which are brought in pairs) are valid if they come from a single species, a burnt offering (which is not brought in a pair [but is brought all by itself]) surely should be valid if it is of the same species as [the species of the other beast which accompanies it]!

   E. "No, if you have stated that rule in the case of the two lambs brought for Pentecost—concerning which Scripture imposed fewer requirements in connection with bringing them, and so validated them even if they come from a single species—will you say the same of the burnt offering, in which case Scripture has imposed more requirements in connection with the offering? Therefore it should not be valid unless it [and the beast accompanying it] derive from two different species.

   F. "Now the goats brought on the Day of Atonement and those brought on the New Month should prove the contrary. For Scripture has imposed on those offerings multiple requirements, and yet they are valid if they all come of a single species. So they should provide a valid analogy for the burnt offering, so that, even though it comes along with numerous requirements, it too should be valid if it [and the beasts accompanying it] come from a single species.

G. "No, if you have stated that rule concerning the goats brought on the Day of Atonement and those brought on the New Month, for even though Scripture has imposed on those offerings multiple requirements, they are not brought on every day of the year [but only on specified occasions], and therefore they all may derive from a single species. But will you say the same of the burnt offering, for, even though it comes along with numerous requirements, it may be offered on every day of the year? Therefore it should be valid only if it is accompanied by beasts of other species.

H. "Lo, a sin offering will prove to the contrary. For in its regard Scripture has imposed numerous requirements, and it may be offered on every day of the year, and it may come only if it is from a single species. So that should prove the rule for the burnt offering, in which case—even though Scripture has imposed numerous requirements, and even though it is brought every day of the year—it should be valid only if it derives from a single species.

I. "No, if you have stated that rule concerning the sin offering—on which Scripture has imposed limitations, since it may not be brought by reason of a vow or a freewill offering, and therefore it is valid only if it derives from a single species—will you say the same of the burnt offering, which is available for a variety of purposes, since it may be brought in fulfilment of a vow or as a freewill offering? Therefore it should be valid only if it derives from a single species.

J. "Why then is it necessary for Scripture to specify: '. . . To the Lord from the herd or from the flock . . . to make a pleasing odor to the Lord,' meaning 'from this species by itself or from that species by itself.'"

God Rewards Righteousness

The story of God's punishing Miriam for gossiping against her brother, Moses, lays stress on God's role in the process. Miriam sinned, but she was forgiven. Not only so, but—our sages notice—the entire nation waited while Miriam worked out her penance, and only afterward did the nation break camp and proceed on its pilgrimage to the promised land. So the people did not leave behind the sinner but awaited her penance and reconciliation with God. Our sages ask why this was so. They answer in a remarkably relevant way: Because Miriam, in her time, waited on her brother Moses to make certain that—when he was in the ark in the river—he was picked up and brought to safety, so the nation, Israel, waited on her. And this leads to the further truth that God rewards righteousness, as much as punishing sin. The teaching is stated as follows: By the measure that one metes out to others one himself is measured as well. That is to say, there is a measure of divine justice that takes account of human righteousness. We are what we do, and what we do matters to God.

CVI:II

1. A. "Let her be shut up" (Num. 12:14):
   B. The Holy One, blessed be he, shut her up; the Holy One, blessed be he, declared her unclean; and the Holy One, blessed be he, finally declared her clean.
2. A. ". . . Seven days, and the people did not set out on the march" (Num. 12:15):
   B. This teaches that by the measure that one metes out to others one himself is measured as well.
   C. Miriam waited for Moses a single hour, as it is said: "And his sister stood off at a distance" (Exod. 2:4). Therefore the Omnipresent held up the Presence of God and the ark, the priests and the Levites and the Israelites and the seven clouds of glory, as it is said: "And the people did not set out on the march till Miriam was brought in again."

    D. Joseph had the merit of attending to the bones of his father, and among his brothers there was no greater than he, as it is said: "And Joseph went up to bury his father, and with him went up chariots and horsemen" (Gen. 50:7-9). Who among us is greater than Joseph, and Moses alone in his own person took charge of his [Joseph's] bones.

    E. Moses had the merit of attending to the bones of Joseph, and in Israel there was no greater than he, as it is said: "And Moses took the bones of Joseph" (Exod. 13:19).

    F. Whom do we have greater than Moses, of whose bones only the Holy One, blessed be he, took care, as it is said: "And he buried him in the valley in the land of Nebo" (Deut. 34:6).

3. A. R. Judah says, "Were it not stated in an explicit verse of Scripture, it would not be possible to make such a statement at all:

    B. "Lo, Scripture says: 'Go up this mount Abarim, Mount Nebo in Moab . . . On this mountain you shall die . . .' (Deut. 32:49-50). That mountain fell into the inheritance of the sons of Reuben, as it is said: 'The Reubenites built Heshbon, Elealeh, Kiriathaim, Nebo' (Num. 32:37).

    C. "But Moses was in fact buried only in the inheritance of Gad, as it is said: 'Of Gad he said, "Blessed be Gad in his wide domain. He couches like a lion, tearing an arm or a scalp. He chose the best for himself, for to him was allotted a ruler's portion, when the chiefs of the people were assembled together. [He did what the Lord deemed right, observing his ordinances for Israel]'" (Deut. 33:20-21).

    D. "This teaches that Moses was carried in the hand of the Holy One, blessed be he, for four miles from the portion of Reuben to the portion of Gad, and the ministering angels praised him, saying, '"He did what the Lord deemed right, observing his ordinances for Israel"' (Deut. 33:20-21).

    E. "And not only so, but all the righteous does the Holy One, blessed be he, gather in, as it is said: 'Your own righteousness shall be your vanguard and the glory of the Lord your rearguard' (Isa. 58:8)."

When Verses Conflict

Christians serious about the Bible read the text with care. They therefore notice passages in which Scripture seems to contain contradictions, saying one thing in one place and the opposite in some other. Our sages faced the same problem and they systematically and in a critical spirit confronted it. In what follows we see how our sages contrast two verses of Scripture that seem to contradict one another. For example, the blessing of the priest asks God "to lift up his countenance upon you." But Scripture elsewhere says, "Who will not lift up one's countenance." The sense in the latter passage is that God will not show favoritism. But the sense of the former is that God is asked to show favor. The two are reconciled: when Israel does God's will, then God will show God's "countenance," or "face," in the sense we met earlier. When Israel does not, then God will not "lift up a face," in the Hebrew sense of showing favor or even favoritism. The fixed pattern runs through nearly the whole of the composition, making one point time and again. The distinctions form the center of interest—before, after the decree—and the exegesis of the base verse and of the intersecting verse plays scarcely any role. That same point then is worked out at some length, this time through other distinctions and modes of harmonization. God judges humanity. Before the decree has come forth, there can be prayer or mercy or favor. But afterward, God's will be done: Amen. And, as we see in the unfolding of this rich passage, the greatest good that God can give is peace. In this context, it is the peace that comes from knowing the harmony and the cogency of Scripture—one complete message. For the essay on "peace" is also an account of the meaning of what is whole, complete, and, ultimately, without flaw or blemish. That accounts for the joining of two distinct themes in the passage before us: the first, the harmonizing of contradiction; the second, the meaning of that wholeness that, in Hebrew, is the meaning of the word peace.

XLII:I

1. A. "[The Lord said to Moses, 'Say to Aaron and his sons: "Thus shall you bless the people of Israel." You shall say to them: "The

Lord bless you and keep you, the Lord make his face to shine
upon you and be gracious to you,] the Lord lift up his countenance upon you [and give you peace." So shall they put my
name upon the people of Israel, and I will bless them]'" (Num.
6:22-27):

B. ". . . The Lord lift up his countenance upon you" when you
stand and pray, as it is said: "And he said to him, 'Lo, I have
lifted up your face'" (Gen. 19:21) [The context requires this
translation].

C. And lo, it is a matter of an argument a fortiori:

D. "Now if to Lot, I have lifted up my face on account of Abraham,
whom I love, will I not lift up my face on your account and on
account of your ancestors?"

E. This is the sense of the verse of Scripture: ". . . The Lord lift up
his countenance upon you."

2. A. One verse of Scripture says: ". . . The Lord lift up his countenance upon you,"

B. and another verse of Scripture says: ". . . Who will not lift up a
face [and show favoritism]" (Deut. 10:17).

C. How can both of these verses of Scripture be carried out?

D. When the Israelites carry out the will of the Omnipresent, then
". . . the Lord lift up his countenance upon you."

E. But when the Israelites do not carry out the will of the Omnipresent, then ". . . who will not lift up a face [and show
favoritism]" (Deut. 10:17). [So Israel's deeds make the difference.]

3. A. Another explanation: Before the decree is sealed, ". . . the Lord
lift up his countenance upon you,"

B. and after the decree is sealed, ". . . who will not lift up a face
[and show favoritism]" (Deut. 10:17).

4. A. One verse of Scripture says: "O you who hears prayer, to you
shall all flesh come on account of sins" (Ps. 65:2-3 [Hebrew vv.
3-4]).

B. And another verse of Scripture says: "You have wrapped yourself with a cloud so that no prayer can pass through" (Lam.
3:44).

C. How can both of these verses of Scripture be carried out?

D. Before the decree is sealed: "O you who hears prayer, to you
shall all flesh come on account of sins" (Ps. 65:2-3 [Hebrew vv.
3-4]).

    E. After the decree is sealed: "You have wrapped yourself with a cloud so that no prayer can pass through" (Lam. 3:44).

5. A. One verse of Scripture says: "The Lord is near to all who call upon upon him, to all who call upon him in truth" (Ps. 145:18).

    B. And another verse of Scripture says: "Why, O Lord, should you stand at a distance?" (Ps. 10:1).

    C. How can both of these verses of Scripture be carried out?

    D. Before the decree is sealed: "The Lord is near to all who call upon upon him, to all who call upon him in truth" (Ps. 145:18).

    E. After the decree is sealed: "Why, O Lord, should you stand at a distance?" (Ps. 10:1).

6. A. One verse of Scripture says: "Is it not from the mouth of the Most High that good and evil come?" (Lam. 3:38).

    B. And another verse of Scripture says: "And the Lord watches over the evil" (Dan. 9:14).

    C. One verse of Scripture says: "O Jerusalem, wash your heart from wickedness, that you may be saved" (Jer. 4:4).

    D. And another verse of Scripture says: "Though you wash yourself with lye and use much soap, the stain of your guilt is still before me, says the Lord God" (Jer. 2:22).

    E. One verse of Scripture says: "Return, straying children" (Jer. 3:22).

    F. And another verse of Scripture says: "If one turns away does he not return?" (Jer. 8:4).

    G. How can both of these verses of Scripture be carried out?

    H. Before the decree has been sealed: "Return, straying children" (Jer. 3:22).

    I. And after the decree has been sealed: "If one turns away does he not return?" (Jer. 8:4).

7. A. One verse of Scripture says: "Seek the Lord when he may be found" (Isa. 55:6).

    B. And another verse of Scripture says: "As I live, if I shall seek you" (Ezek. 20:3).

    C. How can both of these verses of Scripture be carried out?

    D. Before the decree has been sealed: "Seek the Lord when he may be found" (Isa. 55:6).

    E. After the decree has been sealed: "As I live, if I shall seek you" (Ezek. 20:2).

8. A. One verse of Scripture says: "For I do not desire the death of any one" (Ezek. 18:32).

B. And another verse of Scripture says: "For the Lord desires to kill them" (1 Sam. 2:25).

C. One verse of Scripture says: "The Lord lift up his countenance upon you."

D. And another verse of Scripture says: ". . . Who will not lift up a face [and show favoritism]" (Deut. 10:17).

E. How can both of these verses of Scripture be carried out?

F. "The Lord lift up his countenance upon you": In this world.

G. ". . . Who will not lift up a face [and show favoritism]" (Deut. 10:17): In the world to come.

9. A. "The Lord lift up his countenance upon you"

B. Removing his anger from you.

XLII:II

1. A. ". . . And give you peace":

B. When you come in, peace, and when you go out, peace, peace with every person.

C. R. Hananiah, prefect of the priests, says, "'. . . And give you peace': In your house."

D. R. Nathan says, "'. . . And give you peace': This refers to the peace of the house of David, as it is said: 'Of the increase of his government and of peace there will be no end' (Isa. 9:7 [Hebrew v. 6])."

2. A. ". . . And give you peace": This refers to the peace of the Torah.

B. For it is said: "The Lord give strength to his people, the Lord bless his people with peace" (Ps. 29:11).

3. A. Great is peace, for on that account the tale involving Sarah was revised.

B. For it is said: "And I have grown old" (Gen. 18:13).

C. Great is peace, for the Holy One changed the tale on account of keeping the peace.

D. Great is peace, for the angel changed the story on account of keeping the peace.

E. Great is peace, for a name of God that is written in a state of consecration is blotted out by the water so as to bring peace between a man and his wife.

F. R. Eleazar says, "Great is peace, for the prophets planted in peoples' mouths only the word peace."

G. R. Simeon b. Halapta says, "Great is peace, for the only utensil that holds a blessing is peace, as it is said: 'The Lord give strength to his people, the Lord bless his people with peace' (Ps. 29:11)."

H. R. Eleazar Haqqappar says, "Great is peace, for the seal of all blessings is only peace, as it is said: '[The Lord bless you and keep you, the Lord make his face to shine upon you and be gracious to you,] the Lord lift up his countenance upon you [and give you peace].'"

I. R. Eleazar, son of R. Eleazar Haqqappar, says, "Great is peace, for even if the Israelites worship idols but keep the peace among them it is as if the Omnipresent says, 'Satan shall never touch them,' as it is said: 'Ephraim is joined to idols, let him alone' (Hos. 4:17).

J. "But when they are divided by dissension: 'They love shame more than their glory' (Hos. 4:18 [RSV])."

K. "Lo, great is peace and despised is dissension."

L. Great is peace, for even in a time of war people need peace, as it is said: "When you draw near a city to do battle against it, you will offer peace terms to it" (Deut. 20:10).

M. "So I sent messengers from the wilderness of Kedemoth to Sihon the king of Heshbon with words of peace" (Deut. 2:26).

N. "Then Jephthah sent messengers to the king of the Ammonites and said, 'What have you against me that you have come to me to fight against my land?' And the king of the Ammonites answered the messengers of Jephthah, 'Because Israel on coming from Egypt took away my land from the Arnon to the Jabbok and to the Jordan; now therefore restore it peaceably'" (Judg. 11:12-13).

O. Great is peace, for even the dead need it, as it is said: "And you shall go to your fathers in peace" (Gen. 15:15).

P. And it says: "You will die in peace and with the burnings of your fathers" (Jer. 34:5).

Q. Great is peace, for it is given to those who repent, as it is said: "He who creates the expression of the lips: 'Peace, peace to the one who is far and the one who is near'" (Isa. 57:18-19).

R. Great is peace, for it is given as the portion of the righteous, as it is said: "May he come in peace, resting on their resting place" (Isa. 57:2).

S. Great is peace, for it is not given as the portion of the wicked, as it is said: "There is no peace, says the Lord, to the wicked" (Isa. 57:21).

T. Great is peace, for it is given to those who love the Torah, as it is said: "Great peace goes to those who love your Torah" (Ps. 119:165).

U. Great is peace, for it is given to those who study the Torah, as it is said: "And all your children will be learned of the Lord, and great will be the peace of your children" (Isa. 54:13).

V. Great is peace, for it is given to the humble, as it is said: "The humble will inherit the earth and derive pleasure from the abundance of peace" (Ps. 37:11).

W. Great is peace, for it is given to those who carry out deeds of righteousness, as it is said: "And the work of righteousness will be peace" (Isa. 32:17).

X. Great is peace, for it is the name of the Holy One, blessed be he, as it is said: "And he called the Lord, 'peace'" (Judg. 6:24).

Y. R. Hananiah, prefect of the priests, says, "Great is peace, for it outweighs all the works of creation, as it is said: 'Who creates light and forms darkness and makes peace' (Isa. 45:7)."

Z. Great is peace, for those who dwell in the high places need peace, as it is said: "Dominion and fear are with God; he makes peace in his high heaven" (Job 25:2).

AA. Now it is a matter of an argument a fortiori: If in a place where there are no envy, competition, and hatred and conflict the creatures of the upper world need peace, in a place in which all of these qualities are found all the more so [do people need peace].

BB. And so Scripture says: "Be ashamed, O Sidon, for the sea has spoken, the stronghold of the sea, saying, 'I have neither travailed nor given birth, I have neither reared young men nor brought up virgins'" (Isa. 23:4).

CC. Said the sea, "Now what am I, that I am not afraid of giving birth and producing sons and daughters. And am I going to bury bridegrooms and brides? And what is said in my connection? 'Do you not fear me?' says the Lord; 'Do you not tremble before me? I placed the sand as the bound for the sea, a perpetual barrier which it cannot pass' (Jer. 5:22)."

DD. Said the sea, "Now if I, who have none of these traits, carry out the will of my Creator, all the more so those who are ashamed in Sidon!"

Remembering God through Carrying Out Religious Duties

If I had to state in one sentence the message derived by our sages from Scripture, it would be as follows: "In all your ways, know God." That is to say, the critical issue of faith works itself out in everyday life, and to know, serve, and love God is to carry out God's will and commandments in the here and now. But what that means, with reference to the particular world of religious duties that Scripture constructs, remains to be seen.

To show how, in the book of Numbers, our sages find the answer to the question of "knowing God" in every way of life, we turn to the commandment that is very specific on that question. It has to do with the clothing that one wears (just as the commandment we considered in the book of Leviticus concerning the food that one eats). We recall that the book of Numbers contains the commandment to affix a show-fringe (Hebrew *sisit*) on one's garment. Today, Orthodox Jews do so by wearing an undershirt that bears the requisite show-fringes. Conservative and many Reform Jews do so by wearing a prayer shawl when they recite their prayers. What is interesting in our sages' reading of the matter, however, is not the detail but the main point. They insist that the point of the show-fringes is public, not private. That is to say, what one does in secret—symbolized by the clothing one wears beneath the outer garments—comes to the surface and shows what we really are. The Egyptians acted in secret. God made public the deeds that they did in secret. The show-fringes testify all the time to Israel's status as God's servants. At the end we come to a stunning story. It is relevant both on its own and for what it symbolizes. On its own it tells how a faithful, and yet sinful, man succumbed to his lust. But as he prepared to commit the sin of adultery, he removed his show-fringes and was reminded of who he was and what his duties were. He then desisted. The broader point of relevance is blatant.

To repeat here what I said in the beginning of this book, Scripture forms a commentary on everyday life—as much as everyday life brings with it fresh understanding of Scripture. There is a constant interplay, an on-going interchange, between everyday affairs and the word of God in

the Torah (Scripture). What we see reminds us of what Scripture says—
and what Scripture says informs our understanding of the things we see
and do in everyday life. That is, in my view, the meaning of the critical
verse of Scripture: "In all thy ways, know Him." And the deep structure
of human existence, framed by Scripture and formed out of God's will,
forms the foundation of our everyday life. Here and now, in the life of the
hour, we can and do know God. So everyday life forms a commentary on
revealed Scripture (on the Torah), and Scripture (the Torah) provides a
commentary on everyday life. Life flows in both directions.

CXV:V

1. A. "So you shall remember and do [all my commandments and be
       holy to your God. I am the Lord your God who brought you out
       of the land of Egypt to be your God. I am the Lord your God]"
       (Num. 15:37-41):
    B. [The phrasing, 'remember and do,' serves to] treat remembering
       as tantamount to doing.
2. A. ". . . And be holy to your God":
    B. This refers to the sanctity of all of the religious duties [every one
       of which falls into the classification of remembering and doing,
       thus of sanctifying Israel].
    C. You say that this refers to the sanctity of all of the religious
       duties. But perhaps reference here is made solely to the religious
       duty of attaching fringes to the corners of the garments?
    D. You may argue as follows: What is the context in which dis-
       course takes place? It is the sanctity of all the religious duties
       [not only that of the fringes].
    E. Rabbi says, "This refers in particular to the sanctity only of the
       religious duty of the fringes.
    F. "You say that this refers in particular to the sanctity only of the
       religious duty of the fringes. But perhaps it makes reference to
       the sanctity of all of the religious duties equally?
    G. "When Scripture says: 'You shall be holy' (Lev. 19:2), lo, under
       discussion is the sanctity of all the religious duties equally. So
       when Scripture says: '. . . And be holy to your God,' this refers
       only to the religious duty of affixing show-fringes to the gar-
       ments.
    H. "The upshot is that the commandment involving fringes serves
       to add to the sanctity of Israel."

3. A. "I am the Lord your God who brought you out of the land of Egypt":

   B. What relevance does the Exodus from Egypt have to the present context?

   C. It is so that someone should not say, "Lo, I shall put in dyestuff or vegetable matter [rather than the proper dye for the color blue, which comes from a mollusk and is difficult to get], for they produce a color similar to the required blue. And who is going to tell on me in public?"

   D. "'I am the Lord your God who brought you out of the land of Egypt,' and know what I did to the Egyptians, who acted in secret. I made public [the things that they did in secret]."

   E. Now this produces an argument a fortiori: Now if in the case of the divine attribute of inflicting punishment—which is the lesser—he who incurs a penalty in secret finds that the Omnipresent makes the matter public, all the more so when it comes to the divine attribute of dispensing good—which is the greater of the two. [God will surely grant a public reward to one who incurs divine pleasure in a private deed.]

4. A. ["I am the Lord your God who brought you out of the land of Egypt to be your God"]:

   B. Why make mention of the Exodus from Egypt in the setting of discourse on each and every one of the religious duties?

   C. The matter may be compared to the case of a king whose ally was taken captive. When the king paid the ransom [and so redeemed him], he did not redeem him as a free man but as a slave, so that if the king made a decree and the other did not accept it, he might say to him, "You are my slave."

   D. When he came into a city, he said to him, "Tie my shoelatch, carry my clothing before me, and bring them to the bathhouse." [Doing these services marks a man as the slave of the one for whom he does them.]

   E. The ally began to complain. The king produced the bond and said to him, "You are my slave."

   F. So when the Holy One, blessed be he, redeemed the seed of Abraham, his ally, he redeemed them not as sons but as slaves. When he makes a decree and they do not accept it, he may say to them, "You are my slaves."

   G. When the people had gone forth to the wilderness, he began to make decrees for them involving part of the lesser religious duties as well as part of the more stringent religious duties—for example, the Sabbath, the prohibition against consanguineous marriages, the fringes, and the requirement to don *tefillin* [prayer shawls]. The Israelites began to complain. He said to them, "You are my slaves. It was on that stipulation that I redeemed you, on the condition that I may make a decree and you must carry it out."

5. A. "[So you shall remember and do [all my commandments and be holy to your God. I am the Lord your God who brought you out of the land of Egypt to be your God.] I am the Lord your God" (Num. 15:37-41):

    B. Why repeat the phrase, "I am the Lord your God"?

    C. Is it not already stated, "I am the Lord your God who brought you out of the land of Egypt to be your God"?

    D. Why then repeat the phrase, "I am the Lord your God"?

    E. It is so that the Israelites should not say, "Why has the Omnipresent given us commandments? Let us not do them and not collect a reward."

    F. They do not do them, and they shall not collect a reward.

    G. This is in line with what the Israelites said to Ezekiel: "Some of the elders of Israel came to consult the Lord [and were sitting with me. Then this word came to me from the Lord: 'Man, say to the elders of Israel, This is the word of the Lord God: Do you come to consult me? As I live, I will not be consulted by you. This is the very word of the Lord God]'" (Ezek. 20:1-3).

    H. They said to Ezekiel, "In the case of a slave whose master has sold him off, has not the slave left the master's dominion?"

    I. He said to them, "Yes."

    J. They said to him, "Since the Omnipresent has sold us to the nations of the world, we have left his dominion."

    K. He said to them, "Lo, in the case of a slave whose master has sold him only on the stipulation that later on the slave will return, has the slave left the dominion of the master? [Surely not.]"

    L. "'When you say to yourselves, "Let us become like the nations and tribes of other lands and worship wood and stone," you are thinking of something that can never be. As I live, says the Lord God, I will reign over you with a strong hand, with arm outstretched and wrath outpoured'" (Ezek. 20:32-33).

M. ". . . With a strong hand": This refers to pestilence, as it is said: "Lo, the hand of the Lord is upon your cattle in the field" (Exod. 9:3).

N. ". . . With arm outstretched": This refers to the sword, as it is said: "And his sword is unsheathed in his hand, stretched forth against Jerusalem" (1 Chr. 21:16).

O. ". . . And wrath outpoured": This refers to famine.

P. "After I have brought against you these three forms of punishment, one after the other, then 'I will reign over you'—despite yourselves."

Q. That is why it is said a second time, "I am the Lord your God."

6. A. R. Nathan says, "You have not a single religious duty that is listed in the Torah, the reward of the doing of which is not made explicit right alongside.

B. "Go and learn the lesson from the religious duty of the fringes." [What follows spells this out.]

7. A. There is the case of a man who was meticulous about carrying out the religious duty of the fringes. He heard that there was a certain harlot in one of the coastal towns, who would collect a fee of four hundred gold coins. He sent her four hundred gold coins and made a date with her.

D. When his time came, he came along and took a seat at the door of her house. Her maid came and told her, "That man with whom you made a date, lo, he is sitting at the door of the house."

E. She said to her, "Let him come in."

F. When he came in, she spread out for him seven silver mattresses and one gold one, and she was on the top, and between each one were silver stools, and on the top were gold ones. When he came to do the deed, the four fringes fell out [of his garment] and appeared to him like four witnesses. The man slapped himself in the face and immediately withdrew and took a seat on the ground.

G. The harlot too withdrew and took a seat on the ground.

H. She said to him, "By the winged god of Rome! I shall not let you go until you tell me what blemish you have found in me."

I. He said to her, "By the Temple service! I did not find any blemish at all in you, for in the whole world there is none so beautiful as you. But the Lord, our God, has imposed upon me a rather small duty, but concerning [even that minor matter] he wrote: 'I am the Lord your God who brought you out of the land of Egypt to be your God. I am the Lord your God,'—two times.

J. "'I am the Lord your God': I am destined to pay a good reward.

K. "'I am the Lord your God': I am destined to exact punishment.'"

L. She said to him, "By the Temple service! I shall not let you go until you write me your name, the name of your town, and the name of your school in which you study Torah."

M. So he wrote for her his name, the name of his town, and the name of his master, and the name of the school in which he had studied Torah.

N. She went and split up her entire wealth, a third to the government, a third to the poor, and a third she took with her and came and stood at the schoolhouse of R. Hiyya.

O. She said to him, "My lord, accept me as a proselyte."

P. He said to her, "Is it possible that you have laid eyes on one of the disciples [and are converting in order to marry him]?"

Q. She took the slip out that was in her hand.

R. He said to [the disciple who had paid the money but not gone through with the act], "Stand up and acquire possession of what you have purchased. Those spreads that she spread out for you in violation of a prohibition she will now spread out for you in full remission of the prohibition.

S. "As to this one, the recompense is paid out in this world, and as to the world to come, I do not know how much [more he will receive]!"

Index

GENERAL INDEX

INDEX TO BIBLICAL AND TALMUDIC REFERENCES